Henry James Coleridge

The Prisoners of the King

Thoughts on the Catholic Doctrine of Purgatory

Henry James Coleridge

The Prisoners of the King
Thoughts on the Catholic Doctrine of Purgatory

ISBN/EAN: 9783744797139

Printed in Europe, USA, Canada, Australia, Japan

Cover: Foto ©Thomas Meinert / pixelio.de

More available books at **www.hansebooks.com**

THE PRISONERS OF THE KING

THOUGHTS ON THE CATHOLIC DOCTRINE OF PURGATORY

BY

HENRY JAMES COLERIDGE

OF THE SOCIETY OF JESUS

THIRD EDITION

LONDON

BURNS AND OATES

GRANVILLE MANSIONS W

1884

✠

ANIMÆ

IN DOMINO QUIESCENTI

CÆCILIÆ

MARCHIONISSÆ DE LOTHIAN

PREFACE.

The form in which these thoughts on the doctrine of Purgatory are set forth in this volume is accidental, and I am well aware that it cannot claim to present to the reader a well-arranged treatise on the great subject with which it deals. Two or three years ago it fell to my lot, in conjunction with a dear friend and brother in religion, who is now, I trust, at rest with God, to preach during the Octave with which the Society of the Helpers of the Holy Souls is accustomed to celebrate the annual Commemoration of the Faithful Departed. It occurred to me that some of the miracles of our Lord might be usefully applied in illustration of the doctrine of Purgatory, and thus the substance of some few of the chapters of this book was put together. At the beginning of the present year I began a series of papers on the same subject in the *Messenger of the Sacred Heart*—a religious magazine the existence of which we owe to the zeal and exertions of the widely loved and valued priest of whom I have already spoken. The work has grown under my hands, and it seemed better to finish it at cnce, in order that it might perhaps be of some little use in promoting the devotion of which it mainly treats during the month which Catholics constantly consecrate to the relief of the Holy Souls. About a third of the contents of this volume has appeared in the *Messenger of the Sacred Heart.*

Although the form in which this book is cast almost of necessity precludes the regular and orderly treatment of the doctrine of Purgatory, I am in hopes that no considerable point connected with that doctrine has been altogether passed over. I have found much help from two books which are not very widely known to readers on the subject— the two *Sagri Trigesimi* on Purgatory preached by Pope Benedict XIII. when Cardinal Archbishop of Bologna—in which the whole doctrine of St. Thomas is illustrated with great erudition—and the *Patrocinium Defunctorum* of Father Hautin. I have not thought it necessary to specify all my obligations to these and other writers, in a work the object of which is simply to promote intelligent devotion, written at intervals of time and under circumstances which forbade any unnecessary exertion.

What is new in this volume is chiefly the application of the successive miracles of our Lord to various points of the doctrine of Purgatory. Our Lord's miracles were almost universally acts of mercy as well as proofs of authority, and thus it is natural to find that they are full of teaching as to the various spiritual miseries of souls and His tenderness in succouring them. The Holy Souls are sufferers to a degree and in a manner which are but faintly pictured in the bodily maladies which our Lord so lovingly relieved, and they are sufferers whose case He has left very much to the charity of the children of the Militant Church. His Sacred Heart looked further than the outward disease or privation for which He used His healing or restoring power, and, if it is most natural to consider all bodily evils as shadows and images by which spiritual infirmities are represented, it is not any exaggerated extension of the same principle of accommodation to consider the sufferings of Purgatory, all of which are caused by sin or negligence, as included under it. And no phase or department of Christian devotion can ever lose by being connected in any way with considerations on the acts and sayings of our Lord.

H. J. C.

Feast of our Most Holy Redeemer, 1878.

CONTENTS.

CHAPTER I.

*The desire of our Lord that the Holy Souls should be
released from Purgatory even before the time.*

1. THE wonderful series of our Lord's miracles of
mercy began, as we well know, at the marriage
festival at Cana in Galilee, only a few days after
the time when He had first called to Himself some
few of His future disciples and Apostles, on the
banks of the Jordan, where St. John Baptist had
trained them in the school of penance, and spoken
to them of the Lamb of God Who was to take
away the sins of the world. The blessed Evangelist
St. John, who was himself, we cannot doubt, one'
of these first disciples, and who must certainly have
been present at the marriage feast at which the
miracle was wrought, has left us the history on which
so many of the saints of God have meditated
lovingly, seeing in it a great deal more than the
narrative of a passing incident of our Lord's life.
They have considered that the beginning of miracles,
or "signs," as St. John calls it, must have been so
ordained by God that all its circumstances must
have very deep spiritual significance, and that the
first action of our Lord of this kind which has been
selected for relation by the author of the last and

most sacramental Gospel, must contain in itself prophecy and doctrine, as well as the external display of power and mercy. The Mother of our Lord was present, he tells us, at this marriage feast, and our Lord and His disciples were invited. After a time the wine failed, and then our Blessed Lady, who was perhaps related to the bridegroom or bride, appealed to our Lord in the well-known words, " They have no wine." Our Lord replied, " Lady, what is to Me and to Thee ? " Words which are not wrongly interpreted by the other version, " What have I to do with thee ? " which conveys more pointedly the sense of a kind of acknowledgment of influence which our Lady was exerting over Him, without which He would not do what He was about to do. Our Lord added, " Mine hour is not yet come"—as if thus also to imply that the time for His first display of miraculous power had not arrived, except inasmuch as it was advanced and hastened on by her interference. Thus our Blessed Lady seems to have understood Him, for she told the servants who were waiting at the table, " Whatsoever He saith to you do, do it ; " and thus it was that when He bade them fill the six water vessels, which stood by for purposes of purification, with water, they did so at once without hesitation. Then He bade them pour out the contents of the waterpots to the guests, beginning with the person who filled the office of the ruler of the feast. They did this, and the water was found to be changed into wine, of so excellent a quality that the ruler of the feast called the bridegroom, and told him that people usually gave their best wine first, and then that which was less good, whereas he had kept the good wine for the last.

2. It is also clear that the obedience and simple faith of the servants at the feast, who, without any

hesitation or question, filled the waterpots with water, and then poured out their contents to the ruler of the feast and others, had a certain part in the miracle—a part which we. find constantly required by our Lord on such occasions. It is not our purpose to consider here all the circumstances of the miracle, nor all the lessons which may be drawn from it for our own instruction. But we may select certain points in the conduct of our Blessed Lady and others, and use them for our own guidance and encouragement in the great work of intercession and satisfaction for the Holy Souls of Purgatory, the successful accomplishment of which will give so much glory to God, so much joy to our Lord and to His Blessed Mother, and shed a glow of happiness over the whole company who are banqueting in the Marriage Supper of the Lamb, far more intense and lasting than that which followed at this feast of Cana, when the water had been made wine for the satisfaction and consolation of the hosts and their guests.

3. We may venture, then, in the first place, to enter into the Heart of the Immaculate Mother of our Lord, and ask ourselves what are the virtues which she here practises, and what may have been, in a more special way, her motives for this great act of clemency. We see at once that in her motherly care for the bride and bridegroom she anticipated their wants, and that in the mightiness of her faith she sought the .remedy at the hands of our Lord, when nothing less than a miracle could supply it. Others might have hesitated, either as to His power to perform so wonderful a work, or as to the seemliness of appealing to Him in such a matter, or lastly, as to His willingness to use His Divine power, when asked, for so slight a cause. Again, we may see

that our Blessed Lady was overflowing with zeal for the glory of God and for the honour of her Divine Son, for the manifestation of His power in such a way as to enlighten the minds and confirm the faith of His Apostles concerning Him, and that she discerned with a clear spiritual instinct how well all these great ends might be served by His working such a miracle, even upon this homely occasion, and in the midst of a number of simple country people gathered together for a wedding feast. Again, we may see in this tender condescending consideration of our Lady for the accidental defect of preparation for their guests on the part of those who gave the banquet, a lesson as to her extreme tenderness of heart for even the smallest spiritual needs and sufferings of her children. She was such a mother to those poor people that she could not bear to see them want their full measure of wine: and this lets us see how eager she must be that no one of those who have been redeemed by our Blessed Lord, and made her children by Him on the Cross, should lack the fullest measure of spiritual graces and blessings which He has destined for them. No temporal loss or sufferings, however great and poignant, can be compared to the least possible loss or suffering in the order of grace, and if she was so ready to exert her power at once at the sight of a slight material inconvenience, how can we ever fathom the depths of her all but infinite compassion for the needs of the soul, and the miseries which may issue in the eternal loss of God? Again, we may contemplate the marvellous prudence and humility of her prayer, the penetration with which she understood what our Lord meant when He pleaded that the time was not yet come, the confidence with which she expected the granting of her prayer, and her careful warning to the servants to do whatsoever He told them. In the whole scene we' seem to see the great reverence which at this time waited on our Lord wherever He went, as the homage due to a Person as to Whom there was an indefinable instinct that He was more than man. But our Blessed Lady was anxious that the human part, the exercise of faith and obedience, which was essential for the working of the miracle according to the ordinary laws on which our Lord iusisted, might not be wanting, and so the whole of her loving design for His glory and the relief of the poor couple might not be frustrated.

4. The respect in which they held our Blessed Lady, the reverence with which they regarded our Blessed Lord, their own good-will to the bridegroom and bride, the simplicity of their faith and their natural docility, aided, as we cannot doubt, by the prayers of our Lady and the grace of God, prevented the servants at the feast from falling into the danger of not heeding the charge which had been given to them. It was their business to obey, even against all appearance of reasonableness in the command which they received, and even although they might have been exposed to mockery and reproof if the miracle had failed of its effect. They were told, " Whatsoever He shall say unto you do, do it," and so they did not hesitate to fill the six waterpots with water, and to bear them to the ruler of the feast. Thus they had indeed that part in the miracle which belongs to those who obey against appearance of reason, and so fulfil the conditions which, as has been said, our Lord ordinarily exacted on such occasions. Our Lord, then, in the great readiness which He always 'shows in rewarding faith and obedience, as also in His own

very great compassion, greater even than that of His Mother, for human needs and miseries of every kind, full also as He was of the desire to see the Father glorified, to manifest His own Name, especially to those who were, after Him, to manifest it to the world, rejoicing, moreover, interiorly in the beauty of the graces shown in His Mother's condescension and prayer, and desiring, among other things, to exalt her name also and let it be connected for ever in the history of His kingdom with the beginning of His chain of miracles, brought about in His own sweet and prudent way the wonderful change of the water into the wine. so full of deep spiritual significance, especially as to the marvellous Sacrament of sacraments which He was afterwards to leave behind Him in the Church. Although the time was not yet come, that is, He was not then to have begun His miracles unless the time had been anticipated and forced on by the prayers and actions of His Blessed Mother, still He is not so bound down to times and reasons as that He cannot alter them; and in the infinite foreknowledge of God both times are fixed, when things might happen, as well as when they do happen, when the power of Mary's intercession and of the prayers of the Church are brought to bear upon them. For to God all things are present, what might have been and what might be, as well as what has been and what shall be. It would indeed be very strange, and inconsistent with a true intelligence of our Lord's Sacred Heart, to imagine that He wrought this miracle unwillingly or grudgingly, or with any other feeling than that of great joy at the deep faith and ardent charity of His Blessed Mother, which had, as we may say, loosened His hands before the time, and enabled Him to

grant for her sake and to her prayer, and to the
obedience of the servants, what He would not
otherwise have granted to the needs of the bridegroom and bride. On the contrary, our Lord loves
to be constrained by prayer, He delights in the
importunities of His children, and is grateful to
them when they give Him an occasion of allowing
His justice to yield to His mercy by interposing
the blessed influence of intercession, which has its
lawful weight in His government, on account of
His merits and of our union with Him. Thus it is
equally true to say that God has appointed a certain
course of things, as in the case of the chastisements
which in this world or the next He inflicts upon sin,
and also to say that He desires that His arrangements may be modified and altered by the power of
prayer, and that, taking that power and its exercise
into account, He may appoint a certain other course
of things in which those arrangements are so modified, with an increase of glory to Himself. For it is
more to His glory that He should grant to prayer
favours which He would not have granted without
it, than that no prayer should be made to Him for
the obtaining of those favours.

5. Let us now apply the instruction which is thus
contained in the narrative of this miracle to the
particular subject of these considerations, that is,
to the Christian doctrine concerning Purgatory,
both as to the lessons which we may learn for our
own use therefrom, and as to the means which may
be used for the relief of the sufferers there. Our
desire is, to consider the case of those Holy Souls,
or the decrees of our Lord as to their help, or the
various manners in which they may be helped by us,
as in some way, more or less, represented to us in
each link of that beautiful chain of His miracles of

mercy and power which has been woven for us in the narratives of the four Evangelists. The miracle with which we are now concerned has been left to the Evangelist of the Christian mysteries to relate, and it stands, in a very true sense, at the head of the whole series, placing the prerogative of our Blessed Lady in the clearest light, much as the sanctification of St. John Baptist in the womb of his mother, at the sound of the voice of Mary, stands at the head of our Lord's works of interior grace. It is not at all difficult to apply the main teaching of this wonderful miracle to the doctrine of Purgatory. The persons who were in need at the marriage supper at Cana, and who were relieved by our Lord's condescension to the prayer of His Mother, were the guests at the banquet and, in the first instance, the entertainers themselves, on whom might have fallen the sorrow of being unable to give their guests what was meet and right at the time. But, after all, what are such human needs as these, when we compare them with those which our faith represents to us in the case of the holy prisoners in Purgatory! They are souls who have a right, by virtue of the redemption which has been applied to them, their adoption as children of God, and the grace in which they have left this world, to a seat at the eternal banquet of ineffable delights which is spoken of in Holy Scripture as the marriage supper of the Lamb. Their craving for this enjoyment is far more intense than any hunger or thirst which can be felt or even imagined in this world. Their numbers are undoubtedly very great; for they include, not only the great majority of Catholics who die in a state of grace, but an immense multitude whose magnitude can only be measured by that of the manifold mercy and compassionate wisdom of God, Who provides in so many ways, that far outrun our imaginations, for hundreds of thousands of souls who die outside the pale of the visible Church, in good faith, with true sorrow for their sins, or with only venial sins, on their souls, and with a desire which He accepts, to know and to do all His will, though unrevealed to them formally, or hidden from them by the clouds of education, false instruction, and mis-representations of the Church. The Creator of all these souls has exercised a marvellous care over them in His Providence, shielding them from many dangers, leading them to the practice of many virtues, and, we cannot doubt, unlocking the more secret and marvellous stores of His mercy for them at the last. When we know how much may be gathered from the lives and revelations of the saints as to the length of time during which some souls may be detained in Purgatory, it is not easy to conceive of the number that may be there at any given time as any thing but very large. Especially may this be the case with those whose friends do not believe in or do not practise the many holy methods of aiding the departed which are familiar to Catholics. And each generation in the Church may say to itself, that there are there its own more immediate ancestors and predecessors, those to whom it owes the transmission of the precious deposit of the Christian faith and the sacraments, and all the spiritual benefits which it enjoys. All these are so many thoughts which may spur us on to exertion in the cause of the deliverance of these " guests " of the Great Father of all from the prison in which His justice now detains them. Just as we hear nothing, in the narrative of the miracle before us, of any complaint or petition made by the guests themselves or by their hosts, so is it the rule of the justice of God that the Holy Souls of Purgatory cannot merit or pray for themselves. Their patient, intense, wistful, longing suffering is indeed a prayer which strikes on the mercy of God and the compassionate Hearts of Jesus and Mary with immense force. But their resignation also is perfect, and the union of their will with that of God : and so they leave it to others to say for them, " They have no wine "—simple words, which when we consider what it is from which they are debarred, how deep and burning is their thirst for it, have a depth and fulness of meaning which it would require a long contemplation to unfold.

6. We must also spend a few moments in considering who are the hosts in the marriage supper from which the Holy Souls of Purgatory are, for the time, excluded. We can imagine the deep joy and gratitude of the simple bridegroom and bride when they saw the miracle which had been wrought in their favour. The contemplative writers lead us to suppose that the great act of Divine power struck them so deeply, that they at once consecrated themselves to God in the way that was open to them, vowing to live during their married life in the holy state of virginal continence. But in the banquet of eternity the Host is God Himself, the Father, the Son, and the Holy Ghost, and, wonderful as it seems to say so, we can make Him bound to us by a debt of gratitude far greater than that which bound the bride and bridegroom of whom we are speaking to those who brought about the miracle, by using the means which the Ever Blessed Trinity has placed in our hands of opening the door of the marriage supper to those who have a right to be there, but who are now excluded from it. In a thousand

ways in His ordinary Providence, and also in the great economy of salvation through Jesus Christ, has God put Himself and the execution of the designs of His love into the hands of His children. In a very great measure indeed has He done this in the execution of the counsels of His mercy with regard to the suffering souls of Purgatory. He can feed the hungry and clothe the naked upon earth by the ministry of His angels, if He will, but He has intrusted them, in His ordinary Providence, to human charity. And, in the same way, He is not precluded from pardoning as He pleases the souls who are so dear to Him, still less from hearing in their behalf the prayers of His Blessed Mother, or the saints, or the guardian Angels and others. But in a great measure He has left them, in the wisdom of His charity, to the good offices of the children of the Church, who are in their turn some day to take their places as sufferers in that blessed prison. And as God is infinite in everything, in wisdom, in mercy, in justice, in power, so is He unbounded in His gratitude, and He will repay a thousand and a thousand fold the charity which He thus puts it in our power to practise, which rejoices so intensely His own Heart, the Sacred Heart of Jesus, His Blessed Mother, and the saints and Angels, which adds so much to the glories and joys of Heaven, and of which He has given us the opportunity for the very purpose that it may flow back again upon ourselves, according to the laws of His eternal kingdom, in over-abundant streams, according to our own needs, like that measure " heaped up and pressed together and running over "[1] of which our Lord speaks in the Gospel.

7. Again, there is much instruction for us in eco-

[1] St. Luke vi.

nection with the subject of Purgatory and the charity which is exercised towards its inhabitants, in the part which is played by the servants in the marriage feast, and in the charge which is addressed to them by our Blessed Lady : " Whatsoever He shall say unto you do, do it." It is here that we shall find most practical teaching for ourselves. In the first place, it is clear that the accomplishment of our Lord's most loving purpose in the miracle depended in no slight degree on the ready faith and obedience of the servants. It is conceivable that if they had failed the miracle might have been deferred ; and it is, at all events, certain that in the case of the deliverance of the Holy Souls a very great deal does actually and continually depend upon the vivid faith of the children of the Church understanding the needs of the Holy Souls and their own power of helping them, as well as on the activity of their charity in using that power to the utmost. As a matter of fact, it is probable that very few indeed of us are as much alive as we ought to be to our duties and opportunities of this kind, and that even fewer are as persistent and energetic in their exertions as God would fain have them to be. It may be that many and many a soul would reach Heaven much sooner, but for the languor of our faith and the coldness of our charity, and the considerations which have been already urged might lead us to a practical self-examination as to our use of our manifold and rich opportunities of succouring the departed and so consoling the Sacred Heart of our Lord. In the second place, we may apply the words of our Lady to the servants in the sense of a special charge to ourselves with regard to the performance of our duties to the Holy Souls. Thus, " Whatsoever He shall say unto you do, do it," may mean to us that we are to follow out every inspiration that our Lord sends us as to this work of charity, that we are to consider, in their bearing on this matter, all the charges and promises which He has left behind Him as to charity to our neighbour in general, and that we are to use all the means of gaining indulgences or performing works of satisfaction that fall in our way, without neglecting any. We are to endeavour to fulfil to the utmost the merciful counsel of our Lord in His Providence to us in this respect—to do every act of charity to the departed which He, seeing all our circumstances and opportunities, would have us perform. There is also another sense in which we may understand these words—a sense in which they may help us very much towards cancelling our own debt to the justice of God, as well as towards helping others in the same way. For, if we perform perfectly all the duties and obligations which our Lord lays upon us, if we faithfully and fully discharge the daily duties of our calling in life, we shall by this faithfulness to grace and duty heap up day by day a very considerable treasure in the way of satisfaction for our daily faults, and at the same time we shall gain power to aid Him, as He desires, in the accomplishment of His merciful intentions towards these Holy Souls. For every good work has, besides other qualities, a quality of satisfaction for sin, and the constant sacrifice to God of a perfect life according to our vocation is impetratory of immense graces and gives wonderful power to our prayers. All these things, the satisfactory character of our good actions of every kind, the increase of grace and favour with God which advance in perfection implies, and the power of intercession, when winged, as it were, with the soaring efficacy of a good life, may be turned by us at will to the help of the Holy Souls.

8. Above all, it is well to begin these our considerations on the doctrine of Purgatory with this reflection—that as surely as our Blessed Lady fulfilled her proper office in the Kingdom of her Son by this act of intercession, whereby our Lord was induced, or as we may say in other words, enabled, to anticipate that beginning of His miracles which must have been an object of very great longing desire to His Sacred Heart, so surely do we fulfil our office and duty in the Church by forcing on, if we may so speak, the time of the deliverance of the Holy Souls, by means of the suffrages, and prayers, and sacrifices and penances, and satisfactions, to which He has been pleased to attach so great a power for this very purpose. In one sense we may say of Him, as to these Holy Souls, His time has not yet come ; but in another, He has made it depend on us whether it has come or not. Indeed, the thought that the time has not come for His justice to set them free without the help of His children, involves and contains the other thought, that the time for our exertions, which He so much desires, has come already, if we will but enter into the counsels of His love. For His justice can be satisfied by our charity as well as by their sufferings, and it is more for His glory that the satisfaction should be made in the first way than in the other. At the wedding feast, our Lord's time had not come, but Mary's time had come—and so in regard of the Holy Souls, our time for relieving them has come, and is always present, as long as we have the power to lighten and shorten them.

CHAPTER II.

*Purity required by God in those who see Him in
Heaven.*

(THE CLEANSING OF THE TEMPLE.)

St. John iii. 13—19.

1. THE cleansing of the Temple, an action which
was twice performed by our Blessed Lord, at the
beginning and at the very end of His Public Ministry,
is not, strictly speaking, reckoned among His
miracles. It was a moral, rather than a material,
miracle, and the result was produced by the effect
of His wonderful majesty and dignity, by the panic
which fell upon the merchants in the Temple,
produced, no doubt, in part by their own unquiet
consciences and the reverence which they knew to
be due to the Holy Place, and perhaps by other
spiritual influences working upon them. And yet
St. Jerome reckons this action as among the greatest
of our Lord's miracles, using the word in the widest
sense which it usually bears. For certainly, few
things could be more wonderful than to see a crowd
of busy money-getters, bent on their own enrichment
and tolerated by the authorities of the Temple,
suddenly driven in fear and confusion from its
courts by a single Man, armed with no authority
but that inherent to His own Person, with no
visible assistance, and no weapon in His hand
more formidable than a scourge of small cords.

The malice and obstinacy of men, the hardness of heart which is produced by a life given up to sensuality or to the eager pursuit of wealth—these are forces which seem more difficult to tame and cow than the physical elements or the diseases which assail the body. In this sense, then, this action was a great miracle, and, being so, we shall find that it affords us more than one point which may be profitably studied by us in our considerations with relation to Purgatory, and which may help us both to avoid those punishments ourselves, and to deliver from them others who are now undergoing them.

2. St. John tells us, then, that soon after the miracle at Cana, our Lord went up with His disciples to the feast of the Pasch at Jerusalem. He found the Temple crowded, not only with worshippers from all parts of the Holy Land, and, indeed, of the Roman world, but also by other occupants who had established a custom which sanctioned their presence. " He found in the Temple those who sold oxen and sheep and the changers of money sitting." Upon this our Lord made a sort of scourge of small cords, " and drove them all out of the Temple, the oxen and the sheep also, and He poured out the money of the money-changers, and overturned their tables, and to those who sold doves He said, Take these things hence, and make not the house of my Father a house of traffic." St. John adds an authentic commentary on this remarkable action of our Blessed Lord, when He says that His disciples afterwards applied to it the saying of the Psalmist, " The zeal of Thy house hath eaten me up."[1] The motive, therefore, which prompted our Lord was the zeal for the purity and honour of the house of His Father,—as, indeed,

---

[1] Psalm lxviii. 10.

is shown by His own words to the sellers of doves, " Make not the house of My Father a house of traffic" —words which are still further illustrated by what He said on the second occasion on which He cleansed the Temple, when He quoted the prophecy, that " My house shall be called the house of prayer to all nations."[1] It was inconsistent with the reverence which was befitting a place in which God was so specially worshipped, and in which He vouchsafed to dwell with a peculiar kind of presence, such as was to be found nowhere else in the whole world, that traffic should be carried on in its courts, even though it was traffic which was, more or less, necessary on account of the sacrifices and offerings which were there made by the many devout persons from all parts of the world who came thither to honour God. Such persons required that the money which they brought with them should be changed for coin which could be offered in the Temple—many of the coins which they brought from abroad being idolatrous in their inscriptions—and also that they should find at some convenient place near at hand the victims which were prescribed for the various kinds of sacrifice which their circumstances or their piety prompted them to offer. This traffic, therefore, was not in itself sinful, except in so far as it was carried on in an unjust spirit of extortion by the dealers whom our Lord drove out. But it was something profane in the place in which it was carried on—something inconsistent with the perfect silence and reverence, the spirit of worship, adoration, recollection, the intimate feeling of God's near presence, which became the courts of that solemn Temple, and our Lord's burning love for His Father's honour would not suffer it. It was now that was fulfilled of Him

[1] St. Mark xi. 17 ; Isaias lvi. 7.

that prophecy of Malachias, which is also applied to His presence in the Temple at the purification of His Blessed Mother, " Presently the Lord Whom you seek, and the Angel of the Testament, Whom you desire, shall come to His Temple. Behold, He cometh, saith the Lord of Hosts. And who shall be able to think of the day of His coming? and who shall stand to see Him? For He is like a refining fire."[8] His zeal for God's honour made Him lay aside the meekness and gentleness which were His ordinary characteristics. They made Him take the law into His own hands, though in all other matters He refused to resume the office of a judge or of an executioner of justice. They made Him use a sort of violence, although even this was tempered by considerateness and equity, for He was less severe on those who sold doves, the offerings of the poor, and simply bade them remove the cages in which they were confined from the courts of the Temple.

3. We have therefore, in this action of our Lord, as has been said, an instance of His zeal for the honour of His Father, and of His high sense of the ineffable purity and holiness which must be required in all that dwells or passes in His sanctuary. Our thoughts pass very easily from this consideration to that in which this significant action becomes an image of the severity with which our Lord's Heart must burn at the sight of anything that is unworthy or unbecoming in those who are to live in the presence of God, and in whom He has, as the Scripture tells us, taken up His abode. St. Paul tells us that our bodies are the temples of the Holy Ghost, and we know from many other passages in Sacred Scripture that the hearts and souls of Christians are the chosen sanctuaries in which God

8 Mal. iii. 1, 2.

delights to dwell. If, then, our Lord, when as yet His mission was one of mercy, when He came in meekness, lowliness, and humility, not breaking the bruised reed or quenching the smoking flax, yet felt Himself constrained to lay aside His gentleness in order to cleanse the Temple with a scourge, how much more terribly will His zeal for the honour of His Father burn " like a refining fire " when He comes to the soul which has been the chosen dwellingplace of God at its last day, when He comes, not as Saviour only, but as Judge, and when the very reason of His coming, is that He may exact a most minute account of all our shortcomings, and punish with due severity everything which He finds unworthy of the presence of God? It is not a material temple, which is doomed to perish, which He will then come to cleanse and purge of all that He finds unbecoming in, it. It is not a temple in which God will dwell for a time only, and then depart. The souls of Christians which are presented to Him by their Guardian Angels at the moment of the Particular Judgment are intended by His immense mercy to live in His presence and sanctuary throughout all eternity, and He is to take up His abode in them and never to depart from them. They are to be for ever the homes of most holy thoughts, most burning affections of the purest and sublimest charity ; they are to be filled with the supernatural knowledge of Him and of all His works and ways, and to be flooded, without being destroyed thereby, by the ineffable ecstatic love which is the fruit of the Beatific Vision. No presence of God in an earthly temple can be compared with the close and intimate union between Him and them in Heaven. How can He, Who was full of zeal for the external purity of the material Temple at

Jerusalem, bear, in souls like these, which He has purchased with His own Blood and fed upon the graces which flow therefrom, with anything that is soiled, or crooked, or mean, or earthly, the miserable results of passion, or carelessness—with anything, in short, which may fairly move Him to anger on account of His zeal for the justice of God and the holiness of all that are to belong to Him?

4. On the other hand, when we consider what we may well suppose to be true as to the state in which many souls meet our Lord as their Judge, souls which nevertheless die in His faith and in His grace, we may well say to ourselves that He must find in them far more things to offend His most pure eyes and to provoke His anger than He found on this occasion in the Temple at Jerusalem. For such things are all the arrears of penance undone for sins confessed and absolved; all the penalties of sins, lighter in comparison with mortal sins, but still very displeasing to Him in themselves, which through carelessness and want of self-knowledge have never been retracted and made the subjects of sorrow—sins of habit, sins caused in others by bad example or negligence, sins of others in which we have shared, besides the immense and overwhelming multitude of sins of omission. The holy Psalmist cries out: "Who can understand sins? From my secret ones cleanse me, O Lord, and from those of others spare Thy servant."[4] No doubt many of these debts to the justice of God may have been cancelled in various ways before the moment of death; but here, again, we are met by the thought of our extreme carelessness in doing penance, in the practice of good works which may satisfy God's justice, in gaining indulgences, and the like. When we put

<hr>

[4] Psalm xviii. 13.

together the thought of the intense purity which is required for God's presence and the thought of the blindness and carelessness of many Christians as to the debt which they owe to His justice, we are certainly led to the fear that our Lord, when in this sense, He comes to His living temples, will usually be obliged to exercise very great severity, and we find it easy to understand that those who pass from His judgment-seat to their thrones in Heaven without experiencing the pains of Purgatory are few indeed.

5. Indeed, if it were not for the blessed knowledge which our faith assures to us of the ineffable mercy of God in the Incarnation of His Son and the Redemption of the world through Him, the thought of the infinite justice of God might well make us wonder how any one can stand in that terrible moment of the Particular Judgment. And in the same way, the glimpse of our Lord's severity, in His zeal for the honour of His Father, which is afforded us in this action on which we are meditating, might very well help us to understand the teaching of Scripture and of the Saints as to the very great sufferings to which the souls in Purgatory are subjected, in order to the full expiation of their faults and that perfect purification which is necessary to them to make them fit to stand before God for ever. The more fully we are enabled by the teaching of the Holy Ghost to understand, in part at least, the holiness of God, the more shall we be prepared to believe in the intensity of the pains of Purgatory. But now—to take up the thought which presented itself so naturally to us in the first of these considerations—there is indeed no vestige in the sacred history on which we are meditating of any help or even encouragement furnished to our

Lord in His work of purification by the bystanders or witnesses of His action of zeal. But, when we turn our minds to that other purification of which we are considering this cleansing of the Temple to have been a figure, we find that it is in our power very materially to assist our Lord, to share, as it were, His work with Him, and by so doing to gain His gratitude and the abundant blessings which flow from His Sacred Heart on all who in any way advance what He is engaged upon. Surely it would have been a most blessed-work and a service to our Lord which He would have repaid in His own magnificent way, if the disciples, or the priests and officers of the Temple, had thrown themselves into the work which He had begun, and removed with their own hands the articles and animals which offended His eyes. This is what we can do. For we can make the accomplishment of the work of purgation of the Holy Souls more easy and more rapid, by the many means which He has placed at our disposal of helping those blessed victims of His justice, who are, at the same time, the objects of His tenderest love. Their immense sufferings, far greater than any that we can either feel or imagine upon earth, may well enough move us to compassion, and make us exert ourselves for them as we do when we see our fellow-creatures in the agonies of death from hunger, or disease, or pain of any kind. At such a time we do not hesitate to sacrifice ease, comfort our own resources, even what may now or hereafter be most necessary for ourselves—the extreme needs of those who are bound to us by so many ties of nature and grace overpower all other claims. But it is not compassion for the suffering souls alone which is suggested to us as the motive of our charity by the action of our Lord of which we are considering. It is also a desire to see His zeal for the glory of His Father and the holiness required in everything that belongs to Him, satisfied —a desire that everything that is unbecoming may be swept away at once from the sanctuary of God, that the temple, in which He is to delight to dwell for ever, may be at once made fit for His Presence —"not having spot, or wrinkle, or any such thing," [5] as St. Paul says of the Church.

6. And, with regard to ourselves, it is impossible but that the kindling in our hearts of the flame of zeal for the purity of God's abode should very greatly help us to make our own hearts fit dwellings, as far as may be, for the Holy Ghost. The very consideration of the holiness of God and of the very great dishonour to Him which may be brought by the careless and indifferent lives of those who belong to Him, must in itself furnish a powerful motive for the avoidance of such negligence on our own part, and for the immediate cancelling, by means of the holy sacraments, prayer, penance, almsdeeds, and the like, of the debt which we ourselves may have contracted to His justice. The consideration that the soul of the Christian is, in truth, the chosen temple and abode of God cannot be deeply rooted in the soul, without, by the assistance of His grace, producing in us a readiness in that holy exercise of the Presence of God which is of such immense importance in the process of sanctification. These two fruits are, as it were, naturally engendered by the zeal and devotion for the relief of the Holy Souls. But we have not only to deal with the fruits which are given up to this devotion. We may also reckon on the bountiful goodness and graciousness of our

[5] Ephes. v. 27.

Blessed Lord, Whose part, as it were, we take when we aid in the purification of these holy prisoners. We may also look for an especial blessing and assistance from His own Royal Mother, the Queen of Purgatory, the first, as we saw in the former meditation, to exert herself in a cause like that of the sufferers there. We may expect that their patron saints, and indeed the whole company of the Blessed, will assist us in keeping our own souls free from stain, or in getting rid of any stains which may now infect them, as well as on the intense and burning gratitude of the Holy Souls themselves—a gratitude only to be measured by their sense of the awful holiness of God and of the severity of His judgments.

CHAPTER III.

The Devotion to Purgatory as an Exercise of Faith.

(THE HEALING OF THE RULER'S SON.)
St. John iv. 46—53.

1. THE miracles which we have already considered in relation to the Catholic doctrine concerning Purgatory, have shown us the great claims which the Holy Souls have upon our charity, the great delight which our Lord takes in hearing our prayers for them, and the extreme severity of the justice of God in consequence of which they suffer as they do. The next miracle in the Gospel history adds another general consideration to those which we have already set before us, for it impresses on us very strongly the value which our Lord attaches to the exercise of faith, which has so large a part in all our thoughts

and conduct concerning Purgatory, whether as to the relief of those who suffer there, or as to the pains which we may take to save ourselves from the same chastisements. This third miracle is related by St. John, in the place named above, and it took place within a few weeks of that visit of our Lord to Jerusalem at which He cleared the Temple for the first time. On His return into Galilee, He went to Cana, where the first miracle had been performed, and while there He received the visit of a man of rank and authority who lived at Caphar-naum, whose son lay at the point of death. The father had heard of the wonders which our Lord had worked at Jerusalem, and came to beg Him to come and visit his son, hoping that He would cure him, as He had already cured so many others. Our Lord, as we know, was always full of the most gracious condescension in such cases, and allowed Himself to be called hither and thither by those who had need of Him for themselves or others. But on this occasion He did not at once comply, just as He had not at once complied with the prayer of His Blessed Mother at the marriage-feast. He put the father off, as it were, with the remark, "Except you see signs and wonders you will not believe!" This was not a simple reproach—it was at least half a question. It was a hint to the father's faith, by means of which our Lord sought to raise it higher than it was—to make it as firm and penetrating as the faith of the centurion afterwards, who may have been a friend of the ruler, and who, instead of begging our Lord to come to him and heal his servant, told Him that he was himself unworthy that He should enter under his roof, and that if He only spoke the word his servant would be healed. The ruler does not seem at once to have understood our Lord, and he renewed his prayer that He would come down to Capharnaum ere his child was dead. But our Lord's first words had no doubt stimulated his faith, and had been accompanied by grace which raised it to a higher level. So, when our Lord told him to go, that his son was living and restored to health, he believed, as St. John says, the word that Jesus said to him, and went his way. He was met on the road by some servants of his household, who told him of his son's recovery at the very time when our Lord's words had been spoken. And the fruit of his faith and gratitude was greater than it might otherwise have been, for he became a believing disciple of our Lord with all his household.

2. The characteristic, then, of this miracle is that it is a practical lesson of that same truth which our Lord afterwards expressed in His words to St. Thomas, " Because thou hast seen Me, thou hast believed; blessed are they that have not seen and have believed."[1] If He had not wished to lead the father, in the miracle before us, on to this more blessed grade of faith, He would probably have granted his request at once, and gone with him to Capharnaum. We see here, then, the great joy which our Lord takes in the higher degrees and forms of faith, inasmuch as He took the pains to lead this anxious suppliant on at the cost of the trial which the first apparent denial of his petition must have involved. And we cannot doubt that the miracle is recorded for us with this intention, among others, that we may understand and practically use the truth of the immense importance to our souls of all the highest exercises of faith of which we are capable. It is better to believe without sight, than to see and believe. The most profitable exercise of this holy

<hr>

[1] St. John xx. 29.

virtue is that in which there is the least sensible evidence—that in which we have the Word of God for what we believe, and nothing else but the Word of God. It is in this spirit that the Church, when she commends the soul of a departing Christian to God, pleads for him his faith in the highest mysteries of the Creed, "for although he has sinned," she says, "yet he has always firmly believed in the Father, Son, and Holy Ghost ; " and in the same way the great Sacrament of the Altar, by means of which the greatest grace of all is conveyed to us, is essentially and pre-eminently the mystery of faith, of which St. Thomas sings—

> Sight and taste and touch are all in Thee deceived,
> But the hearing only safely is believed,

—the merit of faith being all the greater in proportion as the thing which we believe is not only simply difficult to nature and sense, but even, as it seems, contrary to them. We know, on the other hand, how often our Lord had to complain of the want of a perfect and, as it were, full-grown and robust faith, even in the Apostles and in others who were not His enemies. The unbelief of the Nazarenes stopped the full flow of His gracious miracles in His own town.[2] When He was asleep in the boat during the storm, and His disciples woke Him up in alarm, He rebuked them for their want of faith.[3] When St. Peter attempted to walk on the waters, and began to sink, he also was chidden as one of little faith.[4] And in these two last instances our Lord seems to find fault with His Apostles for the absence of a very high degree of faith, such as might hardly have been expected in them as a · matter of course. The very high promises which He makes elsewhere to faith in prayer, and such

[2] St. Matt. vi. 5.　[3] St. Matt. iv. 40.　[4] St. Matt. xiv. 31.

expressions of His as that in which He told them that if they had faith as a grain of mustard-seed they should move mountains, may be also cited as a proof towards the same conclusion. And, indeed, it seems only reasonable that God should give immense privileges to the exercise of faith, by which the intellectual part of our nature, the most excellent quality which we possess, is brought into subjection to Him at the command of a loving will.

3. It seems to follow from this that we may expect a special blessing upon devotions and acts of virtue in which the exercise of faith has a specially large part and influence, in which the things of sight and natural considerations are less mixed up than in others. Many beautiful sayings are found in the writings of holy men in special commendation of the Holy Souls in Purgatory, on account of the excellence of the charity which manifests itself in that devotion, and the like. But the point which, more than any other, belongs to the subject before us in the miracle now under consideration, is that which relates particularly to the very great exercise of faith which that devotion implies. In the case of the corporal works of mercy, and in others of the spiritual works of the same virtue, we have before our eyes the sufferers for whom we exert ourselves. Their miseries appeal to us sensibly, and a hard heart indeed is required to enable us to steel ourselves against the appeal to our natural compassion which is made by the sight of the hungry, the sick, the prisoners, and the many kinds of affliction which the Providence of God brings home to us in such cases. Again, there is a sensible satisfaction and pleasure in ·the act of giving such relief and help as are in our power to bestow. We see the misery, and we see and feel the healing

of that misery which the act of charity brings about.
We may, indeed, be able to resist the temptation
to self-gratulation, which sometimes arises at such
times, and our intention may be so pure, and our
Christian prudence and humility so well grounded,
as to make it easy for us, if we do not escape the
praises of men, at least to be indifferent to them.
We may accustom ourselves to turn all these acts
of charity into exercises of faith and of love to our
Blessed Lord, Who has so tenderly committed
misery in all its visible forms to our care, and tells
us that whatever we do to the least of those who
belong to Him is done to Himself. But in the
compassion which we practise towards the holy suffering Souls, there is nothing visible or sensible at
all to move sympathies, and there is no danger at
all that the mercy which we work should fall under
the eyes of men, and so, in some measure, have its
reward here. The doctrine concerning Purgatory
is not against reason—on the contrary, it is the natural offspring of a right and reasonable conception
concerning the justice and holiness, as well as the
mercifulness, of God. But it is faith that teaches
us the truth of what we might conjecture as reasonable concerning the existence of Purgatory. It is
faith that teaches us what we know concerning the
pains which are there suffered, and the expiation
which is wrought out by means of those pains. It
is faith that teaches us that we possess, by God's
infinite mercy, the power of relieving those pains
by means of our own prayers, suffrages, sacrifices,
and satisfactions, and the great benefits to ourselves
which we may earn by this exercise of charity.
The results which we may obtain by this devotion
are as unseen as the sufferings themselves which
we strive to relieve ; and although our hearts are

naturally moved to aid this or that particular soul which is dear to us on account of the ties of nature or love, we still cannot tell what the state of that soul may be, whether it is in need of our assistance or not. We have no visible success to encourage us, nothing tangible to be the reward of our toil. In these and other particulars the prayers and penances and alms and indulgences which we offer for the Holy Souls are a constant exercise of faith, in a manner and degree which cannot be affirmed of the other works of compassion and mercy.

4. It is clear that one great object which our Lord had in view when He seemed to decline the request of the father in this miracle, was not so much the good of the child who was sick as that of the father himself and of his family. He sought to procure for them the spiritual reward of a higher exercise of faith, and not only to find an opportunity of relieving the poor suffering child from the disease which affected him. We may see that there is the same end to be gained in the exercise of faith which our Lord requires of us in the devotion to the Holy Souls. It is pre-eminently a spiritual devotion—one which blesses those who practise it as well as those for whose sake it is practised, and especially in the way of perfecting their faith, and giving them, as it were, a firm hold of its truths and a clear perception of the realities of the unseen world. Those who are drawn especially to this devotion live in an atmosphere in which the great truths of the holiness of God, the heinousness of sin, the keen penetrating severity of the Divine justice, the purity which is required for Heaven, the value of time and grace, the power of prayer, the unfailing efficacy of the Precious Blood, the Sacraments, the Holy Sacrifice, and the Cross, are

seen more clearly and more nearly, with none of
the clouds of earth, the mists of sense, or the false
lights of the world, to veil them or distort them.
Many persons have learnt the true emptiness and
nothingness of the world, its pleasures and gains
and honours, by being forced either to suffer themselves, or to devote themselves to the care of the
sick or afflicted who have claims upon them. The
truth of the miseries of our present condition is
borne in upon them with wonderful power, and
they are enabled to walk along the common paths
of life with a new sense, as it were, of what is is.
It is less easy for such men to be deceived by the
emptiness and hollowness which impose upon the
frivolous and thoughtless worldlings around them.
There is something analogous to this in the case of
those who live very much in the habitual thought
of the sufferers in Purgatory, of the claims which
they have on our charity, and of the means which
are so abundantly supplied to us in the Church of
satisfying those claims to our own immense advantage. It is impossible but that such Christians
should gain daily in delicacy of conscience, in familiarity with spiritual truths, in courage under
suffering, in love of the Cross, and in charity for
souls. They must grow in knowledge of God and
of His ways, in contempt for the things of sense,
in keenness of discernment as to the pettiness of
many things which are commonly hindrances to
perfection, and of the immense power of sacramental grace, and in the spirit and habit of prayer.
Thus a silent change comes over them, and, in
reward for their charity, which has so little that is
sensible to feed on, they insensibly acquire spiritual
instincts almost as keen as those of the holy sufferers themselves.

CHAPTER IV.

Gratitude of the Holy Souls for their deliverance from Hell.

St. Luke iv. 28—30.

1. VERY soon after the miracle of the healing of the nobleman's son, who was ill at Capharnaum, we find that our Lord went to His own home at Nazareth, and there taught in the Synagogue on the Sabbath day. This is not the place to explain at length how it came about that, after charming His whole audience by the gracious words in which He commented on the passage of Isaias, in which His own mission as the Messias was described, He offended them grievously by telling them that He was not about to perform wonderful miracles to gratify them, as if they had a sort of right in Him, and by reminding them how the great prophets, Elias and Eliseus, had been guided by Providence to work miracles in favour of Naaman the Syrian and the widow of Sarepta, rather than their own people. The Nazarenes were " filled with anger," as St. Luke tells us, " and rose up and thrust Him out of the city, and brought Him to the brow of the hill whereon their city was built, that they might cast Him down headlong. But He passing through the midst of them, went His way." The Evangelist does not tell us in what manner it was that the malice of these Nazarenes was

baffled, and how our Lord delivered Himself out of
their hands.　There is a spot shown at Nazareth
which is traditionally said to mark the place where
our Blessed Lady looked on in agony while her Son
was being taken to the " Mount of Precipitation,"—
and we may feel sure that her tender heart must have
been torn with anguish at that time, somewhat like
that which she had afterwards to endure at the foot
of His Cross.　And in proportion to the pain and
and anxiety which she then suffered must have been
her relief and joy when she knew that our Lord was
safe, and that no one had any power to hurt Him
in the least.　This thought will be enough to supply
us with matter for meditation in accordance with
the general subject which we have set before us.

2. We cannot suppose that the deliverance of our
Lord from His enemies, in whatever manner it may
have been effected, can have come to Him as a
matter of surprise, or as something for which He
had not hoped.　But nevertheless it would have
been an occasion for Him to give thanks to His
Father for the care with which He watched over
Him, and the Psalms, which represent so wonderfully to us the affections of the Sacred Heart, are
full of expressions of gratitude for such deliverances.
The lives of the Saints were to be full of such
escapes and instances of God's protection, and for
this reason among others, it may be, that our Lord
chose to have experience of the like in His own life.
We may pass on at once to that which is the special
subject of these chapters, and find something in the
doctrine of Purgatory which may be illustrated from
this incident.　It is certain that at the moment of
death the soul has a sudden light flashed upon it,
which may be considered as an essential part or
condition of the Particular Judgment, by which it

is enabled to see in the light of truth the whole of its past life, and to form a right estimate as to each particular incident of it. Then it sees what God has done for it, and what it has in return done for or against God—the devices of His ineffable mercy and unwearied faithfulness, its own faults and shortcomings, the dangers which it has escaped, and the opportunities of grace which it has missed. The light which then streams in upon the mind will reverse and cancel all human judgments and estimates which it may have formed of these things. We must not consider it as entirely engrossed by any one of the vivid impressions and feelings which will then be brought home to it, to the exclusion of others, and we must always remember that the souls which die in grace are confirmed therein for ever at the moment of death, and that the love of God will take possession of the heart as the queen and ruler of all other affections. Still, we may consider one of these affections by itself, for the purpose of enhancing our own conceptions of its truth ; and so in this way we reflect on the feeling of gratitude with which the soul will then be filled at the sight of so many dangers, of which it was either entirely ignorant or only half aware, averted by special Providence, and favours of which also it had but little thought. Many souls will then wake up, as it were, like persons who have been walking in their sleep along the brink of a precipice, by a narrow winding path, with death on every side of them, and be appalled and aghast at the sight of what that path has been. They will see the dangers of what they thought almost harmless, the snares in which they almost of their own accord entangled themselves, and the malice and cunning of the enemies who were besetting them with temptations, from which they hardly cared to turn away. On the other hand, they will see the immense care of God, either in guiding them away from danger, or in giving them the means and the opportunities of repairing the injuries which they may have done to Him and to themselves; they will understand the power of sacramental grace, the efficacy of angelic guardianship, the might of Christian intercession in Heaven or earth, of the Communion of the Saints, what it is to have been made members of Jesus Christ and "partakers of the Holy Ghost." Especially in the case of those who have even sinned mortally, will there be a most keen sense of what it is to have deserved Hell after having been made heirs of Heaven, what it is to have been saved over and over again, as we may say, from the eager hatred of the enemies of God, in whose power they had placed themselves. It would seem as if this one thought would be enough to generate a love and gratitude to God intense enough to extinguish all desire of shrinking from the temporary punishment which the justice of God has yet to exact from them. The effects of this true view of what their life has been will abide throughout the whole of their time of purification, giving a special intensity to their love of God, even if the details of the picture then presented to them are not allowed to remain upon their memory with undiminished vividness.

3. The consideration which is here suggested may be used to help us to feed our devotion with regard to Purgatory and God's great mercy as displayed there. It will be found that a great number of passages in the Psalms, especially in these which are used in the Office for the Dead, or again, the other Gradual and Penitential Psalms, as well as those which are full of thanksgivigs,

such as the hundred-and-second and and the hundred-and-sixth, will seem wonderfully full of meaning if they are looked on as utterances of the Holy Souls in Purgatory, or of the Church in their name. And although such Psalms contain a great number of penitential and sorrowful expressions, of complaints, as it were, of suffering and the like, still the dominant tone in many is full of confidence, hope, and especially thankfulness. This may help us to understand the truth of which we are now speaking—the immense gratitude of the Holy Souls for their deliverance from the terrible punishments of Hell which they may have deserved, punishments the very worst part of which is that they are not accompanied or sweetened by any love of God or any hope in His mercy. Another feature of the passages of which we speak is the frequent reference to the enemies from whom the Psalmist has been delivered, to their malice and to their power, which have nevertheless been defeated by God's goodness. We shall have occasion to speak of the enemies of God and man from whom the Holy Souls have been delivered in the next chapter, but it may be well to add here a few thoughts concerning the way in which they are so frequently baffled and disappointed, contrary to all their hopes and desires.

4. St. Paul, in the Epistle to the Colossians, speaks in marvellous language of the triumph of our Lord over the evil Angels by means of the Cross, on which He took away and cancelled, as the Apostle tells us what was a sort of title which they had over us on account of our sins. He speaks of our Lord as " blotting out the handwriting of the decree that was against us, which was contrary to us ; and He hath taken the same out of the way, fastening it to

His Cross, and despoiling the principalities and powers, He hath exposed them confidently in open show, triumphing over them in Himself."[1] His words remind us of the image which our Lord used on more than one occasion, of the " strong armed man," who keeps his court and his goods in peace, until a stronger than he comes upon him and overcomes him, and takes away all his armour in which he trusted and distributes his spoils.[2] The intense pride and arrogance of the devils made it most difficult for them to understand how they were to be conquered and baulked by the humiliations of our Lord, and, in the same way, they are for ever being disappointed and spoiled of their prey in the case of Christian souls which are rescued from their very jaws by the grace which is the fruit of those humiliations. These victories tend immensely to the glory of God and of our Lord, and are perpetual occasions of fresh discomfitures to His enemies. Thousands of souls, for instance, are saved from them by the last Sacraments duly received, even after a long course of sin ; thousands more by interior graces, such as the power to make an act of contrition at the last moment, which are, no doubt, special favours on which no one could be so foolish as to reckon without almost certainly, by that very presumption, debarring himself from them, but which still are granted in a measure of which we have no knowledge to many sinners who would be lost without them, on account of the intercession of our Lady or the Saints, or in reward for some good work or service to God and the Church done long before, it may be, by the person or by some one to whom he belongs. Again, it may be considered as certain that God takes

<hr>

[1] Coloss. ii. 14, 15.   [2] St. Luke xi. 21, 22.

the soul out of the world at a moment when He sees it to be merciful to do so, knowing that if it lives on it will not be better, or that if its life is not shortened it may be worse. For the moment of the death of each one of us is entirely in the hands of God. In these and in other ways the malice of the enemies of our souls is constantly defeated, to their great indignation and confusion and disappointment, and to the great glory of God. All this part of His Providence, in their own case, is clear to the Holy Souls of Purgatory. This knowledge must be the foundation of most intense acts of love and gratitude, such as we find expressed in the passages of the Psalms to which reference has been made.

5. It must certainly be their wish, and also to the glory of God, that we should help them to discharge this debt of gratitude, by mingling thanksgivings for their deliverance with our prayers for their perfect and speedy purification. It is possible, also, that in many cases a want of thankfulness to God for benefits of which they were conscious, and a general unfaithfulness as to the full discharge of the duty of thanksgiving, may be among the causes of their detention from Heaven. When St. Paul instructs his disciple, St. Timothy, as to the practices to be observed in the Church over which he was set to rule, he says, " I desire, first of all, that supplications, prayers, intercessions, and thanksgivings, may be made for all men,"[8] and although the last-mentioned kind of prayer may more especially signify the offering of the Holy Sacrifice, this would certainly not take away the force of the injunction as to making thanksgiving in all other ways also for all men. We cer-

[8] 1 Tim. ii. 1.

tainly learn from the Psalms the lesson of uniting thanksgiving with supplication, and we may help, as well as gladden the Holy Souls, by giving earnest thánks to God for His great mercies towards them.

CHAPTER V.

The Holy Souls and the Evil Spirits.

(THE DEMONIAC IN THE SYNAGOGUE.)
St. Mark i. 23—29.   St. Luke iv. 33—37.

1. Two of the Evangelists, St. Mark and St. Luke, place at the beginning of our Lord's public preaching in Galilee a series of miracles—of which some are related by St. Matthew also—and which were worked by Him on the Sabbath Day in Capharnaum, the city in which, more than any other, He dwelt during His Public Ministry. It is impossible not to be struck by the contrast between the events of this Sabbath and those of that which may have immediately preceded it in order of time. Our Lord had almost openly declared to the people of Nazareth that He was not sent to them to work miracles, but to the inhabitants of Capharnaum. It is often found in the lives of His saints that a great danger and a signal deliverance are the immediate antecedents of great exertions on their part for His glory, and of remarkable successes in His service. Something of this kind may be noticed as to the wonders which occurred on this Sabbath, which came so soon after the attempt made on our Lord's life by the Nazarenes. The first of these miracles attracted very great attention, and was the

immediate cause why His name came to be pub-
lished abroad throughout the whole of the region
of Galilee.   This miracle is that which was wrought
on the demoniac in the synagogue.   The case does
not appear to have been one of those in which the
demoniac was ordinarily so violent as to make it
impossible for him to remain in his usual home and
among the society of men, such as we meet with
afterwards in the account of our Lord's visit to the
country of the Gadarenes.   He was allowed to
attend the services in the synagogue, and that is
enough to show that he was not in the habit of
disturbing . them.   But the great majesty and
authority of the teaching of our Lord produced an
unusual impression on all who heard Him, an impression for good or for bad as the case might be,
according to the state of their hearts.   To the
impure spirit who had been allowed by the permission of God to possess himself of this poor man, the
presence of our Lord was altogether intolerable.
His hatred of God and of all God's creatures, above
all, his hatred of any thing or person that bore a
close connection with the great mystery of Redemption, made him writhe in extreme spiritual tortures
at the near presence of the Incarnate Son Who had·
come to work out the salvation of the world. So the
rage of the devil overpowered him, and he broke
out while our Lord was teaching in a loud voice,
using the organs of the poor man whom he possessed:
" What have we to do with Thee, Jesus of Nazareth !
art Thou come to destroy us ? I know Who Thou
art, the Holy One of God."   Our Lord, Who so
constantly forbade the persons whom He healed to
make Him known, would not allow the enemy of
God and man to bear witness to Him in this way,
so " He threatened him, saying: Speak no more,

and go out of the man ! And the unclean spirit, tearing him and crying with a loud voice, having thrown him in the midst ;" as St. Luke adds, "but without doing him any harm, went out of him."

2. The great astonishment of the congregation who witnessed this display of our Lord's authority, of which each of the Evangelists speak, shows that they were entirely unaccustomed to such exertions of power. We know that instances of possession were by no means uncommon, either among the Jews or among heathen nations, and that there were exorcisms occasionally used by the Jews to which our Lord referred when He was accused of casting out devils by the power of their own prince. But, even though exorcisms were more frequent among them than we can suppose, there would still be something far more striking about the authority of a Teacher Who in His own name, and without any ceremonies, cast out the devils at His word. This seems to have been the impression produced upon the people, of whom St. Mark tells us that "they were all amazed, insomuch that they questioned among themselves, saying, What thing is this ? What is this new doctrine ? for with power He commandeth the unclean spirits, and they obey Him." It is difficult to think that even those who might live with frequent experiences of these horrible phenomena could soon become so accustomed to them as to be without terror and consternation at such sights. . For such facts bring home to us in the most appalling manner the truth that we live exposed to the assaults, and to a certain extent in the power, of malignant and relentless spirits, far more intelligent and far stronger by nature than we are, who hate us with a hatred which has no parallel in the creation of God, and who could at any moment inflict on us the most

fearful physical evils, if they were permitted to exert all their force against us. When they are allowed, in God's inscrutable Providence, to usurp that all but entire dominion over human beings like ourselves, which is seen in the case of possession, we might be tempted to think that our Creator had altogether abandoned His creature, and handed it over to its most deadly enemies, whom it has no chance of escaping or power of resisting. Faith tells us that this is not the case, and that even in possession the will may remain unbent and unconsenting to the awful wickedness which the devil may put into the mouth, or the terrible mischief for which he may use the hands. Still, we can imagine nothing in nature more absolutely appalling than the sight or hearing of a human being under the influence of possession. And then, when all this fearful tempest of diabolical passion is calmed at a word, and the seemingly irresistible might of the evil one is paralysed in a moment, so that he becomes at once weaker than a child, and reduced to the most abject obedience, the power of God is certainly shown in a way which has few parallels, and we receive a most wonderful assurance of His loving care and protection over us. We might think and know less of His absolute sovereignty over the spiritual creation, if we had not experience of the temptations, obsessions, and possessions, which He sometimes permits to His enemies and ours, all of which are quelled by a word from Him, or from His Saints, or by the ordinary and appointed rites of the Catholic Church.

3. The consideration of this miracle, therefore, naturally suggests to us the whole large subject of the extent to which God allows us to be assailed and tried by our spiritual enemies, the greatness of

their natural powers, and the victories which He gains over them in the weakness and humility of His children. The whole mystery of the Incarnation, and of Satan's defeat thereby, is the typical instance of a victory of this kind, and we know how much this thought of our great deliverance from our spiritual enemies seems to occupy the mind of our Blessed Lady and of St. Zachary in the *Magnificat* and the *Benedictus*. But we are now to ask ourselves what bearing the points of doctrine which here rise to the surface, as it were, in our consideration of the miracle before us, may have upon the special subject of the sufferings of Purgatory. Does the permission which God accords to the evil spirits in this life, to molest and annoy us, extend to the world beyond the grave? Are they to be our tormentors in Purgatory, as they are allowed to be the tormentors of the lost souls in Hell? It has been thought by some Catholic writers that the presence and sight of the devils form a part of the sufferings of the Holy Souls; indeed, it seems to have been held by some that the devils had a part in the infliction of these torments. We have no certain authority speaking on these subjects, although the lives of the saints and the chronicles of religious orders contain several visions which seem to support this view. On the other hand, other writers have thought it best altogether to deny that God will permit His enemies either to afflict, or insult, or distress by their presence and their blasphemies against Him the souls which are in that holy prison. These writers rely on the dignity of the souls there detained, and on the immense love with which God regards them, for arguments in support of their opinion. They say that the Holy Souls are, after all, victors in their conflict with the powers of evil, and that it is not becoming that the vanquished foes should be allowed to insult or annoy their conquerors.

4. Perhaps the truth may be that, as we shall have occasion to consider hereafter, there are very many and very great differences between various classes of souls in Purgatory, as, indeed, there are great and wide differences between various souls in Heaven and in Hell. In the case of those who have been saved by a late penitence, assisted by the sacraments of the Church, after a long period of sin, during which they have been, more or less, led captive by the devil at will, as the Apostle speaks, it need not be thought impossible that the devils should be allowed to be visible to them during their detention in Purgatory, perhaps to upbraid and revile them, or to afflict them by the blasphemies which they are continually hurling againat God. The torments caused by their presence alone would be very great and intense. Some of the saints, as St. Catharine of Siena, have been allowed for a moment to see the utter deformity and hideousness of these enemies of God, and the effect has been that they have felt that they would rather walk along a path of fire until the Day of Judgment than again endure such a sight. Inasmuch as Purgatory is the place of God's justice, a justice which is most particular and accurate and discriminating in allotting to every offence the punishment which it deserves, it does not seem unnatural that, as everything which has been used as an instrument or an occasion of sin is here made an occasion or instrument of punishment, the devils also may be made in some special manner such instruments to those who have been their willing dupes and slaves during life. There are some sins which are in a manner

more diabolical than others, such as pride, calumny, blasphemy, and the many various forms of unlawful intercourse with the unseen world. Even if we consider that the mercy of God shields other sufferers in Purgatory from the terrible anguish of such sufferings, it may be supposed that in such cases as those mentioned it is not always so.

5. At the same time it may be remembered, that even although the visible presence and activity of the evil spirits may not be among the ordinary pains of Purgatory, there is a sense in which all who are there detained may have to suffer intensely on their account. For among the pains which are there suffered those are certainly not the least which are the results of the neglect of grace, the misuse of opportunities, the yielding to temptations, and the like. The souls who are there suffering have been enabled to look upon the whole of their former lives and on the course of God's Providence towards them in the light of truth, caught from the close presence of our Lord at the Particular Judgment. Conscience then wakes up, and discerns everything as it has never discerned anything before, and if they have an altogether new intelligence concerning the mercies and bounties of God towards them, they have the same new intelligence as to the means of grace, the value of the opportunities of merit, the importance of every moment of time, which have been vouchsafed to them. The same clear light must of necessity show their sins and negligences and omissions in colours of heinousness such as they did not before perceive; and it will be by a gleam of the same illumination that they will understand, not only the true malice and hatefulness of the spiritual foes who have assailed them, their intense activity and

cunning, the perseverance with which they have plied their work, but also the treachery and disloyalty of their own want of vigilance and faithfulness in the service of the Master Whose sovereign goodness was assailed in every temptation and evil suggestion with which they were themselves beset. They are enabled thus to see that what seemed at the time the promptings of natural weakness or indolence were in truth the suggestions of the evil spirits, who despise nothing in their warfare against men, and count it a gain worthy of all their exertions if they can make Him be served imperfectly by those whom they cannot persuade to offend Him openly and grievously. In proportion as the Holy Souls are filled with His love and raised above the delusions of the world of sense, in the same measure must the thought of having so often been the occasion of unholy triumph to His enemies have grieved and cut them to the heart when it was presented to them at the moment of the judgment, and of their confirmation in the grace in which they have left this world. The saints of God even in this life, have a wonderful quickness in discerning the action of the evil spirits in matters in which no thought of them at all occurs to less enlightened Christians. It is Satan's great desire to hide himself, and he is content not to be known if he can only be successful. At the moment of death, at all events, the veil which has so often concealed him will be torn away, and it cannot but be an intense grief to those who suffer there to see how often he may have deceived them.

6. Thoughts of this kind may enable us to understand that everything that is a source of grief to the Holy Souls, in consequence of the details of their past lives, may be connected in their sorrow

with the evil spirits, who have always gained something whenever they have themselves failed in
perfect faithfulness to God, and whose malignity
and loathsomeness they have learnt for the first
time fully to conceive. We may elsewhere have to
draw out more in particular what some of the chief
sources of their regret may have been—a regret
based not merely on the offences which they may
have committed, but also on the loss of grace which
has entailed an eternal loss of degrees of glory to
which they might have attained. God's goodness
is so great that in Heaven every one feels the most
absolute contentment with his own lot, though it
may not be the highest lot to which he might have
attained. The Holy Souls are confirmed in charity,
and they too are so perfectly united to the will of God
that their state is one of content. But the love of
God which penetrates them does not destroy their
pain, which is founded on the knowledge which lit
up their minds at the hour of death and judgment
as to their own sins against that Infinite Love.
To deliver them altogether from this pain by hastening on their perfect purification is one of the
great acts of charity which it is in our power to
accomplish by our prayers and by the other means
which are given to us of helping them. And we
shall certainly advance our own claims on the
mercy of God and on their gratitude very greatly
by labouring for them in this way, while the thought
of the pain which they may be suffering at the recollection of the miserable satisfaction which they
must, from time to time, have given to the evil
spirits, cannot but make us more watchful, more
discerning, more ready to meet their attacks, more
perfectly awake to the truth of which the Apostle
speaks when he says that our warfare is not " against

flesh and blood, but against principalities and powers, against the rulers of the world of this darkness, against the spirits of wickedness in the high places."[1]

7. It would indeed be well for us if we could gain, as a reward for any exertions which we may make or pains which we undergo for the sake of the relief of the Holy Souls, something like the keen perceptions which they possess of the truths and facts which surround our spiritual existence and our state of trial. This would be an increase of faith, both in intensity and in the range of truths which it embraces, such as that which the Apostles once begged of our Lord. The knowledge with which theology supplies us as to the power and malice af the evil spirits, of the extent to which they are permitted to try us, and of their extreme activity and cunning, would then become a practical influence on our daily conduct, giving us a manliness, a courage, a disregard of trifles and frivolities, a readiness to suffer and even an eagerness to fight, such as become soldiers of Jesus Christ who have no time for softness, for effeminacy, for dalliance with the things of sense and with anything that can weaken us or fetter us in the warfare in which we are engaged. This is the true fruit which we ought to draw from the consideration of the great power and malignity of our spiritual enemies, when that consideration is balanced by the other truths which God has made known to us as to the assistance which He will afford us in the conflict. Taken by itself, the knowledge that we are the constant objects of the hateful machinations of the citizens of Hell might well appal us; but we know also that we have Him on our side of Whom it was

____
[1] Ephes. vi. 12.

said that " With power He commandeth even the unclean spirits, and they obey Him." Thus it is that
after the words which have just been quoted from
St. Paul as to the " spirits of wickedness in the high
places," we find the Apostle breaking out into his
famous exhortation about all the weapons with
which the Christian warrior is to arm himself.
St. Paul is speaking, as it appears, in the first
instance to the clergy of the community to which
he is writing, but his words are applicable to all
Christians. " Therefore, take unto you the whole
armour of God, that you may be able to resist in
the evil day, and to stand in all things perfect.
Stand, therefore, having your loins girt about with
truth "—the continual meditation of the great truths
—" and having on the breastplate of justice "—the
practice of all Christian virtue—" and your feet
shod with the preparation of the gospel of peace "
—for the preaching and advancement of the Gospel
is the first duty of all Christian priests, and, in
their degree, of laymen also—" in all things taking
the shield of faith, wherewith you may be able to
extinguish all the fiery darts of the most wicked
one "—using faith as a shield against all temptations
—" and take unto you the helmet of salvation and
the sword of the Spirit, which is the Word of God,
by all prayer and supplication praying at all times
in the Spirit, and in the same watching with all
instance and supplication for all the saints." [5]

[5] Ephes. vi. 13-18.

CHAPTER VI.

The Holy Souls and the Saints.

(HEALING OF ST. PETER'S WIFE'S MOTHER.)

St. Matt. viii. 14, 15; St. Mark i. 21—31; St. Luke iv. 38, 39.

1. IMMEDIATELY after the miracle by which the
devil was driven out in the synagogue from the man
whom he had possessed, the Evangelists tell us how
our Lord, when the congregation had broken up and
the people returned to their homes, went Himself to
the home of St. Peter and St. Andrew, taking with
Him St. James and St. John, and there healed the
mother of St. Peter's wife of a violent fever which
had attacked her. The circumstances which are
specially mentioned as to this miracle are these:
that the disciples told our Lord of the case, and
entreated Him to heal the sick woman; that He
went to the place where she was lying, stood over
her, took her by the hand, commanded the fever to
leave her, and lifted her up in such perfect health
and strength that she was able at once to minister
to our Lord and His companions at the meal which
followed. There are many points in this simple
narrative on which the meditative soul may well
delight to linger, such as the perfection of the cure,
the condescension of our Lord in His Incarnation,
and the necessity of communion with Him, as taught
by the power of the touch of His hand on this

woman, and the like. But, as it is our business here not to attempt to exhaust all the holy teaching which may be found in each one of our Lord's miracles, but to fasten more particularly on some point in each which may help us in our charity towards the Holy Souls and in our own preparation against Purgatory, we need go no further than the first circumstance which meets us as we consider the story in detail.

2. All the Evangelists who relate this miracle especially mention the connection between St. Peter and the person who was healed by our Lord, and it seems unlikely that this would have been the case unless there had been in their minds the thought that the favour was granted, in some measure, out of regard to St. Peter, as the favour at the marriage feast at Cana had been granted out of regard to our Blessed Lady. Our Lord may have desired in a particular manner to encourage and deepen the faith of His Chief Apostle, and He may also have intended the miracle as a mark of His favour towards him, and as a reward for the faithfulness with which he had hitherto followed Him and His word. He was about to set forth on the morrow of this day on the first of His great missionary circuits throughout Galilee, and He was about to require the attendance of at least the four of the future Apostles who are named in the history of the miracle. The home which Peter and Andrew were to leave behind them was in distress and anxiety on account of the alarming illness of the mother-in-law of the first-named Apostle, and it was in keeping with that immense tenderness of consideration which our Lord showed at the very same time that He showed His masterful authority and absolute power in commanding those whom He chose to follow Him

without delay, to leave that home of the Apostles full of joy and gratitude in the place of sorrow and mourning. Thus, if we pass from this particular instance of our Lord's most thoughtful and grateful mercifulness to the consideration of that mercifulness in general, the circumstances of this miracle suggest to us how great is the love which our Lord bears to His saints and His servants, and how ready He is to lavish His more extraordinary bounties out of consideration for them.

3. The power which God has accorded to His saints in Heaven, the great glory which He desires to derive from the honour which is paid to Him, through and in them, the importance in the scheme of His kingdom which belongs to the "Communion of Saints," and the charity which is, as it were, its life-blood, and the immense benefits which He intends to impart to the members of the Church who are not yet in Heaven by means of those who are reigning there, would furnish subjects for far longer meditations than any for which we can find space. The language which is so constantly used by our Lord in His Parables and in other parts of His teaching concerning the reward of His faithful servants is enough to assure us of all these truths, at least when that language is taken in connection with the belief and practice of the Catholic Church in all ages. For our Lord constantly speaks of power and authority conferred as the reward for faithful service. In one of His parables the faithful steward is to be " set over all that his Lord possesseth."[1] In another, that of the talents, the servants who have trafficked well with the sums confided to them are not rewarded in kind, as it were, by riches, but by the promise, " I will set thee over many

<hr>

[1] St. Luke xii. 44.

things; enter thou into the joy of thy Lord."[2]　In another, that of the pounds, it is the same thing; the servant who has gained ten and the servant who has gained five are both rewarded, not by having more pounds intrusted to them, but by power. "Thou shalt be having power over ten" or "five cities."[3]　In another place, our Lord describes the reward of His servants by saying that their Master "will gird Himself, and make them sit down to meat, and passing will minister to them."[4]　And thus we find that the memories of the Saints were presented to God from the first, even in the Holy Sacrifice of the Altar, and that their names are repeated before Him in the sacred Canon itself, as if He would have His own peculiar honour accompanied by honourable mention of their names also. We come to the same conclusion as to the immense power of the Saints from the consideration of the Calendar of the Church, whose offices and services day after day throughout the year are almost uniformly connected with them, the only breaks in such uniformity being the great feasts or seasons which commemorate the most important mysteries of the Life, Death, Resurrection, and Ascension of our Lord Himself, the coming of the Holy Ghost, and the great mysteries of the life of our Blessed Lady.　For the offices and liturgy of the Catholic Church are framed, indeed, with a view to our instruction and edification, by the examples of our Lord and the saints which are successively set before us, and by the continual commemoration of the mysteries of our Redemption.　But they also are framed so as to honour God in the way which is most acceptable to His Supreme Majesty, and we should not be taught

[2] St. Matt. xxv. 21.　　　　[3] St. Luke xix. 17–19.
[4] St. Luke xii. 37.

by the Church to honour Him so continually in His Saints, if the Church in Heaven were not honouring Him perpetually in the same way, with adoration and homage and thanksgivings of which ours here below are but the faintest echoes.

4. A question has been raised among Catholic theologians of various schools, as to the extent to which the Saints in Heaven use their powerful intercession in favour of the Holy Souls of Purgatory. To most Christians it would seem a strange announcement that there could be any doubt on such a matter, inasmuch as we know that the whole Church, whether in Heaven, on earth, or in Purgatory, is the kingdom of charity, and that one of the laws of that kingdom is that each member feels most intensely, according to his capacity and condition, for all and each of the rest, and exerts himself to the utmost of his power which God gives him for the relief or help of those who are in any way in need of them. We shall see that one of the reasons adduced on the negative side is founded on the immense force of this charity on the parts of the Saints, as if their prayers for the Holy Souls would continually empty Purgatory, if there were not some restriction to prevent it. The chief argument, however, is that the Saints cannot perform any works of satisfaction, and that therefore they cannot in this way help the holy prisoners of Purgatory. It is undoubtedly true that the Saints cannot satisfy for sin in the way in which the children of the Church upon earth can do this. But they can impetrate mercy and forgiveness, and the merits which they have accumulated in their lifetime may enable them to do so with greater efficacy. Besides this, their prayers can move God to accept for the Holy Souls the satisfaction of living persons; they

can move Him to inspire the living to help the departed, and give them powerful grace to do so : they can obtain from the Divine Mercy that the time of the detention of the Souls in Purgatory may be shortened, perhaps by the pain being made more intense. Moreover, the satisfactory works of the Saints during their lifetime, of which they have themselves no need, may be applied at their prayers to the Holy Souls in Purgatory. Certainly the offices of the Church and the prayers in use among her children imply that the power of the intercession of the Saints for the Souls in Purgatory is beyond all question. The difficulty about the emptying of Purgatory is easily answered, for the prayers of the Saints have no power of satisfaction, which is what is chiefly and most directly needed for the relief of the Holy Souls, and, moreover, the Saints, like the Holy Souls themselves, are confirmed in grace and perfect in charity, and therefore can desire or ask nothing that is not in perfect conformity with the ordinances of God. But, as has been already said, in the chapter on our Lord's first miracle, it is often the especial desire of God that the ordinances of His justice should be overridden by those of His mercy, which is set in motion by prayer. [5]

5. Although we cannot be certain to what extent the holy suffering Souls are already illuminated as to the glories and happiness of Heaven, still we may well suppose that they are able to see, in some measure at least, the innumerable blessings and mercies which they have received in the course of their life from the good Providence of God, and among these, the many benefits which He has

---

[5] See on the subject of this paragraph, Benedict XIII. *Trig. I. sopra il Purgatorio*, Sermon xxiv., where the references to Soto, St. Thomas, Suarez, and other writers will be found.

granted to them by means of the intercession and protection of the saints. They have also seen at the time of their judgment, how many more favours might have been won by them from God if they had been more devout to His servants reigning with Him, whose power to help us is so often made to depend for its exercise on the faithfulness with which we invoke them and honour God in them. In this way, while the Holy Souls are filled with immense gratitude to their heavenly patrons, and are burning with desire for the moment when they are to become their companions in the enjoyment of the Beatific Vision, in that ineffable charity which unites all the blessed to God and to each other in Him, and in the great work of praise, adoration, and intercession on which they are for ever occupied, they have also been grieved and pained at the little use which they have made of the charity and power of the saints, to the glory of God and the perfection of their own souls. The regret which they have felt at their own neglect of all the means of grace causes immense sorrow to these holy sufferers, because they know that it has deprived God of so much glory, and themselves of so much grace, that it has delayed their entrance into Heaven, and that it has made them for ever incapable of reaching that high place there which they might have attained by greater faithfulness. In this sense even the saints and Angels, and the Blessed Mother of God herself, and our Lord Jesus Christ have been causes of pain to the Souls in Purgatory—pain made up of a sense of ingratitude to benefactors so powerful and so loving, of the knowledge of their own immense loss, and that the measure of the joy and love which they are to give and receive in that blessed companionship in Heaven is for ever.

shortened by their fault. This is a pain which must be very keen to noble, generous, grateful, and loving hearts—a pain which, in the case of which we speak, may not be entirely cured till they enjoy that perfect contentment and ineffable love of God which reigns in every single soul that sees His face, whether its place in Heaven be high or low.

6. We may very well make this regret of the Holy Souls a reason for an increase, both in fervour and in frequency, in our own devotion to and honour of the saints of God. All Catholics, by God's mercy, know what it is to honour the saints, and very few indeed can be found who have not experienced the tenderness of their charity and the greatness of their power in various ways. But so it is with the other means of grace—there may be few good Catholics who do not use them at all, and there may also be very few who use them to the full extent to which God intends them to be used ; and thus the glory of God and of His saints is curtailed, and our own souls are deprived of countless blessings and graces. A great, thorough, intelligent, and familiar devotion to any one of the saints is a rare gift, which produces untold benefits to the soul; and the saints whom God would have us honour and love, and whom the Church proposes to our veneration and imitation, are multitudinous in number as well as indefinitely various in the special character of their sanctity and in the powers which they may exercise with God. A duty such as that which is here set before us—for our duties to the saints flow naturally from the position towards God and us, which He has allotted to them in His kingdom—should not be left to accident, but be a matter of study and consideration, and it is for this reason, as we may suppose, among others, that the

Church raises them to her altars, and sets saint after saint before us as the days of the year pass on. The names we bear, the places or countries in which we are born or are educated or live, the paths of life which we follow according to our several vocations, the lines of our studies or professions, even what seem the accidents of our career, which bring us to this shrine or to that, or make us need this or that particular grace—these, and a score of other circumstances, are so many suggestions on the part of God's Providence to attach our devotion to one or other of His saints. The ways, too, in which they may be honoured are many and various, such as invoking them, imitating them, visiting their shrines, venerating their relics, propagating the charities to which they have been specially devoted, helping the orders which they have founded, or making known any works which they have left behind them. All these things vary according to the circumstances of their lives and the peculiar services which God has received from them. In all these, and in other ways, we must pay to them the debt of gratitude and reverence which the Holy Souls have owed, as well as that which we owe to them ourselves, and we may thus secure their powerful intercession and protection in their favour as well as in our own.

CHAPTER VII.

Promptitude in Assisting the Holy Souls.

(CURES WROUGHT ON THE EVENING OF THE SABBATH.)

St. Matt. viii. 16-18; St. Mark i. 32-34; St. Luke iv. 40, 41.

1. THE miracles wrought in the deliverance of the demoniac in the synagogue, and in the healing of the mother of St. Peter's wife, do not exhaust the gracious works of mercy which made this first Sabbath of our Lord's preaching at Capharnaum so memorable in the Gospel history. The Evangelists tell us that, in the short evening of that day, after the sunset, " they brought all to Him that were diseased, and that were possessed with devils: and all the city was gathered together at the door." St. Luke, speaking of the sick, says that " He, laying His hands on every one of them, healed them." As to the demoniacs, St. Matthew says that " He cast out the spirits with His word; " and St. Luke and St. Mark add that, when the devils cried out, " Thou art the Son of God, He rebuked them, and would not suffer them to speak."

2. These miracles have one characteristic circum‐stance, which each of the Evangelists mentions, and which will be sufficient for our present consideration. In each narrative we are told that these poor sufferers were brought to our Lord as soon as it was

evening, after the sun had set.   The reason for this, in the minds of the people of Capharnaum, was that the rest of the Sabbath lasted from sunset to sunset, and that they were consequently free to do so much of work in the way of charity as was required for the bringing of the sick, some of whom no doubt had to be carried on beds or pallets to the door of the house in which our Lord was, as soon as the sun had set.   The twilight in those countries is usually very short, and there was, therefore, very little time for the transport of the sick from one part of the city to another, and for the leisurely healing of them by our Lord, as He laid His hands on each one singly.   But the charitable zeal of the good people of Capharnaum would not wait for the morning, and it may have been that this wonderful exercise of our Lord's mercy was carried on when, but for that, the whole city would have been wrapped in sleep, under the bright light of the summer moon, and it must have lasted far into the night ere the last poor sufferers had been relieved.   And it was well for them that their friends had been so eager and even so impatient to secure their speedy cure.   For we are told by the Evangelists that very early indeed on the following morning our Lord rose and went out of the city into a desert place to pray.   He was pursued by Simon Peter and the other disciples, who entreated Him to return, as every one was seeking Him.   But He bade them come with Him on the journey which He at once began, to go through the other cities and villages of Galilee preaching, and it does not seem that He even went back for a moment into Capharnaum.   As it appears, the sufferers would have been unrelieved, but for the eagerness and promptitude of their friends, who would not delay a moment in bringing them to our Lord, notwithstanding the lateness of the hour and the great throng at the door, so great that St. Mark, speaking from the recollection of St. Peter, an eye-witness, says that "all that city" was collected there. It was probably a warm summer night in June, and it cost them but little to wait patiently for their turn in that immense crowd, and when in the morning they learnt that the wonderful Teacher and Healer was already far on His way to other places, they must have thanked with all their hearts the quick charity which had taken them at once to His feet.

3. These people of Capharnaum, therefore, are in this narrative set before us as examples of promptitude in acts of mercy and charity, and we cannot be surprised if our Lord, in His joy at their faith and eagerness, poured out for them a very large measure of His bounty. The language of the Evangelists would almost justify us in saying that He left no one unhealed who could be brought to Him, and that a very large number of the sick and the demoniacs that were there to be found were brought to Him. It was the beginning of the great display of miracles by which His public preaching throughout the country of Galilee was heralded, and it is often the way of God to give at the beginning of His merciful dispensations more freely and largely than afterwards, in return for the fresh ready faith with which those dispensations are welcomed. However the facts of the case may have been, it is certain that the conduct of the people of Capharnaum, which was met by our Lord with so rich and magnificent a series of miracles, may be taken as a typical instance of that very beautiful virtue of promptitude which is so dear to God. Like other graces, it has a natural representative and image in the natural quickness in which some persons excel others so

much—a quality not always virtuous, but which enables those who possess it to do so much more in the business and conflict of life than others who are by nature slower. The promptitude which is a grace of God, and which may be said in some measure to reflect His own rapid way of working great effects and changes in a moment, is accompanied with the most perfect calm and tranquillity, which also are qualities which characterise the most mighty and the most instantaneous works of God. In some respects God appears to us to be infinitely patient and deliberate in His works, biding His time, as we say, and letting years or centuries pass away until the moment which He has chosen arrives. And then—swiftly, silently, and in a moment—His works are done. We are to imitate His patience and deliberateness, so to speak, by never acting until our path is plain and until we are clear as to His will, and then we are to reflect His swiftness in brooking no further delay, and carrying out at once the good work which we have conceived. For all that we have to do must be done in time, and time is a thing which we can never command— the moment passes away, the opportunity is lost. All the good that we can do depends for its performance and for its perfection on the assistance of His grace, and grace is another thing which we can never depend upon at a future moment if we do not use it while we have it. We cannot bid it wait or come again to-morrow. Thus, one of the great beauties in the perfection of the work of the saints is the swiftness and promptitude of their actions, which are guided by Him of Whom a Father says— "Nescit tarda molimina Spiritûs Sancti gratia." This quickness runs through the whole range of their virtues, and consists in perfect correspondence to

Divine grace in the use of the occasions of virtue which present themselves. It has nothing of impetuosity or hurry or fussiness about it. For just as the good use of the tongue consists as much in silence as in speech, so swiftness and promptitude consist as much in not doing things before their time as in doing them at the right time, and not later. The Preacher counsels us—"Whatsoever thy hand is able to do, do it earnestly,"[1] as if we had nothing else to do for the time but that; and our Lord bids us "take no thought for the morrow," as if to do so were to occupy our minds anxiously on things which have not yet come to our hand, and as to which we are not certain that they ever will come.

4. Among all the exercises and acts of virtue which are to be done swiftly and at once, after the pattern of God's works, there are some which fall under this head in an especial way, such as works of justice, of charity, and of fidelity. Thus not to pay wages or debts at the right time, to delay the fulfilment of a promise which we have made, or to put off an act of charity which concerns God, our own souls, or our neighbour's good, are acts on which the failure of promptitude may have very serious consequences. Thus we find St. James reproaching the rich and threatening them with severe punishment for keeping back the wages of their labourers.[2] Any debt that we owe to man or God, such as the debt of penance and satisfaction, or of a vow or promise, and the like, comes under that urgent instruction of our Lord in the Sermon on the Mount, where He bids us, "Be at agreement with thy adversary betimes, whilst thou art in the way with him; lest perhaps the adversary deliver

----

[1] Eccles. ix. 10.   [2] St. James v. 4.

thee to the judge, and the judge deliver thee to the officer, and thou be cast into prison. Amen, I say to thee, thou shalt not go out from thence till thou repay the last farthing."[1] And we know that when our brethren are in need or in pain, and it is in our power to relieve them, we are bound in all charity not to delay a moment, if possible to relieve their affliction. To delay help is at all events to increase their suffering, to add to its duration, and to run the risk of not relieving it at all.

5. These thoughts very naturally lead us to the application of the lesson here set before us as to our duties in regard to the Holy Souls of Purgatory. For in the first place, very many of them may be suffering there for a lack of this promptitude in the discharge of obligations, whether of justice or of charity, of which we have spoken. Many an act of devotion or of charity, or of restitution, or of satisfaction for sin, may have been delayed by them, and death may have found them with that debt undischarged. It is impossible that persons who have not habitually this grace of promptitude and exactness should have nothing to make up in the next world in consequence—and when we re- member that death, however much it might have been looked forward to in an ordinary way, is unexpected when it actually comes to the majority of Christians, we may be certain that most men will be found, in this sense, unprepared for it. But, putting this consideration aside, it is certain that our charity to God and to the Holy Souls, and to ourselves, binds us, even when there is no obligation of justice, not only to assist them in all the ways in our power, but also to assist them as quickly as possible. The obligation of justice, of course, is

[1] St. Matt. v. 25, 26.

still more serious, as binding those who are children or heirs of the departed, those who have received benefits and kindness from them, those whom they have instructed and helped, the priests who have received alms in order that they may say mass for them, or any who have lived upon the foundations which they have made. But where the obligation is strictly an obligation of Christian charity, the circumstances of the case of the Holy Souls plead for their help without a moment's delay. It is a very great difference indeed whether God is deprived or not of His glory by their complete deliverance even a little later or a little sooner. If it was an immense gain to one of these poor sufferers from disease or demoniacal possession 'at Capharnaum to have been healed or set free by our Lord on that Sabbath night rather than on the next day, much more is it an incalculable gain to a soul in Purgatory if its detention in that prison be cut short even by an hour or by a minute. It is not the certainty that they will be delivered some time or other that is enough to satisfy the charity of any one who is at all enlightened as to the pains of sense and of loss which are to be undergone there. We count it very poor charity indeed, in the case of human sickness or affliction of any kind, that is content with the knowledge that, after an indefinite period, that affliction will cease. And when we remember that our Lord has told us that we shall be dealt with by Him as we have dealt with others, we may be quite certain that, if by His merits and mercy we escape the flames of Hell, it will still be a terrible aggravation to our lot in the fires of Purgatory if we have any slowness or delay in relieving others with which to reproach ourselves.

CHAPTER VIII.

The Church on Earth and the Holy Souls.

(THE MIRACULOUS DRAUGHT OF FISHES.)

St. Luke v. 1-11.

1. THE two preceding chapters have shown us the truth that, although the saints of God in Heaven are so full of charity and also so powerful in His kingdom, as to appear almost to share His almightiness, they are yet in a certain way fettered as to the exercise of their influence in favour of the Holy Souls in Purgatory, by their inability to use that which is the most direct way of relieving those sufferers, because they are unable to make satisfaction for them. We also saw, in the last chapter, the special importance to them of seizing without delay every opportunity which may occur for their relief. We may use the next miracle of our Lord in illustration of a further and kindred truth, the thought of which is suggested by the foregoing considerations. What the saints in Heaven cannot do for the Holy Souls, in the way of satisfaction, which is their most direct need, that the Church on earth alone has the power of doing. It seems from many truths which meet us in these considerations, as if it were no exaggeration to say that the Holy Souls are in a special and direct manner commended and even left by God to the charity of the Church on

earth, all of whose children have the power of aiding them by prayer, penances, almsdeeds, fastings, and by the offering of the Holy Sacrifice of the Mass for them, while her Pontiffs have also the power of applying the treasure of the satisfactions of our Lord and the saints to them by way of indulgences. Much as the saints and Angels can do for them, still the official duty of their liberation, if we may so speak, rests upon the Militant Church rather than on the Triumphant Church, and the time during which they can be helped by us so efficiently, as well as with so wonderful benefit to ourselves, is just this short time of our life here, while we are in the possession of the means of grace and merit. This is the arrangement of God and our Lord in His kingdom, and that it is so is a great and urgent reason for us to exert ourselves to the utmost in their behalf. We may use, as has been said, the next in order of our Lord's miracles as enabling us to draw out this truth.

2. It was mentioned in the last chapter that our Lord, immediately after that Sabbath at Caphar-naum, which He made so notable by the many and various miracles which He had wrought on that day and on the following night, left the city and pro-ceeded, with a few followers, some of the future Apostles, on the first of His great missionary circuits throughout the region of Galilee. His chief occupation, during the busy weeks and months that ensued, was preaching, instructing, comforting, and guiding the many souls who came to Him, either in crowds or singly, for the precious lessons which He was commissioned to deliver. Great multitudes always thronged to hear Him, and large crowds, it is probable, followed Him from city to city, and formed a sort of continual pilgrimage that

waited upon Him. It was to such a multitude as this, that, after He had been for some considerable time employed in His missionary work, He delivered His great discourse which is known to us as the Sermon on the Mount. But although our Lord's chief employment at this time was the discharge of the office of Teacher and Healer of souls, He never neglected the exterior works of mercy and compassion. His miracles at this time were probably countless and very magnificent, but they were of necessity more or less of the same kind everywhere, and thus they have not been specially recorded by the Evangelists. Thus it is, that in our attempt at tracing His great recorded miracles one by one, we have to pass over this long period of activity, or, at least, the greater part of it. The next miracle, the circumstances of which we find specially recorded, is that which has been named above—the first of the two which our Lord wrought on the Sea of Galilee, is what is commonly called the miraculous draught of fishes.

3. The future Apostles were not at this time, as afterwards, collected into a sort of religious community, so as never to be separated from our Lord and from each other. Thus it was that at some short interval in the course of our Lord's active missionary labours—very probably after the delivery of the Sermon on the Mount—St. Peter and St. Andrew, with St. James and St. John, had spent the night in their former occupation as fishermen, and had taken nothing in their nets. On the morning after this our Lord came to teach the people by the sea-shore, as was sometimes His habit, and finding that the pressure of the throng was very great, He had entered one of the fishermen's boats, and delivered His instruction from

the water at a distance of a few yards from the
land. When the time of teaching was over, He
bade Simon Peter, the owner of the boat, to launch
out into the sea, and let down his nets. St. Peter
replied that they had already laboured in vain all
night, but that at our Lord's word he would let
his nets down. The result was that the nets now
inclosed an immense multitude of fishes, so great
that the nets were in danger of breaking, and when
the partners of Simon Peter and his brother,
St. James and St. John, whose boat was also close
by, were called to help, both the boats were so laden
with the fishes as to be near sinking. St. Peter
turned to our Lord in his deep astonishment, awe,
and thankful humility, with the famous words:
" Depart from me, Lord, for I am a sinner." Then
our Lord answered him : Fear not : from henceforth
thou shalt be catching men. They drew their boats
to the shore, and left all, and followed Him." That
is, as it appears, they once more started in His
company on a great expedition over the country,
the object of which was the preachiug of the
Gospel.

4. This miracle has many very remarkable features, and it is not our purpose at present to dwell
on them one by one. It is one of the unsolicited
miracles of our Lord—in which, for that very
reason that they were unsolicited and unexpected,
we naturally look for some deep prophetical meaning
and instruction. Indeed, it is clear that our Lord's
object was to encourage His Apostles, and especially
St. Peter, for the work which he was about to com-
mit to them. The failure of their toil during the
whole night before, when they had not our Lord with
them, and did not let down their nets at His word,
was providentially arranged in order that the

success of their fishing when these circumstances were changed might strike them more forcibly. The connection between our Lord's preaching to the crowds and the fishing of the Apostles was also providential, and the miraculous draught showed in a figure how fruitful and multitudinous was the effect of His Divine words on the souls of His hearers. He shows Himself, in the multitude of the fishes, as the Master of the whole creation, possessing power and dominion which nothing can gainsay, and disposing of His irrational creatures according to the behests of His sovereign will. In the spiritual truth which is represented by this external dominion, He is seen as the Lord and Master of the human heart, which it has been His will to make free, and to endow with the responsibility on which its eternal lot is to hang, and which yet is in His hands to draw as He chooses when He addresses it with the solicitations of His interior grace, and the external ministrations by which He chooses to work upon it. In both cases we see Him arranging, according to His absolute will, both the material and the spiritual creation; and thus we are led to the remembrance of the wonderful wisdom and lordly freedom with which He has ordered the whole of the universe, and the various functions and offices and mutual relations of the beings, His creatures, who compose it.

5. This order of the universe is one of the marvels the contemplation of which furnishes endless delight and instruction and thankfulness to the Blessed in Heaven, who understand how everything is in its place, how all creatures serve Him, how each contributes in its own way to the carrying out of the eternal counsel which He has decreed to follow. At His word all things were made, on His word the

Angels wait to perform their various tasks, on His will the whole creation depends. So at His word Peter let down the net, certain that He could give no command which was not the command of a sovereign Whom all things are bound to obey. It is His word and decree that has endowed the Church on earth with the great array of powers which she possesses for the benefit of the holy departed, and when we do all that lies in us to make this array available and fruitful, we are but carrying out His behests, with His word for the guarantee that we shall not labour in vain. He has committed this work to the Church, which has always been considered as represented by the barque of Peter, and with His word to encourage us, we may venture to undertake what is not in the same way committed to Angels or saints in Heaven, just as to them it is not committed to consecrate the Adorable Sacrifice or to absolve men from their sins in the Sacrament of Penance.

6. One point in the miracle on which our thoughts may fasten in connection with the subject which runs through all these considerations, may be that which filled the future Apostles with deep astonishment and awe, so as to frighten them by a close sense of the presence of Divine Power in our Lord, as it were, touching them, and by its very nearness casting them down at His feet, in the consciousness of their own unworthiness to be assisted and blessed by the Pure and Ineffable Majesty of His Godhead. It was the prodigious multitude of the prey that had fallen into their hands, that caused this effect, and the immediate connection between His simple word of command and the success which rewarded their obedience. This wonderful and preternatural efficacy of the labour undertaken at our Lord's word, when contrasted with the utter barrenness of

their former exertions, struck them, as it were, to the heart, and was, we cannot doubt a most efficacious lesson in preparing them for the Apostolical labours which were foreshadowed in this fishing. For success in all such labours, of whatever kind, depends altogether, not on any human exertions, though these must not be wanting to the very utmost of our power, that we may not do the work of the Lord negligently—but on the word or will of our Lord, Who reserves it to Himself either to prosper the work or not, according to His own inscrutable counsel. But there is one security for His prospering it, and that is to be found in His command. Now the commands of our Lord are expressed to us in various ways—sometimes by the injunctions of our Superiors in the Church, and sometimes by the ordinary instructions and rules and practices of that Church, all of which come from Him. To know that He has attached certain graces and promises to prayers or good works for a particular object in His Kingdom, which cannot but be very dear to the Sacred Heart, is to know that He desires and enjoins us, in the degree in which it lies in our power, to labour for that end with the prayers and good works which He has so blessed. And in the case of the Holy Souls we have so far an injunction from Him to do this— though it may not be expressed in so many words in any one place—that consciously to neglect it can hardly be less than an act of disloyalty to Him.

7. Our faith tells us that the holy realm of Purgatory never gave up its prisoners to the enjoyment of the Beatific Vision in Heaven until after our Lord's Passion and descent into Limbus. In this respect we may compare the great work of the full deliverance of the Holy Souls, to the draught of

fishes which rewarded the faith and obedience of the Apostles, when our Lord bade them cast their nets, and we may contrast that success with the comparative fruitlessness of all efforts that might have been made before the accomplishment of the work of redemption on the Cross. It is only at the word of our Lord that this work of zeal and charity can be carried out, because it is by the merits of His Passion alone that the gates of Heaven are thrown open to the faithful departed. The pious prayers which were made for the dead under the older dispensations of God might profit them so far as to procure their relief from the pain of sense, and their translation to the peaceful abode in which our Lord found the saints of the Old Covenant, when He descended among them from His Cross. But they could not win for them that perfect deliverance which it is now in our power to procure for them, and which in His Providence He mainly looks to us to procure, because good works wrought on earth have a power of satisfaction which does not belong even to the prayers of the saints in Heaven. To know this Catholic doctrine is to know the power which our Lord has placed in our hands with regard to the holy dead, and to know our power is the same thing as to know that He wishes us to exercise it. Thus, then, the word has been spoken to us by our Lord to let down our nets, to labour in every way that is in our power, systematically, continuously, thoughtfully, seriously, and at the cost of any sacrifice to ourselves, in the great ransoming of souls so dear to Him. He bids us all, according to our opportunities and capacities, to take up this work, not as a spiritual superfluity which we may indulge in or not, according to our tastes, but as a duty imposed upon us by the grea law of charity, and by the special power which He has placed in our hands for its performance. St. John says, "He that hath the substance of this world, and shall see his brother in need, and shall shut up his bowels from him, how doth the charity of God abide in him?"[1] And on the principle of this argument it may be said, that the knowledge of the need of the Holy Souls on the one hand, and our special power of helping them on the other, make it imperative on us, if we have the love of God, to labour in the great work of their release.

8. But the Apostles were amazed and struck dumb, as we may say, on the occasion of which we are speaking, not simply at the fact that their labours when undertaken at our Lord's bidding were successful, but at the amount and marvellous abundance of the prey which they had taken. Now there are good reasons for thinking that the great abundance which rewarded them in their fishing would seem as nothing if it were placed by the side of the multitudinous fruitfulness which, by God's blessing, will attend the labours of those who give themselves with all their heart to the great work of Christian charity of which we are speaking. In the first place, the prayers which are made for the relief of the Holy Souls are not impeded in their effect by any indisposition on the part of those for whom they are made. Such indisposition is the great reason why prayers for the conversion of sinners or heretics, or for the advancement of those who are already serving God to a higher kind of service and greater spiritual perfection, are often rendered comparatively fruitless in those for whom they are made. In the second place, every good work of every kind has a quality of satisfaction

---

[1] 1 St. John iii. 17.

belonging to it, and as this may be applied, if we so choose to offer it, for the benefit of the Holy Souls, they may receive daily and hourly succour from us, and our whole Christian life may be continually fruitful in this holy work. Again, the number of works which may be specially directed to this object is very great indeed, and very various, and embraces all the chief acts and duties of our religious life, fasting, mortification, almsgiving of every kind, prayer, the Holy Mass, Communion, the Rosary, the Litanies, meditation, the Divine Office, or the Office for the Dead, and a thousand other such good deeds. And besides the direct power of impetration and satisfaction which belongs to all these good works as such, the Vicars of Jesus Christ, especially in these later centuries, have been moved by the guidance of the Holy Ghost to endow almost every Christian work of the kind of which we have been speaking ¡with very rich and copious indulgences, which are generally declared to be applicable to the holy departed.

9. When we consider the abundance of the means for this work which are thus placed in our hands, and which by that very fact, we are plainly encouraged to use, we may well suppose that a faithful Christian who has made it one of his daily aims to help the Holy Souls to the best of his power by good works, prayers, and the gaining of indulgences for them, may be seized at the Last Day with a holy and most blessed astonishment, like that of St. Peter in the boat, when he sees the multitudes upon multitudes of happy souls in whose deliverance he has had a share. Nor will he need, then, to ask our Lord to depart from him as one unworthy. For the charity with which he has laboured for the glory and content of God and for

the happiness of these Holy Souls, will surely have
covered a multitude of his own sins, or perhaps have
won for him the still higher grace of escaping
from their committal. Nor will he have to be told
that from henceforth he shall be catching men and
not fishes, for the prey which he will have brought
into the net of God's ineffable and entrancing love
will be the noblest of the human race, the souls for
whom our Lord became Incarnate and died, and to
whom He has, in His infinite charity and wisdom,
decreed that the full fruit of His atoning sacrifice
should be applied by means of men like themselves
—whose love will be rewarded by a never-dying and
most tender gratitude from Him as well as from
them, which will abide as a special bond between
them, even among all the joys of eternity.

CHAPTER IX.

Duration of the Pains of Purgatory.

(THE HEALING OF THE LEPER.)

St. Matt. viii. 2—4 ; St. Mark i. 40—45 ; St. Luke v. 12—16.

1. AFTER the miracle of the draught of fishes,
our Lord as it appears, left Capharnaum and its
neighbourhood again for a time, in order to preach
in other parts of Galilee. We have only one
incident preserved to us by the Evangelists which
seems to belong to the period of this new missionary
expedition. But this one miracle was very remarkable indeed, both in itself, in the effect which
it produced upon the people who heard of it, and
in its spiritual and doctrinal meaning. Without

attempting here to draw out all that it signified with relation to our Lord's Person and powers, we shall, as before, shortly relate it, and then draw from it the lessons which seem most appropriate to the great range of truths concerning Purgatory and the Holy Souls there detained.

2. The miracle before us has been related by the three historical Evangelists, whose narratives supplement each other so as to give us a full picture of the incidents. It is remarkable, also, as illustrating the great importance of this miracle, that St. Matthew selects it as the first of a long chain of miracles of various kinds, by relating which he evidently intends to point out how our Lord showed His marvellous healing power on every possible form of disease, on persons afflicted by demoniacal possession, on the elements of matter, as in the case of the stilling of the tempest, and even over the maladies of the soul; such is the great lesson, as we may see hereafter, of the healing of the paralytic. The position which St. Matthew thus assigns to the miracle on the leper, of which we are now speaking, shows that the Evangelist considered it as of very exceptional importance and significance. Our Lord was in " one of the cities," St Luke tells us—one of those through which He passed in His tour of preaching—" and behold a man full of leprosy, seeing Him, and falling on his face," " bending his knee and adoring Him," as the other Evangelists say, " besought Him saying, Lord, if Thou wilt, Thou canst cleanse me!" Our Lord " had compassion on him, and stretching out His hand touched him, saying, I will, be thou cleansed!" The leprosy " immediately departed from him." Our Lord then laid on Him a very strict injunction, which St. Mark tells us He enforced even by threats. He was to

tell no one of the cure which had been wrought on him, but to go at once to the High Priest—who could only be found at Jerusalem—show himself to him, and then make the offerings and sacrifices which the law ordained in such cases, in order that the fact of his cure might be established by the surest of testimonies. It does not belong to our present purpose to draw out the intention with which our Lord gave this strict commandment. But the poor leper who had been healed was unable to keep his cure to himself. The blessing was too great, too sudden, too perfect, his gratitude too deep and intense, for him to be able to hold his tongue. So he began, as soon as he left our Lord's presence, to proclaim and spread about everywhere the miracle which had been wrought upon him, and in consequence of the notoriety which thus surrounded Him, our Lord was obliged for a time to keep away from the cities, and remain in the less inhabited and cultivated parts of the country. Even there multitudes came to Him from all parts, while the rest of the time, which remained to Him from preaching to them and healing them, was spent by Him, as St. Luke tells us, in prayer.

3. It is clear that the healing of a man from the terrible malady of leprosy, was considered by the people as an instance of supernatural power even greater than that which our Lord showed in the cure of other diseases. Leprosy was, and is, where it still exists, a disease belonging, in certain respects, to a class of its own, and it had a kind of sacred character among the Jews, on account of the merciful and significant provisions which had been made for it in the Law of Moses. To heal it was not only to do what was ordinarily impossible to medical science—as, for instance, to give sight to

a man born blind—but to cure a disease which was considered as especially an infliction of God, and, as such, reserved by Him to Himself to alleviate or take away. Thus it seems to have been that this, the first instance of the healing of a leper by our Lord, was considered as a sign of His Power more wonderful than the miracles which had preceded it in point of time. The peculiarities of the disease of leprosy, which made it so particularly fitted to be the special type of sin, were many, and have been spoken of by many Christian writers on this place. It was, for instance, a disease which proceeded from within, and affected the whole part of the body where it existed, making it outwardly hideous and loathsome from its corruption as well as the seat of a latent evil. In consequence of this, and of the other circumstance, that it was incurable and yet often lasted for many years before death ensued, being, in short, a kind of living death, it involved a more complete separation from the usual homes and friends of the patients afflicted by it than was the case with other diseases. We need go no further than these particulars in order to find a very useful lesson for ourselves in regard to the truths which we believe concerning Purgatory.

4. We are often very much startled by the manner in which the sufferings of Purgatory are represented to us in the writings of ascetical authors, or in the visions which are recorded of the saints and servants of God. The reason why we are so startled lies, perhaps, in great measure, in our neglect to take the whole of the teaching which is thus set before us, one part of which is needed in order to balance another ; and it lies partly also in our forgetting that visions must of necessity take the form of pictures addressed to the eye of the mind, in which

every detail has to be filled up in harmony with the principal point as to which it is the purpose of the vision to convey instruction to us. The points in the common teaching concerning Purgatory which are the most difficult for us to take in, are the extreme severity of the pains of sense—which are often represented in visions by the most painful pictures—and the very long duration of those pains. It is with regard to this latter point that the case of the leper may help us to understand the justice of God in dealing with the Holy Souls. The great misery of the leper consisted in his loathsomeness to his fellows, to the members of his own family, his wife, brethren, sisters, and children, in the separation from them which was made necessary, whether by that loathsomeness alone or also by fear of infectiousness in the disease; and in the great length of time, often the greater number of years in a long life, during which his affliction lasted. In all these respects the leper may be considered as an image of the Holy Souls of Purgatory, especially if we consider the doctrine which St. Thomas has laid down concerning the duration of the pains which are endured there. The Angelical Doctor teaches us that the severity of the pains of Purgatory answers to the quantity of the faults which are to be there expiated, but that the length of time during which these pains last answers to the greater or less degree of what he calls the " radication " of the fault in the subject—that is, the degree to which the soul has been attached to an unlawful object, and to which that love has been engrained in the soul. And thus, he tells us, it may be, that one person may be punished for a longer time than another, and yet to a less degree, and the converse. For the soul is more attached to some venial sins than to others, and thus some have to suffer a longer time than others, because when there has been greater adhesion to what is wrong, then there is a slower purgation.[1] This doctrine certainly explains to us how it is that many persons who die in a state of grace may have to remain a long time in Purgatory, even when the sins for which they are there detained are not more than venial. For the lesser faults to which we are inordinately attached are those which are habitual to us, those as to which we often hardly think of making a serious resolution of amendment when we confess them, and yet from the fact that they are habitual, they must amount to a very large number in the course of a long life. And yet these venial sins, though far greater in number than the mortal sins which have been confessed and absolved, are still not so heinous in the eye of God, nor deserving of so severe a punishment in the prison of Purgatory.

5. It may be useful to sum up very shortly the chief arguments which have been adduced by the writers who take the more severe side as to the question of the duration of the pains of Purgatory. Some of these have argued from the famous and very difficult passage in the First Epistle of St. Peter,[2] in which the Apostle speaks of our Lord's preaching to the spirits in prison, whom they suppose to have been the Antediluvians, who disbelieved the warnings of Noe. These must have been for very many hundreds of years in Purgatory. But it is easy to see that in any case this preaching of our Lord must have been addressed to those who were in Purgatory, if at all, before His Passion.

[1] St. Thomas *in Sent.* 4, dist. 21, qu. i. art. 3.
[2] 1 St. Peter iii. 19.

Moreover, the greater length of human life before the Flood must have made it possible to accumulate an immense amount of sins to be expiated there. Another argument which has more force is that drawn from passages in ancient Liturgies, in which prayers are offered for all who have died since the beginning of the world, and from the practice of the Church of allowing and encouraging the foundation of Masses for the souls of those who have been very long dead. Again, the same conclusion is drawn from the great length of the public penances inflicted in ancient times upon sinners while alive; and, again, from the very large indulgences which have sometimes been conceded. These indulgences, of course, correspond to so much canonical penance, and so are a fresh witness to the idea in the mind of the authorities who granted them, as to the length of penance that might be necessary for forgiven sins. The same writers argue also from the great intrinsic enormity of any single mortal sin, which deserves eternal punishment, and they conclude from this that when its guilt is forgiven, it cannot be wonderful that its punishment in Purgatory should be very long indeed. They add that many souls may pass out of this life in a state of grace, after living for a long time in a state of sin, and so with a great accumulation of mortal sins on their souls, which may have to be expiated in Purgatory. Then, each venial sin requires some punishment, and of these there may be almost a countless multitude, making up an all but endless debt to the justice of God.

6. They ask, in the last place, what is to be thought as to the question, whether the great majority of Christians do much or little while alive to cancel the debt which they thus owe? It is not

likely that persons who lead careless lives, who make an open profession of thinking it enough to aim at, to keep out of mortal sin, who approach the sacraments but seldom, and then without perfect dispositions, who hardly ever think of doing penance or making up for their sins by almsdeeds and prayers and acts of charity, can do much in the ordinary course of things towards paying the debt of satisfaction which will otherwise be exacted from them in Purgatory. It seems as if the souls who pass out of this world without having some debt still to pay are very few indeed, and there are a great many revelations among the lives of the saints which seem to imply that many, who are thought very perfect here, by reason of their state of life or of their devotion to good works and the service of God, are yet found by the Just Judge of all, before Whom they stand, to be in need of great purification, lasting for a long time. There are doubts as to the power of attrition without the Sacrament of Penance to cancel venial sin, and satisfactions do not apply to sins which have never been retracted. The ordinary manner of Confession of venial sins, especially of the lighter sort, and of those which are habitual, is often very much wanting in sorrow, even in the case of persons who approach the sacraments frequently. And there are many common defects in the use of the sacraments, both of Penance and of Holy Communion, which prevent those great fountains of remission from producing their full effect upon the soul. And the same may be said of the great treasure of indulgences, which also are only applied to sins which have been in some way positively withdrawn and retracted. All these arguments tend to show that there may frequently be a very long Purgatory indeed awaiting persons who are not simply sinners reclaimed to God at the last moment and saved by the sacraments of the Church, but who have spent their lives more or less in the practice of Christian virtues and the service of God.

7. Such pictures as that which is suggested by the foregoing considerations require to be balanced, as it were, by others, which might represent to us the manifold provisions of God for the remission of sins in its fullest sense, provisions which are within the reach of men 'while yet on earth, and which also operate most powerfully—by His gracious arrangement, moving the hearts of His children to the charity towards the departed which it is the great object of these pages to promote—in favour of those who have been careless as to their own best interests during their lifetime. Let the reasons for thinking that Purgatory is often very long indeed be as powerful as they are represented to be, they are only all the more imperative calls on our charity towards those who cannot now help themselves.

8. We may therefore consider the sufferings of these Holy Souls as figured to us in the case of this poor leper, especially in those circumstances of his case which have been mentioned—the loathsomeness and disfigurement which have passed over the soul, so beautiful by nature and so far more beautiful by grace; the pain of separation from the homes to which they belong, where they are loved and longed for with an affection which far exceeds anything that can be found upon earth, and the extreme and weary length to which their banishment may be protracted by the justice of God. It is quite certain that unless that justice be settled in some other way, the sentence of our Lord, that

they are not to come out "until they have paid the last farthing," must be executed. It is certain also that there are many very startling statements made by the saints and the ascetical writers as to the length of time during which many very good souls are sometimes detained. We have already mentioned that some Catholic writers have said that our Lord does not allow to the intercession of the saints the power which it might have, if the laws of His justice and their own intense love for all that He has ordained were not opposed to the immediate and constant emptying of Purgatory by means of their prayers. But it is certain also that our Lord has as great a good-will towards them, and far greater, than that which He showed at the prayer of the poor leper, and that His Heart is constantly saying of them, " I will that they may be set free." Only in this case it is not the sufferers themselves that are to make the petition, for they cannot ask for themselves. It is by means of our prayers and good works offered for them that this yearning desire of the Sacred Heart for the abridgment of their long time of banishment, of that living death which they lead in Purgatory, is to be brought about. And here again comes in the consideration of our own great advantage, which is involved in the charity for which the present life is the appointed time, The exercise of this charity may well win us the grace to be so careful in our own service to God, as to incur but little debt to His justice, or to cancel at once what we do incur. And our Lord will certainly remember His own promise, if He sees us suffering long in Purgatory, by returning to us in abundant measure the mercy which we have shown to others.

CHAPTER X.

The Holy Souls and the Sacrament of Penance.

(THE HEALING OF THE PARALYTIC.)

St. Matt. ix. 1—6 ; St. Mark ii. 1—14 ;   St. Luke v. 17—26.

1. THERE seems to be little doubt that the miracle of which we are now to speak followed very soon after that of the healing of the leper.   And the former miracle may have been intended, in the Providence of God, to prepare the minds of those who witnessed it or heard of it for the next great wonder which was to display, in a still more marvellous manner the power with which the Sacred Humanity of our Lord was endowed.   This miracle is one of the most remarkable in the whole glorious cycle of the works of power and mercy displayed by our Blessed Lord—not so much on account of the actual difficulty of the cure which was wrought, as on account of the circumstances which attended it, both on the part of those who procured the miracle by their faith, and on the part of our Lord, Who made the marvel which was evident to the eye a symbol and a proof of the other wonder which was wrought in the soul of the poor sufferer, who was brought to have his body delivered from paralysis, and who went away, not only in perfect health of body, but also with the sins, by which his soul had been stained, forgiven and absolved.

2. The circumstances to which we refer are stated by the three Evangelists thus. Our Lord had returned, after an absence of some time, to Capharnaum. He was teaching in a house—not, as it seems, the synagogue—and St. Luke describes the occasion as one of unwonted solemnity. He sat teaching, and, "there were also Pharisees and Doctors of the Law sitting by, that were come out of every town of Galilee, and from Judæa, and Jerusalem, and the power of the Lord was to heal them." It may perhaps have been the case, that they had heard of the new Teacher, or even of the miracle on the leper, which had attracted so much notice, and some of them may have been deputed from Jerusalem to examine into the claims He had advanced. "And behold," four men "brought in a bed a man who had the palsy, and they sought means to bring him in and lay him before Him. And when they could not find by what way they might bring him in, because of the multitude, they went up on the roof, and let him down through the tiles with his bed into the midst before Jesus." Our Lord, "seeing their faith, said to the man sick of the palsy, Be of good heart, son, thy sins are forgiven thee." This was a claim hitherto unheard of among the Jews. The priests of the Old Law could offer sacrifices for sin, and purify the people from ceremonial defilements—they could expiate external transgressions of the law, they could examine the leprosy, which was so perfect a type of sin, as we have seen, and declare it to be healed— but they had no power to cleanse the soul and and absolve the sinner. Nor is there any ground for thinking that the bearers of the paralysed man were any different from the rest of the multitude assembled to hear our Lord teach, as to their belief

on this point. It does not seem that they had any thought of what our Lord would do, when they laid the poor sick man before Him, with so much faith. Nor need it be thought that he himself expected more than the relief of his bodily ailments. The words of our Lord alarmed and half scanda-lised the Scribes and Doctors who heard them, but there was not at this time any open and pronounced opposition to Him on their part, and it seems that they said nothing except in their own hearts: "Who is this that speaketh blasphemies? Who can forgive sins, but God alone?" It was for the very purpose of showing them that God had given to the Son of Man power to forgive sins—a power which He was to leave behind Him in His Church, to be administered for the benefit of the faithful by men like themselves—that our Lord had used words which were so startling to them: "Which Jesus presently knowing in His spirit, that they so thought within themselves, He saith to them, Why think you these things in your hearts? Which is easier to say to the sick of the palsy, Thy sins are forgiven thee, or to say, Arise, take up thy bed and walk? But that you may know that the Son of Man hath power on earth to forgive sins, He saith to the sick of the palsy, I say to thee, Arise, take up thy bed and go into thy house. And immediately he arose, and taking up his bed went his way in the sight of all, so that all wondered and glorified God, saying, We never saw the like," or as St. Matthew puts it, " glorified God that gave such power to men."

3. This great miracle contains so many heads of sacred doctrine, that it would be impossible for us to attempt to exhaust its teaching in a few pages. But, as before, we may select one or two points which have a special bearing on the general subject

of these chapters. In the first place, then, it is clear that if the disease of leprosy represents the state of sin in the respect of the loathsomeness which it brings with it, the length of time during which its punishment may be continued in the justice of God, and in the distressing separation, which it inflicts upon those who have to suffer for it, from their homes in Heaven and the loving society which awaits them there, this affliction of paralysis may well be taken as a figure of the state of sin in other respects—especially that of the loss of the power of motion and sensation which it induces, reducing its victims to that helpless condition which is represented here by the man who could not move himself to seek the aid of our Lord's merciful power, so that he had need of the charity of others to make him capable of receiving the benefit which he required. This is especially true of the effect of sin unatoned for in this life, and which has to be paid for in the fires of Purgatory. For it is a part of God's just decree concerning such sufferers, that they cannot even pray for themselves. We therefore are the bearers of these blessed souls of whose aid they have need, in order that the mercy of God may be extended to them. And indeed their state may well be called a state of paralysis, inasmuch as they live indeed to God, and have a number of wonderful capacities of enjoying Him and exercising the functions of the life which is that of the saints and Angels in Heaven, and yet they are for the time as dead persons, incapable of motion or sensation. All the glorious operations of the state of beatitude are theirs as it were in germ, and yet they are not allowed to develop their powers or to enter on their possession. And if it moves us with compassion to see a man in the full bloom and beauty of his age, struck down by paralysis and fastened in utter help-lessness to a sick-bed, unable to move or use the limbs and faculties which yet remain in their entirety to him, surely it is much more pitiable to see souls that might be enjoying God and glorifying Him by that full and perfect intensity of spiritual activity in which the life of the saints consists, unable to move or feel, as it were, themselves deprived of so much strength and enjoyment, and making the whole company of Heaven wait for the glory which God is to derive from their entrance into the state of beatitude which He has prepared for them. We may surely well call those four bearers blessed, who by their faith enabled our Lord to work this miracle, so beautiful in itself and so full of spiritual and doctrinal teaching. And yet is their blessing greater than that which is within the reach of us all, who have so many means of bringing these helpless but most dear victims of God's justice within the range of His merciful indulgence, ever so ready to pour itself out upon them, if we give it the opportunity? Some pious persons, who are moved especially to give themselves to the relief of the Holy Souls, make it a rule, if possible, to exert themselves in favour of these prisoners of the justice of God in four several ways, as if to honour our Lord by com-memorating the four bearers in this miracle—they remember the Holy Souls by offering for them at least a part of the satisfaction of the Mass which they say or hear, or the Holy Communion which they receive, they give them a share in their prayers, in their good works or almsdeeds, and in their penances or sufferings of whatever kind—under which head Indulgences may be included—voluntary or involuntary. And in this way they do something every day towards performing this work of mercy, of which we have so beautiful an image in the act of faith of these four bearers of the paralytic.

4. But it must be remembered that the great object of our Lord in the performance of this miracle seems to have been to unfold to those who witnessed it, many of whom were among the appointed teachers of the holy people, the great doctrine of the power of the remission of sins, which had been conferred on His Sacred Humanity by God the Father. We should not, therefore, apply to the subject of Purgatory the peculiar lesson of this miracle, unless we considered the bearing of that doctrine on the state and sufferings of those who are detained there. We have already said that a great part of the interior sufferings of the Holy Souls must probably consist in their deep regret for the many opportunities of grace which they have let pass without availing themselves of them. Their love of God makes them grieve over all that has separated them from Him, and especially over every neglect of which they have been guilty of His tender provisions for their spiritual benefit. And certainly to none of the blessed ordinances of God can this regret apply with greater force than to the holy Sacrament of Penance. Well indeed may the people who witnessed the miracle, when they considered the power of which it proved the existence, have given glory to God Who had given such power to men ! For it is certain that a right and perfect use of the holy sacrament of which we are speaking would enable us to obtain such absolute forgiveness of our sins, in the sense in which our Lord used the terms, as to reduce to very little indeed the claims of the justice of God against us in the next world. When we meditated on the miracle of the Healing of the

Leper, we had occasion to remind ourselves of the great number of lighter sins, as we count them, of which we may daily make ourselves guilty, and of which we do not receive pardon here in the sense of remission of the pain due for them, because they are sins of habit or character, hardly noticed or not seriously retracted and repented of. For there must be some sorrow where there has been any wilfulness in the sin which is confessed, some distinct and true desire and intention to refrain from it for the future, if it is to be cancelled entirely, both as to its guilt and as to the penalty due to it. But what is the reason why these sins, which we call venial, are not got rid of altogether as to their debt to God's justice by persons who are frequently approaching the sacraments, especially the Sacrament of Penance ? It is because that sacrament is not perfectly used, because it is shorn of some of its effects and of the power which our Lord has imparted to it, on account of the careless or hasty or otherwise imperfect manner in which we use it.

5. It may be well to insist on this with ourselves. It is quite possible that every confession which is made may be so made that the sins which are then brought to the sacred tribunal may be entirely cancelled, not only as to their guilt, but also as to their pain. It is the intention of our Lord that so it should be, partly by virtue of the intensity of the sorrow which is applied to the sins confessed, partly by virtue of the absolution, and the satisfactory power which is communicated to the works enjoined by the priest by way of penance, which power is greatly extended by the general words with which the form of absolution concludes, by which whatever good we do, and whatever evil we bear with

patience, are raised, as it were, to the rank of satisfactory works. If persons who have been in the habit of frequenting the sacraments find themselves with a great debt to pay to the justice of God, it must be on account of the difficulty of using the sacraments perfectly, which comes from our own dulness and want of fervour, and of our neglect to make very frequent and very fervent acts of contrition, and to use the many means, short of the Sacrament of Penance, which God has given us for obtaining the remission of lighter sins. If a man who had daily access to the treasury of a most wealthy king had only taken each day so small a quantity therefrom as just to keep himself alive, instead of taking what might pay off all his obligations and make him altogether free from the debts of the past, he would only have himself to blame, if on a sudden emergency he found himself liable to accumulated demands without the power to meet them. ·Such a man would be a very inadequate image of the Christian soul which has been constantly using the sacraments, and yet has never taken their full benefit. And yet this is the reproach which the Holy Souls of Purgatory must in so many cases have had to make against themselves. They have seen that a little more care in self-examination, a little more earnestness in their contrition for the sins which they confessed, a little more particularity and sincerity in their resolutions against the smaller faults which were habitual to them, a little more zeal in the performance of their satisfactions, and in suffering patiently the chastisements which the hand of Providence brought home to them day by day, would in the course of time have made an immense difference in diminishing gradually and surely the amount which they owed to the justice of God, Who is now forced by them, rather than by His own will, to punish them for a long time and with much severity in Purgatory, for sins which they might most easily have expiated altogether by their familiar use of the Sacrament of Penance.

6. There is also another point, connected with the Sacrament of Penance, to which it may be well to turn our thoughts for a moment while we are meditating on this miracle, although we shall probably have to speak about it at full length in a later chapter. The power of the Church to apply to the cancelling of the pain due to sin the satisfactions of our Lord and the Saints, on which power the whole system of Indulgences depends, must be considered as included in the words of our Lord, when He said that the Son of Man had power on earth to forgive sins; and when Catholic theologians treat of the Sacrament of Penance, they do not conclude the subject without speaking of Indulgences. We may therefore add this thought to those which have been already hinted at—the thought how deeply the Holy Souls must regret the little use which they may have made of this immense benefit, the small space which the goodness of God in allowing it may have occupied in their minds, the scanty gratitude which they may have rendered to Him for it, and the very slight efforts which they have made to understand and appreciate it, and to enrich themselves from the treasury which is thus laid open to them. This is one of the points as to which there is the most difference between the estimate of things which is formed in Purgatory and that which is common even among good Christians on earth. And if the Holy Souls are filled with sorrow and compunction at any neglect of God's merciful provisions of which they may have been themselves guilty, it is clear

that their sorrow must extend to the little thought which they may have given to their own power, while alive, of relieving others, then in Purgatory, by this wonderful means.

7. Thoughts like these help to show us how very profitable to our own souls is the devotion which has for its object the relief of the sufferers in Purgatory. It is hardly possible for any one to take their case to heart without being moved strongly to greater care for himself. The Holy Souls, whom we aid to the best of our power, will also aid us, both when they reach Heaven and before, and in this way also, our charity will turn to our own great benefit. They will pray for us, that we may have greater grace to be most careful in our approaches to the sacraments, and every step that we make in the more perfect use of the means of grace will make us more powerful to aid them, because we shall be nearer and dearer to God, and so able to win more from His ineffable love and mercy.

CHAPTER XI.

The Application of our Suffrages to certain Souls in particular.

(CURE OF THE MAN AT THE PROBATIC POOL.)
St. John v. 1—15.

1. IT appears that, not long after the miracle which has last been mentioned—the healing of the paralytic man who was let down in his bed into the inner court of the house in which our Lord was teaching—He went up to Jerusalem for the feast of the Pasch. It was now, then, just a year since He had taken on Himself publicly the office of Teacher and Prophet in the Holy City itself, by the wonderful exercise of authority which had been shown in the act of cleansing the Temple. By far the greater part of this year had been spent by Him, as we have seen, in Galilee, at a distance from Jerusalem—from the neighbourhood of which He had retired, in order not to provoke too soon or too much the enmity of the Jewish authorities. At the time, however, at which we have now arrived, our Lord was following what we should call a bolder course, and was claiming for Himself both by act and word, an authority which was not likely to be at once recognised by men so full of ambition and pride as the Chief Priests and Pharisees at Jerusalem. A notable example of a claim to authority hitherto

unheard of, is that on which we meditated in the last chapter—His claim to forgive sins upon earth. The miracle of which we are now to speak is another such instance, at least in so far as it asserted an entire independence of the usual interpretation put by the Jews and their teachers on the law of the Sabbath. When our Lord came to explain, in answer to His accusers, the grounds of His conduct, we shall see that He put forward claims which went far beyond this.

2. It was, then, at this great feast, the second in the course of His Public Ministry, that our Lord went on the Sabbath day to a famous pool of water at Jerusalem, around which there were five porticoes or colonnades, under which a large multitude of sick persons, suffering from almost every form of disease, were lying, in expectation of an opportunity which might possibly lead, in the case of any one, to his relief. For an Angel went down at certain times into the pool, and moved the water, and then the first person who stepped into it after the movement was healed of whatever the disease might be which afflicted him. It was but a chance, for only one among so many could be healed, and we may well imagine how that large collection of sufferers must have moved the tender and compassionate Heart of our Lord. If it had been in Galilee they would probably have all called on Him with one voice to aid them as soon as He appeared; but in Jerusalem He was very little known, and He seems to have entered the place quietly and without any crowd of companions which might attract notice. The miracle which He was about to perform was altogether unsolicited. He did not require prayer or faith, except as far as the latter was implied in the

obedience of the man whom He selected as the subject of His miraculous cure. This miracle, then, like many others, was wrought by our Lord for a special purpose of His own, just as He had turned to a like purpose the incidents of the last-mentioned miracle, and made the faith of the bearers of the paralytic give Him an occasion for proving His authority as to the forgiveness of sins. Thus, He did not heal all or many of those who lay around this pool at Jerusalem, but He selected a single sufferer as the object of His compassion. Again, He did not simply heal him, and then pass away; He laid on him a special injunction to take up his bed and carry it to his home—an act which was certain to attract attention at any time, but which on that particular day was also certain to cause a kind of scandal, inasmuch as it was an act which was considered to be forbidden, and a breach of the Divine commandment. This act had the effect which our Lord must have foreseen. It brought upon Him the complaints and hostility of the Jewish rulers, and gave Him an occasion for setting forth to them the proofs of His Divine mission in a long discourse which St. John relates, and for the sake of which, according to His usual principle in the composition of his Gospel, it seems to have been that he inserted the account of the miracle itself.

3. The particular truth which our Lord meant to assert by means of this miracle does not concern us at this moment, for we are engaged in the consideration of His miracles only as far as they may be used as illustrations of the Catholic doctrine of Purgatory. But there is one particular circumstance about the miracle which will furnish us with abundant matter for thought in respect of that doctrine. It has already been said that our Lord, Who might,

if it had so pleased Him, have healed at a word the whole of the crowd of sufferers who were waiting for the movement of the waters, chose one only as the object of His special compassion. We have no right at all to think that this one person was more deserving of so high a favour than many others, on account of any special sanctity, or resignation to God's will, or contrition for the sins, which may have been punished by his Providential affliction. But two circumstances in the case are mentioned, one by himself, and the other by the Evangelist, which seem to distinguish him from the rest of the crowd : and, as these circumstances are specially mentioned, it is not presumptuous to suppose that they may have had weight in his favour in the mind of our Lord Himself. In the first place St. John tells us that he had been afflicted by his infirmity for as many as thirty-eight years, and that our Lord saw him lying there, and knew that he had been a long time. In the second place, the sick man himself furnishes us with another circumstance, when he tells our Lord that he had no man, when the water was troubled, to put him into the pool. Thus he had been a sufferer for a very great number of years, and he was also remarkably helpless and left altogether to himself. It may have been the case that our Lord selected him from the crowd on account of both these circumstances ; certainly it seems as if St. John meant us to understand that the first of them influenced the merciful tenderness of His Sacred Heart. Thus we have in this miracle both the principle of a selection of one from among many for the objects of Christian charity, and also the grounds on which, among others, preference may be given to this or that particular case—the length of time during which the suffering has been protracted, and the helpless and friendless state of some individual sufferer. From each of these heads we may derive instruction as to the application of our spiritual alms in favour of the Holy Souls who are suffering in Purgatory.

4. In the first place, then, it is certain that the satisfactions which may be applied to the relief of these holy sufferers are limited in their efficacy, either in themselves, as is the case with works which are simply our own, though wrought through God's grace, or in the decrees and arrangements of God Himself, as is the case with the satisfactory power of the Holy Sacrifice, infinite in itself, but not so in its application. Thus, when we visit in spirit this pool of holy punishment, by which so great a multitude of souls are lying, as it were, waiting for the movement of the refreshing waters of God's mercy, we may feel like persons who have but one boon to give, and who should therefore be guided in its application by some reasons of justice or wisdom. Our Lord, if he had chosen, might have healed at once all the suffering crowd; but He did not so choose. In like manner, the application of His meritorious satisfactions to the Holy Souls, which is intrusted by Him to us, is limited by His own decree. The choice as to their application is left by Him very much in our hands for many wise and Divine reasons. All these reasons we need not attempt to fathom. It is enough to say, out of other things which might be said, that the thoughtful and careful application of our good works to particular intentions is a thing very pleasing to Him. It helps on devotion, it fosters charity, it gives us many opportunities of making reparation, or of showing gratitude and

love, and every such act strengthens in the soul the virtue of which it is an act, while at the same time it forms a new link in that marvellous chain of charity by which our whole life is in His intention bound together, the full effect of which is to knit us one to another in the Communion of Saints. It is not contrary to this truth that it is often our best wisdom to pray in general for the conversion of sinners, or the advancement of the good in perfection, or for the souls in Purgatory, without any specification of this or that person. These practices work in the same way, and Christian piety has room both for one and for the other. The Church teaches us to be always honouring God in His great mercies to us' through our Lord, but she also sets before us one by one the mysteries of His Life and Passion, and of their fruits. She teaches us to honour all His Saints in one great festival, and day by day throughout the year she sets before us, one by one, the same Saints in order, as if for the moment our desire was to be to honour that particular Saint alone. We gain in devotion if we offer Masses or Communions or Indulgences or good works for the Holy Souls in general, or for those in particular for whom we are especially bound to pray, or for those whom it may please our Lady or some one of the Saints that we should especially succour in this way; and in this last case we knit ourselves each time by a fresh tie of love, not only to the souls for whom we intercede, but also to our Blessed Lady or to the Saints in whose honour we offer that good work. Thus the whole spiritual doctrine of the value of special intentions in all that we do for the honour of God or the good of souls is brought before us by this instance in which our Lord selected one poor sufferer, out of so large a multitude, as the subject of the work of mercy which He was about to do in the course of that great series of manifestations of Himself which was so essential to the accomplishment of His work in the world. It was in accordance with the çounsels of His wisdom that one single person should be selected; but He did not, as an ordinary man might have done, take the first person on whom His eyes might fall and work the miracle on him. He made a selection according to the instincts and judgments of His own ineffably wise and loving Heart.

5. Before we proceed to examine what may have been our Blessed Lord's principle of selection, so to speak, on this particular occasion, we must remind ourselves that we are not always free as to the choices which we have to make in this respect. There are often considerations of justice or of natural equity which may come in to guide us imperatively in this matter. There are souls to whom we owe more than to others; our parents, our near relations, our teachers, those who have laboured for and waited on us, those who have set us good example, those who have had to suffer on our account, those whose benefits and good works we inherit, as the founders of colleges, those who have given alms and made pious foundations of other sorts by which we profit, those, in short, whose debtors we are in any of the almost number-less ways in which such obligations can arise. We need not speak of such obligations as constitute a strict debt of justice, for in that case the obligation could not be neglected without sin. But there may be others who have claims upon us in the sight of God, for whom He would have us pray, as showing thereby the virtue of gratitude which is so extremely pleasing to Him; or again, charity in a particular

manner, as our enemies, or even because in some
cases we have been responsible in His sight for some
of the acts which cause them suffering now. Thus,
if we have ever neglected any duty of example or
warning or correction, if we have ever connived at
faults, or occasioned them, by provocations to anger
or any other sin, delayed others in their conversion
to a better life, or encouraged them to pay little
attention to some Divine call, to put off the settling
of some matter of conscience which was urgent, or,
as happens frequently in the case of persons approaching the Church, used human motives or the
pressure of earthly interests to keep them back from
any sacrifice which God requires of them—then
indeed we have a debt to them which we are bound
to repay to our utmost. Many a high vocation has
been lost, many a call to the relinquishment of
schism or heresy has been corresponded to when it
has been almost but not quite too late, in consequence of the thoughtless way in which people
act to one another when in difficulties of this kind.
And, to turn to another head, we have great
obligations, accruing in the course of our lives,
to a great number of persons of whom perhaps we
think but little in our prayers—men whose books,
or whose sermons, or whose example, have done us
good and helped us on, and who may now be in
need of out assistance in their time of suffering
and expiation. Thoughtfulness in all this matter
cannot but be very pleasing to God—and at all
events we may be sure that it is well sometimes to
offer our Masses or our satisfactions for those for
whom God would have us offer them, in order that
we may practise this virtue of repaying as best
we can the blessings we have received.

6. Having thus far reminded ourselves of the

obligations under which we may lie, and which may guide our selection in the allotment of the spiritual alms which we have to distribute, we may return to the lesson which our Lord gives us, not only as to the thoughtfulness in general with which this selection should be made, but also as to the particular motives which seem to have influenced Him on this occasion. The two circumstances, already mentioned, which were peculiar in the case of the sick man who was selected as the subject of the miracle, were the length of time during which he had suffered, and his entire want of human aid. If we apply this thought to the case of the Holy Souls, we are at once struck with the ease with which the lessons of which we are in search are furnished to us. Something has already been said, in the chapter on the Healing of the Leper, of the great length of time to which the suffering in Purgatory may be extended, and the books of holy writers on the subject are full of very grave warnings upon this point. Thus Christian devotion has often felt itself moved in a special manner to the relief of the souls which have been the longest in Purgatory, or of those who owe the longest debt to God's justice, unless it be cancelled otherwise than by their own sufferings. " Woe is me, that my sojourning is prolonged!" is the cry of such souls, and we cannot think of such words without remembering at the same time that even a comparatively short period of suffering there is felt as immensely long, on account of the intensity of their pain, or of the burning desire which they feel for the enjoyment of God. Both these circumstances have the effect of making what is already long seem even longer than it is. Again, the touching words of the sick man in this miracle, " Lord, I have no man !" apply very beautifully to the case of others among the holy prisoners of Purgatory. It is very sad to know, as we do by experience, how very soon the memory of the departed fades away from the hearts of men. It may be one of the things at which the Angels marvel most. The deadening effect of the impressions of present and sensible interests upon the traces left on our hearts even by the deepest of our affections and the strongest claims on our gratitude, is a thing which makes us sometimes wonder whether we have hearts at all. Sometimes, again, our own want of remembrance of the departed who have claims on our assistance, may be allowed in the just Providence of God to act in our own case, when our time of need may come, in turning away from us the thoughts of those whom we may leave behind us. With the same measure which we have used towards others will the aid which we ourselves need so much be meted out to us.

7. But, to conclude with a practical suggestion, there are often other circumstances which may produce the same effect on the holy sufferers in Purgatory without so much of cause in faults of their own. as of others. For they may pass away into the next world at a time or in a place where many of the ordinary means of help to the departed are comparatively wanting. Thus, for instance, the Catholic parents of the generation in this country which witnessed the change of religion from Catholicism to Protestantism, must have been largely defrauded of what may be called their natural rights in this respect. The same may be said of our own Catholic forefathers during the centuries of persecution, when there were so few priests in the country, and when it was so difficult for Catholics to hear

Mass or to approach the sacraments. To such persons we owe the incalculable debt which their constancy in keeping to the faith has entailed upon us; but they could have had little aid, ordinarily speaking, from those who came immediately after them in the inheritance of that faith. The same thing may be said of a great number of persons who are secretly converted to Catholicism, perhaps on their death-beds, while their families and friends remain Protestants. The same is true of the number of souls, known to God alone, who die outside the visible pale of the Church, but who have been baptized, and have by His mercy either been preserved from mortal-sin, or visited with interior grace sufficient to enable them to reconcile themselves to Him by adequate sorrow before they die, and whose good faith makes them, as the Fathers say, belong to the soul of the Church, though not to its body. In all these cases there are no suffrages offered for the departed. Their friends and kinsfolk may not forget them, but they have never been taught how much they stand in need of prayer. For it is the invariable device of Satan in the introduction of false and imperfect creeds to shut the eyes of men as much as possible to the claims of God's justice, as well as to the provisions of His mercy for the relief of misery of every kind. These thoughts are sufficient to indicate a number of other cases in which the words of the sufferer in this Gospel narrative, " Lord, I have no man ! " are true of certain among the Holy Souls of Purgatory, and thus to point them out as especial objects of the compassionate and thoughtful charity of the children of the Church.

CHAPTER XII.

The Holy Souls especially helped by prayers on Festivals and Anniversaries.

(THE CURE OF THE MAN WITH THE WITHERED HAND.)
St. Matt. xii. 9—14; St. Mark iii. 1—6; St. Luke vi. 6—11.

1. WE have seen that our Lord healed the poor man whom He found lying in one of the porches of the Probatic Pool on the Sabbath day, although the lesson with regard to the doctrine of Purgatory which was drawn from that miracle did not refer to the particular point. The student of the life of our Lord will be aware that, just at the period of which we are speaking, He took occasion more than once or twice, to assert very clearly, by word and action that the Jewish tradition which seemed to forbid the exercise of good works on the Sabbath, if they were ever so little laborious in themselves, was a false tradition, and one by which He was not Himself in any way bound. It was soon after the miracle at the Probatic Pool that the disciples were blamed by the Pharisees for plucking the ears of corn and rubbing them in their hands on the Sabbath. On this occasion our Lord again defended Himself for permitting this, as He had defended Himself most formally and at great length at Jerusalem after the working of the miracle lately mentioned. It seems also to have been a little later,

after His return to Galilee, that He worked the miracle on which we are now to comment, with the same purpose of enlightening men as to the observance of the Sabbath, and with the result—which appears to have been the reason why the three historical Evangelists all mention the occurrence—of driving His enemies to the mad and impious step of making a plot against His life.

2. One circumstance is found the same in all the miracles wrought by our Lord on the Sabbath day —that is, that He worked them unasked, except so far as the simple presence of the poor sufferers was a silent but eloquent prayer to His Sacred Heart. He worked them in different parts of the country, as if it had been a special object with Him to draw attention everywhere to the doctrine which He taught and the authority which He claimed about the Sabbath.   In their narratives of the miracle of which we are speaking, the Evangelists tell us that He went into the synagogue on the Sabbath, and that there was then present a man who had a withered hand.   The Pharisees and others watched Him to see what He would do, for the question raised by His act at Jerusalem at the Probatic Pool had already made a great stir.   St. Matthew tells us that His enemies actually put the question to Him, whether it was lawful to heal on that day. This must refer to some few of the party, for the other Evangelists only mention that they watched Him, and that He knew their thoughts, and asked them the question Himself, whether it was lawful on the Sabbath to do good or bad, to save life or destroy it ? They were silent, and then He probably added, as St. Matthew tells us, the words which imply His own answer, asking them which of them would not help out a sheep which had fallen into

a pit on the Sabbath—how much better was a man than a sheep ! St. Mark tells us that He looked round with anger, being grieved at their blindness of heart. Then our Lord bade the man with the withered hand stand in the midst, and asked them the same question, as if to show that He was about to answer it by deed as well as by word. He bade the man stretch forth his hand ; he did so, and it was made whole.

3. It is not our business here to draw out our Lord's reasons, as far as we can divine them, for thus insisting, in the teeth of opposition, on the Christian liberty of doing good on the Sabbath day. But may gather from it a very profitable and practical head of instructions as to our own special subject of Purgatory, by reminding ourselves that the Sabbath day, in our Lord's Life, represented to Him the great chain of festivals, the anniversaries of His mysteries, and the like, which was afterwards to exist in His Church, and that He was about to enact, as it were, the Law of the Sabbath in a new form, in the institution of all the ecclesiastical festivals and solemnities with which we are so familiar. The Church, acting by the authority over the Sabbath which belonged to Him as the Son of Man, was to transfer the observance from the seventh day of the week to the first, as well as to spiritualise the mode in which the precept of the Sabbatical rest was to be obeyed. Our Lord was looking forward to this feature in His Kingdom in all that He did and said with regard to the Sabbath. It seems to have moved Him even to anger and indignation when He saw His critics so blind of heart as to object to the performance of works of active mercy on that day. But we may venture to think that He might not perhaps have acted or spoken so strongly in

opposition to the religious prejudices of the Jews, unless He had meant to insist on a principle which directly contravened those prejudices—the principle that feasts and holy days and religious solemnities and commemorations were to be times of rejoicing and of spiritual activity, great occasions for the exercise of mercy and charity on the part of Christians, and for the bountiful diffusion of graces and spiritual gifts on the part of God. Thus Christians have always considered that they might hope for special and large gifts of grace on occasion of the great solemnities of the ecclesiastical year, the days on which the chief mysteries of our Lord or of His Blessed Mother or of the Saints are commemorated. The Church encourages this belief in a number of different ways, one of which, which has especial relation to our own subject, is the connecting her greater indulgences with the more solemn feasts. Thus it may be said to be a principle of the new Kingdom of our Lord, that the great acts and mercies of God, whether in the life of our Lord Himself, or in the lives of His Saints, or in the history of the Church, should have each their special commemoration, as the great consummation of the work of Creation had its special commemoration in the observance of the Sabbath. But the observance of the Sabbath was not a simple commemoration, it was also an institution full of benefit to mankind for many various reasons. Indeed, there can be no such institution in the Kingdom of God as a simple commemoration of past mercies, which is not also an occasion for the obtaining of fresh benefits from His inexhaustible and ineffable goodness. And, in the same way, the festivals of our Lord, His Mother, and the Saints, which are occasions of intense joy to the Church in Heaven and on earth, are also intended by God to be opportunities which He may take, in His infinite bountifulness, of pouring out ever fresh and fresh blessings upon those who celebrate them devoutly.

4. There are many reasons for thinking that, among the many ways in which we may please God at such times, that of praying especially for the deliverance of the Holy Souls is not the least. This act of mercy belongs, it may seem, as of right to the great moments of triumph in our Lord's history, and to the anniversaries which celebrate them. It is thought by many holy writers that, on Holy Saturday, after our Lord's descent "into the lower parts of the earth," as St. Paul speaks, He not only set free from their captivity the Saints who were detained in Limbus, but that He also made His presence felt in Purgatory by the deliverance either of all the souls which were then suffering pain, or at least, as St. Thomas seems to think, of all those who by their faith and devotion while alive had merited that He should so deliver them. St. Vincent Ferrer says that if the number of the delivered from Purgatory on that occasion was measured by rigorous justice, it would not extend beyond these last mentioned; but that if it were measured by the sweetness of God's mercy, all would have been set free. It is also the opinion of many Doctors that, when our Blessed Lady was dying, she obtained from her Son the liberation of all that were then in Purgatory, who accompanied her to Heaven in the triumph of her glorious Assumption. It is said by some that she exercises her loving power in favour of the souls of Purgatory on every feast of her Assumption, and even on all her feasts, and of those of the Nativity and Resurrection of her Divine Son. We find also privileges

of the same kind attributed by holy writers to some of the Saints, as St. Laurence, who delivers a soul every Friday, and St. Francis of Assisi, who is allowed to deliver his own religious children on his annual feast day. The number of instances in which some such privileges are mentioned in the Lives of the Saints and in other such books, seems to show us that it is according to the mind of the Church to think that these privileges exist, and that it is usual for the favourite servants of God to be allowed such powers at the times of their feasts. If we put by the side of this the other fact, already mentioned, of the habit of the Church to attach special Indulgences to works of piety on such days, we have quite enough to encourage us to hope that it is greatly pleasing to God that we should make such days occasions for exerting ourselves in some special manner for the relief of the Holy Souls. We may say to ourselves those words of our Lord, " How much is a soul better than a sheep ; " and if at times of rejoicing, and on occasions which remind us of mercies which we have received even in the natural order—birthdays, wedding-days, and the like —we think it well to give alms, or to exercise the rite of hospitality, or the duty of visiting the sick and the afflicted, we may surely hope with great confidence that God will hear our prayers and accept our thanksgivings more readily, if we make it a point never to let a holy day or festival season pass away without endeavouring to make the Saints and the Holy Souls partakers in our feast, the latter by the prayers or good works or Masses which we offer for their deliverance, the former by the accidental glory which redounds to them when such offerings are made in their honour, and when their glorious company in Heaven is increased by fresh arrivals from Purgatory.

CHAPTER XIII.

The Holy Souls specially helped by works for the Service of the Church.

(THE HEALING OF THE CENTURION'S SERVANT.)
St. Matt. viii. 5—15; St. Luke vii. 1—10.

1. THE next of our Lord's miracles in order of time, after the miracle in the synagogue of which we spoke in the last chapter, seems to have been the healing of the centurion's servant. This took place after an interval of at least some weeks, during which our Lord was absent from Capharnaum, and in which we must place the great event of the delivery of His Sermon on the Plain, and the still more important event which immediately preceded it—the election of the twelve Apostles. It is natural to suppose that after some time spent in His usual course of missionary preaching our Lord returned for a short rest to Capharnaum. Here, as the Gospel narrative tells us, He was applied to by the chief Jews, the rulers of the synagogue, and the like, in favour of a person who was too modest to come to Him himself, partly on account of his sense of unworthiness, partly because he did not belong to the sacred nation. He was a Gentile officer, probably a Roman, in command of some small force in the city, and it seems that he must have been a dweller there for some time. He had

1

become acquainted with the Jewish society of the place, he had taken an interest in their religion, to which he had probably become a proselyte, and he had shown his attachment to it and to them by more than one good work, especially by having built them their synagogue at his own expense. He had heard of our Lord—it is very likely that he had heard of him as a teacher, and not only as a worker of miracles, for the story of his application to our Lord seems to show that he knew the nobleman whose son our Lord had healed at a distance, before the formal beginning of His Galilean preaching, and had caught from him the special lesson of faith which had been insisted on in his case. If this is so, it is not likely that the nobleman would have been backward to speak to him of his own belief as to our Lord's Divine mission. The centurion, however, was now anxious about the health of one of his servants, of whom we are not told whether he was or was not a Jew. The servant was lying under a violent attack of paralysis, in great pain, and not far from death. Under these circumstances the master went to the chief Jews, as has been said, and asked them to intercede for him with our Lord. This they did very willingly, representing that he was a lover of their nation, and had built them the synagogue. We need not go through the whole series of details which are related by the two Evangelists. Our Lord said at once that He would come and heal the sufferer, but He was met on the way first by some friends sent by the centurion, and then by the centurion himself, begging Him not to put Himself so much out as to come for he was well aware of his own unworthiness to receive Him under his roof, and also that our Lord could heal as well by a word as by His presence, at a distance as well as on the spot. He was himself, he said, a man both under authority and also with some authority of his own over his inferiors ; he knew what authority was, and he was quite sure that our Lord had only to exercise His authority over disease and health in any way that pleased Him, in order to produce the effect which He desired. " Only say the word, and my servant shall be healed."

2. We need not pause to dwell on the intense delight which this display of faith, and of humility founded on faith, caused in the Sacred Heart of our Lord. In some respects this centurion was an earnest and foretaste to Him of the multitude of souls who were to follow him in his ready and generous faith, and to come, as He said to His disciples, from the east and west, and sit down in the kingdom with Abraham, Isaac, and Jacob. These considerations belong to another time. At present we shall find abundant food for thought in two things which seem to stand out from the story, and to illustrate in very different ways the doctrine to which these chapters are devoted. These two things are suggested, the first by the recommendation with which the Jews sought to move our Lord's compassion in favour of the centurion, when they said that he loved their nation and had built them their synagogue, and the second by the beautiful words of the centurion, which the Church has made her own by taking them into her own mouth at Holy Communion, " Lord, I am not worthy that thou shouldest enter under my roof."

3. The first of these heads contains the whole doctrine, so to speak, of the immense value of good works done for the Church and her children as such, and especially of the particular good work of

building churches and raising altars for the worship of God and the honour of His saints. When the Jews put this forward as their special ground of recommendation to our Lord in favour of the petition of the centurion, they may perhaps have thought that they ought to meet the objection which might be made that the subject of their petition was an alien to the holy people. They may have meant to say that although he was a Gentile, still he had deserved well of the Jewish community. If they meant no more than this, then we may take their words as having more force on our Lord's Heart than they expected. To love the holy nation of the Church, and especially to show that love by raising the sanctuaries of God, gives a higher title to our Lord's goodwill than simply to belong to the holy people. The rewards which our Lord confers on any service done to His kingdom or to the worship of God, are determined and measured by His own most magnificent liberality. He says in His charge to His Apostles, [1] that any one who receives a prophet in the name of a prophet shall receive the reward of a prophet—that is, he shall be dealt with by God as if he had himself done the work of the prophet whom he receives. These words indicate the law of the gratitude of God, if we may so speak, for any services of the kind of which we are speaking. They are of immense consolation to all those who have the means and the goodwill to advance the service of God by the use of wealth, influence, position, authority, and the like. Such persons have opportunities which others have not, of gaining the friendship of the saints and of our Lord Himself, and their opportunities amount to nothing less than the power to gain a share in all the good works

[1] St. Matt. x. 41.

for which they open the way by their munificence. Let us take the case, for instance, of a person who uses his wealth to build a Christian church in which the Holy Sacrifice is continually offered to God, in which the Gospel doctrine is constantly preached, in which the sacraments are administered, in which the Blessed Sacrament dwells on the altar day and night, in which prayer is almost unceasing, and in which a thousand hidden graces are imparted, hour after hour, by our Lord to His faithful worshippers. Let us take the case of a person who founds a convent in which the chosen souls of the Church may retire from the world, and give themselves up without interruption or distraction to that "attendance on our Lord," of which St. Paul speaks;[a] or a college in which the highest mental culture is imparted, under the guidance and blessing of religion, in which learning is pursued for the sake of elucidating Scripture and theology, in which missionaries are trained for the glorious work of carrying the Gospel into heathen countries, and of supplying the wants of the sacred ministry in countries where priests are comparatively few. In all these cases the person who makes this holy use of the worldly goods which God has given him, has a share, according to our Lord's rule, in all the good that is done to His honour in the church or convent or school or college, or in any other work of a like kind, which he has helped to found. And as the work goes on for generation after generation, the founder, or the souls to whose benefit he may wish to apply its satisfactory power, will continue to enjoy his share. If he be in Heaven, he will have an accidental increase of joy for all that is done; if he or they be in Purgatory, it cannot

[a] 1 Cor. vii. 35.

be doubted that his soul or theirs will be greatly and continually relieved, and the time of their deliverance hastened on, by the service to God which is daily and hourly accruing in such places as those of which we have been speaking. God Himself and all the Court of Heaven, the Blessed Virgin and the saints and the Angels, as well as the Church upon earth and her children, are his debtors, who will certainly not forget their obligations, and who are very powerful in their means of payment and very prompt in using them. The best works that can be done for the Church are those which most directly contribute to the worship of God and the preaching of the Gospel, and those also which last on generation after generation. We see in.all this the holy wisdom and considerate charity and prudence of ancient times, when the foundation of convents or colleges or schools, or the building of churches or of chapels in churches, was a favourite work of piety, very often indeed undertaken with a distinct and definite purpose of providing for the relief of the souls in Purgatory.

4. Here, then, is a very practical point of teaching concerning the way in which we may benefit those dear to us, for whose souls we are anxious to obtain the speedy mercy of God. The erection of an altar in their memory, or the foundation of Masses, or the contribution to the maintenance of a priest, especially in parts of the world where the Church is most in need of support from a distance, and in countries where it is possible for a very small annual sum to keep a mission alive, and so to contribute to the service of the altar under circumstances which promise exceptionally large returns for any labour or alms that are spent upon them—these and other similar ways of helping the holy sufferers

are suggested by the miracle before us. It must be remembered that any one who procures the celebration of a Mass which would not otherwise be celebrated, does not benefit alone his own soul or the soul for whom the Mass is offered or that of the priest who offers it, but the whole Church of God in Heaven, on earth, and under the earth. This is a good deed which rejoices God and the Saints and Angels, as well as the living and the dead, and it is no wonder if the prayers and interests of such a person are assisted by the intercessions of all Heaven.

5. But there is another and very beautiful lesson to be learnt from this good centurion, which illustrates one of the most suggestive points in the whole doctrine concerning Purgatory and its prisoners. This lesson is contained in the words to which reference has already been made: " Lord, I am not worthy that Thou shouldest enter under my roof, but only say the word, and my servant shall be healed." These words should be put by the side of other expressions of the same kind, which are among those breathings of the Holy Ghost which seem most clearly to interpret the words of St. Paul, when he says that the Holy Spirit of God prays in us and moulds, as it were, our petitions, so as to make them the prayers which are acceptable to our Heavenly Father. They are to be set by the side of the cry of the publican of whom our Lord speaks, who would not so much as lift his eyes to Heaven, but smote his breast, saying, " God be merciful to me a sinner." They belong to the same class as the words of St. Peter in the ship—" Depart from me, for I am a sinful man, O Lord." They remind us of the answer of the Syrophœnician woman, " Yea, Lord, the dogs eat of the crumbs

which fall from the master's table." These are the petitions which have so much power over our Lord's Sacred Heart. We are told by holy writers on the subject of Purgatory, especially by St. Catharine of Genoa and those who have followed her, that the Holy Souls have so deep a sense of their own unworthiness to meet the eye of God in Heaven, before they are perfectly purged from the imperfections which are consumed in the fire of Purgatory, that they would shrink back from His Presence if it were offered them to pass into their destined Beatitude before the time. So intense is their love of God, and so entirely does that affection overrule or absorb any other, such as the desire of their own happiness, that for His sake and for the sake of the holiness which becometh His courts, they cannot bear to think of anything that is unfit being presented there.

6. We cannot doubt that this beautiful humility of the centurion made our Lord all the more ready and eager to help him ; and that it was one of the fruits of his very keen and penetrating faith, which made him see the dignity of our Lord's Person far more clearly than many others who approached Him with similar petitions. So in the same way, the intense humility of the Holy Souls, which is founded on their charity, is one of the causes for which our Lord's Sacred Heart yearns after them with so extreme a love. We may, then, add this to the other motives which we have already considered as incentives to our own charitable exertions for the relief of these Holy Souls, which all tend to their speedier purification and to the hastening of the moment when the desires of our Lord's Heart may be satisfied in them.

CHAPTER XIV.

Our Blessed Lady and the Holy Souls.

(THE RAISING OF THE WIDOW'S SON.)
St. Luke vii. 11—16.

1. NOT long after the miracle on the centurion's servant, of which we spoke in the last chapter, our Lord exercised, for the first time of which we have any record, His power over life and death, by raising the dead to life. Although we have but three instances, recorded for us in the Gospels in which He raised the dead, we cannot doubt that He used this power much more frequently. In the same way, although this is the earliest of these instances given by the Evangelists, we cannot be certain that no other instance, unrelated by them, had preceded it. But St. Luke had, evidently, a particular reason for inserting it here, and we may fairly consider it, for purposes of meditation, as the first. The story is so familiar to us that it hardly needs repetition. Our Lord with His disciples and a considerable multitude of followers, was on the road near a city called Naim. Just as He came near the gates of the town, a funeral procession met Him. The corpse was that of a young man, the only son of a widow, and a great number of her fellow-citizens were accompanying it and her to the grave. Our Lord was touched

with pity at her bereavement, and bade her not to weep. Then He went up to the bier, touched it, and while the bearers stood still, He bade the young man rise up, and "he that was dead sat up, and began to speak," and our Lord "gave him to his mother."

2. The manner in which we are applying these considerations to the state of the Souls in Purgatory and the methods which may be used for their relief and release, allows us frequently to leave aside the more obvious and direct teaching of a miracle, in order to dwell upon some truth which may be represented rather than directly conveyed by the circumstances of the case. In this anecdote of the raising of the widow's son, it appears that the motive which acted on our Lord's Sacred Heart was that of compassion for .the widowed mother of the young man. Our Lord may have had other motives besides this—but this it is which is specially mentioned by St. Luke. We are told nothing of any intercession, as in the case of the centurion's servant, nor indeed is it certain that the throng who came forth from the gates of the city to follow the young man to his grave had the faith which was requisite in order to make them intreat our Lord to work so great a miracle. The bearers of the bier "stood still," but even this does not show more than a certain amount of deference and reverence to our Lord. The miracle, like so many others, was a most wonderful manifestation of power, and, as such, was an act which suited well the purposes of God in showing to this world the dignity of His Incarnate Son and the power with which His Sacred Humanity was endowed. Many other miracles were wrought by our Lord for the purpose of this manifestation. But in this case we have the

one motive assigned—the compassion of our Lord's
Heart at the sight of the widowed mother following
to the grave the body of her only son.

3. If we turn our thoughts from the scene set
before us by St. Luke, to the subject which has
become so familiar to us in these chapters, that of
the condition of the suffering souls in Purgatory,
we naturally ask ourselves whether there is in their
case any call on the compassionate Heart of our
Blessed Lord which may be compared to the claim
made on His mercy by the sorrowing widow of
Naim. And we see at once that every Christian
soul, and in a special way every soul in Purgatory,
on account of its helplessness and of the lot of
suffering to which it has been sentenced, may be
considered as the child, in a different sense, of two
mothers—the Catholic Church and our Blessed
Lady. It is a serious truth, and not merely a
poetical or fanciful image, that our Lord takes
note of this claim on His compassion, and that
each poor Christian soul, whether on earth or in
Purgatory, receives from Him love and compassion
and help for the sake of its filial relation to the
Church and to His most beloved Mother. In the
present chapter we shall take occasion to dwell for
a few moments on the last of these two relation-
ships. Our Blessed Lady has a special interest in
and power over the Holy Souls in Purgatory, and
we can never treat adequately the subject of the
means by which we may ourselves help them without
taking this power into consideration, and reviving
our own devotion to her as their Mother and
Queen.

4. It would take many chapters to draw out at
full length what can be gathered from Christian
writers as to the particular interest with which our

Blessed Lady regards the Holy Souls. It is probable that, as the saints, in Heaven or on earth, are higher and higher in their intelligence and love of God, in the same proportion do they " understand," as the Psalmist says, " concerning the needy and the poor," and so, in an especial manner concerning the neediest and poorest, in a certain sense, of God's children, the sufferers in Purgatory, who can do nothing for themselves. If this be so, then, as the knowledge of God and of our Lord, and of all that belongs to His glory, which our Blessed Lady possesses, is greater than that of all the saints and Angels together, as her charity is, in the same way, alone more intense than that of all the rest of the dwellers in Heaven, so her desire to aid the Holy Souls would be in proportion greater than that of all others. They may be considered, in one respect, as the choicest and dearest of her children, except the saints themselves, who need nothing and are deprived of nothing. She has been made in a particular manner their Mother by our Lord on the Cross, for in them the fruits of His Precious Blood are secured. Holy writers tell us also that she has received a special power and commission to move the mercy of God in their favour, according to the arrangements of His kingdom, in which she fills a throne, only less lofty than that of her Son. This is altogether in accordance with the laws, if we may so speak, of the Kingdom of the Incarnation. Our Blessed Lady has a special compassion for the sufferings of the Holy Souls, on account of her own great sufferings on earth, in some respects very like those which are endured in Purgatory. She was conceived without original sin, and filled with all the graces from the first, her virtues and merits were ever increasing, she was confirmed in grace, she never committed sin, venial or any other. And yet she suffered most intensely, on account of the sins of the world which her Son had to bear, on account of the treatment with which He met, the very intensity of her knowledge and of her charity caused the intensity of her pain, while yet she was ever in perfect peace and union with the will of God, and she felt more than any other soul could feel the desire to be with God and with her Son, and so the pain of detention from Heaven. On all these accounts there is ground for saying that she feels, more tenderly than all the saints, compassion for the Holy Souls. These and other considerations form the basis of the doctrine which attributes to our Blessed Lady a peculiar prerogative as well as a special care in regard of Purgatory and its prisoners.

5. In accordance with this doctrine, we find the lives of the saints, the chronicles of religious orders, and other such records, full of anecdotes and revelations which all tend to the same conclusion, that our Lady is constantly exercising her power in favour of these Holy Souls, and that, on the other hand, devotions that are practised in her especial honour are among the most efficacious means which the children of the Church on earth possess of helping those blessed sufferers. It will be enough here to speak of the universal devotion of the holy Rosary, with which all Catholics are familiar. Some writers tell us that this, after the holy Sacrifice of the Mass, is the most powerful weapon that can be used to obtain their deliverance. The holy Rosary stands, to the great mass of Christians, much in the same place as the Divine Office of the Church to those who are bound to recite it, or who

have the custom of so doing. The Divine Office is the great public prayer of the Catholic Church, and it remains such even in the case of those who do not recite it in the choir, but privately and singly. And it has great efficacy on that account, for in the Catholic Church there is a special power and blessing on united, universal, and, as it were, official prayer and praise, which cannot be altogether impaired even by the unworthiness of some who are the ministers of the Church for this purpose. The holy Rosary is sometimes called the Psalter of the Blessed Virgin, and the universality of its use renders it, in a sense, the prayer of the whole Church, though not in the same degree as the Divine Office. Intrinsically, moreover, it has an immense impetratory power with God, because it is in fact the pleading before Him of the merits of our Lord and of our Blessed Lady in all the mysteries which it commemorates, and which embrace the whole range of the scheme of our Redemption as accomplished by Him. Then, again, it pleads all these merits, as it were, through the heart and through the lips of Mary herself, and so it adds to the power of the mysteries in themselves that of her perfect prayer and intercession, and the affections and intensity of charity which glow in her bosom. Again, it uses with all its marvellous power the words of our Blessed Lord in the *Pater noster*, and of the Archangel, St. Elisabeth, and the Church, in the *Ave Maria;* being also, at the same time, a chain of most excellent acts of faith, hope, charity, and other supernatural virtues, which are exercised in the consideration of the mysteries.

6. It would be almost impossible to exaggerate the importance which holy writers attach to the practice of this devotion, whether as a means of

intercession for the Holy Souls, or for our own benefit, and, as a matter of history, it is of our Lady, as honoured by this devotion, that the words of the Chnrch seem so particularly true, *cunctas hæreses sola interemisti in universo mundo.* The devotion of the holy Rosary was first propagated by St. Dominic with the express intention of freeing large Catholic populations from the contagion of a frightful heresy, and down to the present day it seems to have this effect. We are speaking of it, in this chapter, as a most powerful means of impetration of mercy for the souls in Purgatory. But in this, as in many other cases, the charity which we practise toward them flows back in abundant streams to the benefit of ourselves in this world and in the next. The various forms which devotion to our Blessed Lady may take are almost innumerable, and we have in this chapter spoken only of this principal and universal devotion of the holy Rosary. Masses in her honour, Masses offered for the souls devout to her, or to whom she may wish to apply them, alms given, or works of mercy practised with the same intention, or again, the recital of her office, the visiting her statues, honouring her pictures, and the like, may all be used for the benefit of the Holy Souls as well as our own. One act of devotion may be specially mentioned here, as having to some extent revived in our days, although there has never been a time in the Church's history when it has been extinct, and although it is not limited in its object to our Blessed Lady. This act of devotion is the making pilgrimages to shrines, whether ancient or new. The facilities of travelling have indeed made pilgrimages less difficult in our own time, and it may be thought by some that they are now more of a pleasant excitement than, as of old, a laborious work of penance and even of danger. But, in the first place, a pilgrimage need not be made to a distant shrine, and a shrine of our Lady—let it be only her picture or statue in some neighbouring church—may be visited on foot, while a truer pilgrimage, costing toil and time, may be made to a greater distance. If, even in a country like ours, shrines of our Blessed Lady were frequently visited in this manner, we cannot doubt that the devotion of the faithful would soon unlock the treasury of her marvellous favours. In the second place, pilgrimages to the more celebrated shrines of modern times, places like Lourdes or La Salette, where our Lady has appeared in our own day to persons, still living, or to the spots more anciently connected with her name, as Loreto and the like, are protestations of Catholic faith very valuable in an age like ours, they cost more in human respect than of old, though less in bodily fatigue, and are therefore very acceptable to her who is essentially " the Faithful Virgin."

CHAPTER XV.

Our Lord's Mission to Purgatory.

(THE MIRACLES WROUGHT BEFORE THE DISCIPLES
OF ST. JOHN BAPTIST.)

St. Matt. xi. 2—6; St. Luke vii. 17—23.

1. ST. MATTHEW and St. Luke tell us of an incident in our Lord's preaching which seems at first sight somewhat difficult to understand. It appears that when our Lord's marvellous miracles came to be spread about by report over the whole country, and soon after the miracle of the raising of the widow's son to life, the fame of these great manifestations of power and mercy reached the little company of the disciples of St. John who were still attendant on their master in his prison at a distance. The disciples told St. John of our Lord's miracles. The Blessed Baptist took the occasion of doing what, more than anything else, might prepare them for the acceptance of our Lord as the Messias. He himself, as we are told by St. John the Evangelist, had worked no miracles at all,[1] and now our Lord was doing what were commonly understood to be " the works of the Christ"—that is, the marvels of healing and power which it belonged to the promised Messias, in particular, to perform. The Baptist, therefore, sent two of his disciples to our Lord with

[1] St. John x. 41, 42.

J

the formal question: "Art Thou He that art to come, or look we for another?" St. Luke tells us that our Lord answered the question in two ways—in deed and in word—" In that same hour He cured many of their diseases, and hurts, and evil spirits, and to many that were blind He gave sight. And answering He said to them, Go and relate to John what you have heard and seen. The blind see, the lame walk, the lepers are made clean, the deaf hear, the dead rise again, to the poor the Gospel is preached, and blessed is he whosoever shall not be scandalised in Me."

2. These words of our Lord may be considered as conveying a double proof of His mission from His Father. In the first place, they were a reference to, almost indeed a quotation from, the Prophet Isaias, in a passage in which it is clear that he was describing the signs of mercy which should wait upon the Messias when He came, and also in another passage which had already been applied by our Lord to Himself in His discourse in the Synagogue at Nazareth at the very opening of His preaching in Galilee.[1] These passages must have been well known to the disciples of St. John, and thus our Lord's answer amounted to an appeal to the fact that in Him the prophecies concerning the Messias were fulfilled. In the second place, putting aside for the moment the prediction of these things concerning Him by a Prophet whom all acknowledged as inspired by God, the things themselves were proofs that He was " He that was to come, and that they did not look for another," because they were the works of healing and mercy, both in body and soul, which might naturally be expected in the deliverer of the human race. The

[1] Isaias xxxv. 5, lxi. 1.

Jews, who knew the prophecies, could understand both these arguments, but if they had not had the prophecies, they would have been able to take in the second. The perfect Christian demonstration, as we know, embraces both these heads of proof, and is made up of the combination of both. For miracles that have been foretold by prophets sent by God are a more secure and infallible proof than miracles alone, even when, as in the case of our Lord's miracles, their character of mercy and love, and the manner in which they present themselves as relieving all the ills of our human condition, give them an authentication as Divine, which simple signs of power, such as the Jews required of our Lord, could never have. This, then, seems to be an explanation sufficient for our present purpose of the incident here recorded. It enables us to see that our Lord's acts and words furnished St. John with the opportunity of bearing witness to his own disciples as to the Divine Mission of our Lord, by pointing out that the latter had now received the Divinely appointed evidence from God that He was the Redeemer of the world. This evidence consisted in the works of power and mercy which marked His footsteps through the world. These works amounted to a witness from God the Father, as our Lord said more than once, that He was indeed He that was to come.

3. We must now leave the disciples of St. John Baptist and turn to a company of sufferers, of whom those whom our Lord now healed were the images and representatives. The passage of Isaias, to which reference has been made, seems to speak almost as directly of the prisoners of Purgatory as of the various forms of earthly wretchedness. Taken as a whole, it describes even more truly, in

all its particulars, the visit of our Lord to the lower parts of the earth, when He set so many souls free from Purgatory, than even His sojourn among men on earth. " The land that was desolate and impassable shall be glad, and the wilderness shall rejoice, and flourish like the lily. · It shall bud forth and blossom, and shall rejoice with joy and praise. The glory of Libanus is given to it, the beauty of Carmel and Saron, they shall see the glory of the Lord and the beauty of our God." Such language paints even more truly the deliverance of the Holy Souls, and their admission to the Beatific Vision, than the earthly miracles of our Lord. " Strengthen ye the feeble hands, and confirm the weak knees. Say to the fainthearted, Take courage and fear not, and behold your God will bring the revenge of recompense, God Himself will come and save you." These words again describe the state of the Souls in Purgatory accurately, as well as those that follow. " Then shall the eyes of the blind be opened, and the ears of the deaf shall be unstopped. Then shall the lame man leap as a hart, and the tongue of the dumb shall be free, for waters are broken out in the desert, and streams in the wilderness, and that which was dry land shall became a pool, and the thirsty land springs of water. By the dens where dragons dwelt before, shall rise up the verdure of the reed and the bulrush. And a path and a way shall be there, and it shall be called the holy way: the unclean shall not pass over it, and this shall be unto you a straight way, so that fools shall not err therein. No lion shall be there, nor shall any mischievous beast go up by it, nor be found there, but they shall walk there that shall be delivered. And the redeemed of the Lord shall return, and shall come into Sion with praise, and everlasting joy shall be upon their heads, they shall obtain joy and gladness, and sorrow and mourning shall flee away."[8] It is not necessary here to do more than indicate the many points in which this passage illustrates the redemption of the Holy Souls from their state of infirmity and bondage, and their passage into the light and joy of Heaven. But even if this be not included in the literal sense of the words of the Prophet, still our faith teaches us that the deliverance of the prisoners of Purgatory was a part of our Lord's work, a part which He began to execute when He went down into the lower world after His Passion, and that this work has been going on ever since, having been committed by Him to His Church on earth, which would fail to carry out the whole of her appointed task and office, if she were to neglect it. And so it may be said of our Lord, in His own Person and in His Church—which is to carry on to the end of time that which He has begun— that we know Him to be He that was to come, and that we do not look for another, as much by His constant beneficence and mercy and the healing and consolation which He brings to the suffering souls, as by the corporal miracles which He wrought while in the flesh upon earth. For " He that was to come" was to be the Redeemer and Restorer and Consoler and Saviour of our poor human nature in all phases and forms of its misery and need, and if He had left any form of wretchedness and suffering unprovided for, especially that keenest and most intense suffering of all which is in Purgatory, then it might be a question whether we should not look for amother. As a matter of fact, the deliverance which our Lord wrought for the Holy Souls

[8] Isaias xxxv.

when He descended into the abode of spirits after His Passion, belongs, according to Catholic belief, to that article of the Creed in which we profess our belief in that descent.

4. Moreover it may be considered certain that the devotion to the Holy Souls, which consists in endeavouring to assist them under their sufferings in every manner open to us, is a part of that original religion of mankind which was given to our first parents to hand on to their children, and which was made the foundation on which the written Law, and, afterwards, the Gospel itself was founded. It is certain that the Jews offered prayers, mortifications, and sacrifices for the dead, and it is probable that, could we trace accurately the distorted and disfigured principles of true religion which are, as it were, embedded in the false systems of the heathen world, we should be able to see how the idea of applying to the departed the satisfactory power of good works and acts of religion, offered to God in the faith of the coming Redeemer of the world, lies underneath the whole system of funeral rites and observances which prevailed among the ancients outside the pale of Judaism. There is no positive precept as to prayers or sacrifices for the dead, either in the Mosaic or the Christian Law, and this is enough to prove, when taken in conjunction with the universal Jewish and Christian practice from the beginning, that that practice was in existence and honour before Moses and before Christianity. Thus we must look upon it as having either sprung up of itself from the natural instincts of the human heart, or as having, like sacrifice, been a part of the original revelation and teaching of mankind by God. The latter is the more probable supposition, especially as it does not altogether exclude the

other. In either case we may consider that our Lord's great work in the relief of Purgatory was foreshadowed in the universal belief and practice of the religious part of mankind, and that in this way also, when He came to fulfil it and to hand it on to the Church, He showed that He was He that was to come, of Whom the prophets spoke, and for Whom the whole world yearned.

5. This enables us to understand how the neglect and disuse of prayers for the dead, and the practical or positive denial of their value or efficacy, is a certain mark, in any religious community, that it has fallen away from the Church of Jesus Christ. These things involve a mutilation, so to speak, of the mission of our Lord, a halving of His beneficent work as the Saviour of mankind, a curtailing of the effects of the merciful counsel of God in bringing about the great work of the Incarnation. It is very significant indeed that the practical dying out of charity for the dead, as of all intercourse by way of invocation with the other great parts of our Lord's family in Heaven and on earth, the saints and Angels, has come about, in Protestant societies like the English Establishment, much more by a sort of mournful instinct and consciousness of separation, than by any actual legislation prohibiting these beautiful exercises of charity. Protestants feel that they cannot help the dead, that they have nothing to do with them, as if they almost in their hearts acknowledged the truth of the Catholic reasons why it is so—that they are themselves cut off from the Body of Jesus Christ, and cannot, in consequence, have any right to carry on the work of mercy which is the application, through the Church, of the merits of His satisfaction for the members of that Body. It is hardly too much to say, that just as we know a

man to be dead to all spiritual grace who does not, according to his opportunities, practise the law of charity to his neighbours, and just as we should know a religion to be un-Christian which forbade the exercise of charity, so we may be certain, without further proof, that a religious communion is cut off from our Lord which proscribes prayers for the dead, or even in which that charity is not practised. Such a communion has found another Lord, and not He that was to come, and in Whom the prophecies and the natural anticipations of mankind were to be fulfilled.

6. But our thoughts must not rest on those religious communities alone in which the doctrine of Purgatory is practically denied. We must think of ourselves, the children of the Catholic Church, and learn from this miracle, looked upon in the light in which it has been set, that we must consider the work of the ransoming and deliverance of these holy captives as one which our Lord expects us to carry on as a commission from Himself, as a legacy which He has left us, as a proof of the truth of His Mission. The Catholic Church is the Spouse and Heir of Him that was to come, and she is known and proved as such by her universal charity, which embraces alike earth and Heaven and Purgatory. The world is always asking whether she is what she claims to be, and her answer is the same as that of our Lord to the disciples of St. John Baptist. But the truth of her answer is proved by the charity and self-devotion of her children as well as by her formal teaching, and it rests upon us to make this proof so conspicuous and so convincing that no one can gainsay it.

CHAPTER XVI.

The Desire of the Holy Souls for the Society of Heaven.

1. OUR LORD on several occasions delivered from the power of the devils, who had possessed them, persons who were afflicted by the loss of one or more of their senses, as of sight, hearing, or speech. In these cases the recovery of the use of the senses in question followed on the casting out of the devils, and this circumstance appears to have produced a great effect on the witnesses of the miracles. Thus we find, both in the account in St. Matthew of the miracle of which we are now about to speak, and in that of a similar, though not identical, cure, mentioned later on in the history by St. Luke, that the people cried out in the one case, " Is not this the Son of David ?" and in the other, that " the crowd marvelled; " while a third, also mentioned by St. Matthew, the people said, " It was never so seen in Israel."[1] On all these three occasions the splendour of the miracle not only moved the admiration of the crowd, but also excited in an unusual degree the malice of our Lord's enemies, who took occasion from these cures to propagate

[1] Cf. St. Matt. ix. 32, 33 ; St. Luke xi. 14.

and repeat their calumny that He cast out devils in consequence of a league with the prince of the devils. We are now to speak of the first instance, in point of time, of a miracle of this class.

2. "Then was offered to Him one that was possessed with a devil, blind and dumb; and He healed him, so that he spake and saw. And all the multitude were amazed, and said: Is not this the Son of David? But the Pharisees, hearing it, said, This Man casteth not out devils but by Beelzebub, the prince of the devils." St. Mark tells us that the Pharisees, or, as he calls them, the Scribes, who uttered this calumny, had come down from Jerusalem. It is clear that the authorities had by this time determined to thwart and persecute our Lord to the utmost of their power, and that they had sent persons of learning and character from Jerusalem into Galilee in order to watch Him and take every opportunity of finding fault with Him and opposing Him.

3. We need not pause to dwell further on their great perversity and malice, nor on the singular pain which this accusation, so often repeated in the subsequent months of our Lord's public teaching, gave to His Sacred Heart. If we were meditating on sin, we might find some useful thoughts in the comparison which the state of this poor sufferer whom our Lord healed suggests between the diseases of the body and the evils of the soul. But as we are considering all these miracles in relation to the Holy Souls of Purgatory, we may be satisfied with the image which is here presented to us of what must be a great part of their suffering. They are not, indeed, like the person before us, under the dominion of the devil. We have seen that they have been rescued from him, that they are full of

gratitude on that account, and that they have been made aware how very near they have been to the danger of becoming his slaves for ever. We have also seen that in Purgatory it need not be supposed to be an ordinary suffering even to see or to be taunted by the devils. But though the Holy Souls are delivered from that kind of bondage to Satan which is involved in a state of sin, or even in exposure to mockery and insult from the devils, they are still, as we saw in the case of the paralytic, deprived of the use of many of their spiritual faculties or capacities for the functions of the blessed life of immortality and joy to which they are destined. The two senses of which this poor man was deprived for a time, while he was under possession by the devil, are those by which we communicate with the world around us, and especially with our fellow-men. If to the loss of speech and sight, the loss of hearing is added—as in the case with many who are dumb—then we become cut off almost entirely from intercourse with men like ourselves. The ingenious charity of Christians has, indeed, found a way of giving a kind of social life and enjoyment of intercourse even to those who are afflicted with the loss of all the three senses here mentioned ; but the loss even of one, much more of two of them, is a very serious privation indeed. If those whom Providence allows to be placed in this unhappy condition are left to themselves, they are certainly almost altogether cut off from all society, and from the employment and the love, as well as from the cultivation of mind and intelligence, which is to be found, in creatures like ourselves, chiefly in society.

4. The sufferers in Purgatory are not only cut off from the Beatific Vision of God, and from all that

it implies in regard to their knowledge and love of Him as possessed by them, but also from that intense happiness which consists in the mutual love and converse of the saints and Angels in Heaven. God has made men for this wonderful happiness; their minds and hearts are formed to know and love one another, and to communicate their thoughts and affections by means of speech. The enjoyment of which we are thus capable is higher and deeper in proportion to our own intellectual and moral perfection, to the degree of the same perfection which those with whom we can converse have attained, and to the mutual goodwill and confidence which exist between us. To know intimately and love tenderly only one very good person who returns our love, opens to us a whole world of delight and profit. Here on earth any enjoyment of this kind must be very limited indeed. It is limited by our own very imperfect knowledge of the hearts even of those who are nearest to us, by the moral defects or imperfections which prevent us from being entirely lovable or entirely unselfish in our love. It is almost the greatest blessing of which we are capable in this respect to have known one or two very holy persons. The great delight which we find in conversation with such persons is a faint reflection of what the joys of Heaven must be in this respect. Every one there is in the highest state of perfection, every one full of knowledge and love, every one able to communicate himself and to understand others in the most intimate manner, every one glowing with the most intense happiness and joy. We are often inclined on account of the narrowness and pettiness of our conceptions concerning the things of God, to make difficulties to ourselves concerning the happiness of Heaven in this respect—how far we shall know one another, and be able to continue and make perfect the holy intercourse of love which has bound us on earth to those to whom we have been united by God's Providence and the like. We are actually sometimes inclined to think of transplanting the jealousies and selfishness of earthly affection into that abode of peace and charity, as if the love and joy that we could have there could be affected by any such childish imperfections. All these foolish fears and fancies vanish before a few simple meditations on the immense blessings which God has prepared for us not only in the possession of Himself, but in that also of all those who are to share with us in the joy of possessing Him, our Blessed Lady, the saints and Angels, our own companions and friends, and the whole innumerable society of Heaven. There indeed is true society, converse, love, and there alone, except in so far as, by the grace of God, we know what is true Christian friendship and affection on earth, and in so far as by our devotion to and childlike confi- dence in the saints and Angels, especially those to whom God has in some particular manner committed us, we are able to anticipate here the blessings of this kind which await us.

5. It would be far from the truth to say that the Holy Souls in Purgatory have no share in the peace and love which must bind all the children of God together, to whatever realm of His Church they may belong. They are confirmed in grace, and full of charity, and so they must love very intensely indeed all that belong to God, the saints and Angels, their companions in Purgatory, and those who are still upon earth. Nor is it doubtful that they are visited and consoled, at least by the Angels, and that they

can have comfort by being allowed to know how the saints love them and pray for them, and the affection which is borne them and the efforts which are made for them by those whom they have left behind here. It may also be considered that they may have some kind of holy converse among themselves, and that their mutual love is a source of peace to them. But still their state is essentially one of pain, and also one of banishment and privation, and on this account it must also be a state of intense longing for the more perfect love and communion which awaits them with those who are to be their companions in the sight of God for ever. Their hearts are full, but they are bound to be mute—their tongues are tied by the justice of God, as the tongue of this demoniac was tied by the possession of the devil.

6. They may have seen, moreover, in the light of the Particular Judgment, that their banishment from the society of Heaven and from that free communion with the saints and Angels for which they so much long, is partly a punishment for some inordinate or blameworthy use of that poor kind of intercourse with others which the gift of speech enabled them to enjoy while on earth. Without speaking here of the innumerable sins of the tongue which may have to be expiated in Purgatory, it may be enough to think of the faults which may infect social intercourse as such, the inordinate affections, the jealousies and rivalries, the small practice of charity, the neglect to resist human respect, the coldness to those whom we might have consoled or assisted, the numberless acts of self-seeking and vanity which may arise in the daily intercourse of life. There may be "silence from good words," and breaches of silence from bad words, which may

be punished by the enforced silence of Purgatory. This is a very large subject for thought, and it is enough here simply to indicate it. Our Lord now, in Heaven, as on this occasion when on earth, is very desirous and ready to relieve this muteness, and to loosen the tongues which are now held back from the praises of God, the exercise of charity, the expression of their joy and thankfulness. We have it in our power to hasten on this deliverance, and by doing this we may perhaps obtain the grace so to use our own gift of speech and our own conversation with our neighbour, as to escape the mournful self-reproach of seeing hereafter that we have prepared ourselves thereby, rather for the prison of Purgatory, than for the happy conversation of the children of God in Heaven.

CHAPTER XVII.

Peace of the Holy Souls.

(STILLING THE TEMPEST.)

St. Matt. viii. 23—27 ; St. Mark iv. 36—40; St. Luke viii. 22—25.

1. THE most striking of our Lord's miracles to those who witnessed them must perhaps have been those in which He displayed His power over the forces of nature, which are usually so far above all human control. For diseases are to a certain extent, and in certain cases, within the reach of science and experience, at least as to some alleviation of their evils : and even when He gave sight to the blind or speech to the dumb, the organs of sight or speech were there in the first instance to make

their miraculous use less startling when it was be-stowed. In the case even of the demoniacs, there was obviously present a personal power at work, different from that of the possessed themselves, which power was quelled and reduced to obedience by the command of our Lord. In the case of which we are about to speak there was nothing of this kind. For the powers of nature, as we call them, seem to us so entirely subject to the unchangeable laws which govern them, as to admit of no inter-ference—at least any interference with them seems to appal and even alarm us, as if the most stable and certain things in all the world in which we live were being shaken. Thus it seems to be predicted by our Lord that, in His good Providence, some most marvellous alterations in the aspect and con-dition of the physical universe will be given by God as the last signs to arouse the wicked world from its sleep before the Day of Judgment. Again, there is nothing in all our experience before which we feel so utterly helpless and prostrate as some of the more violent demonstrations of physical power in the elements, which seem sometimes to unchain themselves, as if for the purpose of showing man how weak and insignificant he is, as in great storms, earthquakes, hurricanes, the eruption of volcanoes, and the like. What must be the power that can tame them? Thus it seems to have been like a new revelation of our Lord's Divine authority, when the disciples and others could say to themselves, "Who is this, that even the winds and the sea obey Him?"

2. The miracle is related by the three historical Evangelists, and the circumstances are placed by them all in the same order, except in one particular. Our Lord is asleep in the stern of the ship, when a violent storm falls on the lake, and there appears to

be imminent danger for His boat and for the others which were in company with it. The disciples come in haste and alarm to wake Him up, and, as St. Mark tells us, with a kind of complaint, as if His sleeping at such a time was a sign of some carelessness as to their fate: " Master, doth it not matter to Thee that we are perishing ? " Our Lord in the first place rises up and rebukes the waves and the winds, bidding them be still. ·Then a great calm comes on as suddenly as the storm which had preceded it, and our Lord turns to the disciples and asks them why they were afraid, calls them men of little faith, and the like. Then follows the exclamation of the whole company, " Who is this, that even the winds and sea obey Him ? "

3. The circumstance in this miracle on which we may fasten in our meditations concerning Purgatory is that of the great calm which came over the lake after our Lord had spoken. This calm was more than natural, because after so great a commotion it is not usual for the sea to become smooth and tranquil all at once. The sudden change seems to have struck the witnesses, as it is specially recorded by the Evangelists. But we may certainly say, without fear of exaggeration, that no sudden calm that ever fell on sea or lake, even when the storm had been·most violent and the change most instantaneous, could compare with the wonderful change to peace and perfect tranquillity which takes place at the moment of death in the case of those who die in the grace of God. This calm and peace is not, in the case of the Holy Souls, a passing, but a permanent state, it lasts as long as they remain in the holy prison of Purgatory ; in some respects it becomes more intense as their period of purification draws towards its close, and then it merges

K

itself in the ineffable repose of the Beatific Vision.
This peace of the holy state of Purgatory is as true
and real an element in the condition of those souls
of whom we are thinking in these chapters, as is
the pain which they suffer and the length of time
for which it may last. It should be our endeavour
to gain a complete view, as far as may be, of their
condition, and for this purpose, it is necessary to
dwell as much on one side of it, so to speak, as on
the other. We may therefore devote this chapter
to some consideration which may serve to illustrate
the peace and calm of which the tranquillity of the
lake of Galilee, after our Lord had stilled the
tempest, may be taken as an image.

4. In the first place, then, it is certain that at the
moment of death those who die in the grace of God
are confirmed in that grace. Here at once is something stable and fixed, free from disturbance and
fluctuation, as when the ever-restless waves of a
lake are formed by the action of freezing into solid
ice, over which the winds, which have before lashed
them at will into perpetual sleepless motion and
agitation, sweep without the least power to dis-
turb their repose. Nothing on earth so nearly
approaches the peace of Heaven as a soul which
is practically and morally, if not literally and
actually, confirmed in grace, as we believe the soul
of our Blessed Lady, and the souls of the Apostles
after the Day of Pentecost to have been. Again,
the Holy Souls are not simply confirmed in grace,
but they love God intensely, according to the
degree of that love which He intends them to have
throughout all eternity, and here again is another
element in their state which enables us to understand how it is a state of the greatest peace. They
love God according to their knowledge of Him and

of His attributes and character, and among other
things in Him which they know and love, is the
infinite justice and holiness which places them
where they are in His kingdom—that is, in a
condition of suffering, which is due to His justice
and to their deserts. The love of God is the true
peace of the soul, and in proportion as the fire of
Purgatory does away with the impediments which
their imperfections have placed in the way of His
perfect reign in their hearts, so does their love of
God grow and become more intense, because it is
no longer kept out of the soul by those impediments.
We know how the love of God has preserved the
saints in tranquillity and peace amidst all the
greatest troubles and anxieties and persecutions of
this world, the most violent sufferings of mind and
body, and thus we are able to understand that the
same love of God may be the source of ineffable
peace to the departed, even amid the severe sufferings which are inflicted in Purgatory.

5. Again, the Psalmist says, *Pax multa diligentibus
legem tuam*—" There is great peace to those who love
Thy law." And the Holy Souls are altogether in
love with the law of God, and would not have it
violated one atom in their own case, even if it were
to lead to their own immediate deliverance from
their punishments. And as to that special law of
God which is His will in every particular matter,
they are most perfectly and absolutely conformed
to it, and would rather suffer for ever as they do
according to His will than be raised at once to the
highest glories and enjoyments in Heaven against
or without His will. In this again we see how
deep their peace must be. No one, moreover, can
be said to be without peace, who is perfectly content with his lot and extremely thankful for it, but

the holy sufferers in Purgatory know that their present condition is the very one condition which suits them best, and is most for their good. They know that God has used towards them infinite mercy in not exacting from them a far greater amount of suffering, that they have deserved far more, and even Hell itself, and on this account they are overflowing with gratitude that their case is not harder than it is.

6. Besides these elements of peace in the Holy Souls there are others which consist in or result from their condition in itself. We all know what are the dangers to peace in this life—dangers so many and so great that it seems almost impossible to be at perfect peace as long as we are as we are. What a blessing we should account it to be free from all external temptation, from all molestation of the evil one, from all provocations to sin from objects external to ourselves, whether they attack us on the side of the irascible part of our nature, or whether their seductions are addressed to our concupiscence! But in the case of the Holy Souls there are no disturbances to their peace from the things which cause us pain or pleasure, which appeal to our ambition, or pride, or anger, or envy, or jealousy. All the beauty in the world cannot be a danger to them, all the riches or honours of the world cannot even seem to them desirable, much less be the occasion of serious temptation. But there is a more interior cause of unrest in us in our present condition, without which the external allurement to sin would not have any power to molest us. This is the interior division in ourselves, the struggle of the spirit against the flesh, of reason and conscience against passion and concupiscence, of the lower part of our nature, as we call it, against

the higher, the struggle which makes us feel that we have traitors in our own camp, and produces a sense of insecurity which is destructive of all perfect.peace. It is in this internal conflict and division that our great danger to sin consists, and so our great cause for perpetual anxiety and watchfulness. But all this is at an end for the Holy Souls. They have no external temptation and no interior conflict, and their state may well be compared to that of the calm lake, which was, as it were, charmed into preternatural repose and absolute tranquillity by the words of our Lord when He commanded the winds and the waves, and they obeyed Him.

7. And again, once more, even if we are tranquil and without fear for our present condition, still, as long as we are in the flesh, we have a very uncertain future before us, and yet a future on which our whole happiness depends. We cannot tell whether we are in the favour of God or not, we cannot be certain as to our perseverance, as to the circumstances under which death will find us, or how it will find us disposed towards God. And as long as this is uncertain, our look to the future must be one of anxiety, not, indeed, untempered by hope and confidence, and even by a kind of moral certainty that we have been trying all our life to serve God, or if we have turned to Him in good earnest, and if He has allowed us to work for Him, to become familiar guests at His table, and well acquainted with His means of grace and the practice of the virtues by which He delights to be honoured, He will not let our hope fail at the last. But still, as long as the future is uncertain, we cannot be free from trembling anticipations as to what we have deserved and what God may do to

us.   But after death all this also is changed; for those who are in God's displeasure then, there can be no more hope, and for those who are in His favour then, there can be no more fear.   Even those who have the heaviest and the longest debt to pay in Purgatory are absolutely certain of their salvation, and they know that the time is fixed in the decrees of Him Who is all powerful, when they shall become fellow-citizens of the saints and Angels in Heaven ; or rather, that they are already their fellow-citizens, and shall infallibly, at God's appointed time, enter on the full possession of their inheritance.   Thus their state may be, as it is, a state of intense pain; it may be a state the sufferings of which surpass all that can be suffered in this world; it may be a state in which every moment seems a long course of years, and which may thus seem to them to pass away with incredible slowness.   But still it must be a state of peace, because doubt and uncertainty and anxiety as to the future can have no place there, any more than they can have place in Heaven itself, the very abode and home of that peace which surpasseth all thought, and excludes even the slightest ruffle of disturbance or disquiet.

CHAPTER XVIII.

Contrast between Purgatory and Hell.

(THE CASTING OUT OF THE LEGION OF DEVILS.)
St. Matt. viii. 28—34, ix. 1 ; St. Mark v. 1—21 ;
St. Luke viii. 26—40.

1. THE consideration of the tranquillity and peace which reign in Purgatory may help to show us how, in a certain sense, the period of their detention there is to the Holy Souls a sort of foretaste of Heaven, and a time when they feel with intense gratitude their deliverance from the stormy and unsettled existence which they have led during their life on earth. The next in order of our Lord's miracles gives us an opportunity of comparing the state of Purgatory with that of the other place of punishment which the justice· of God has established. That other place is Hell, prepared, as our Lord says in His last parable, for the devil and his angels, but which is also to serve for the eternal abode of men such as we are, if they die in mortal sin, and where they will suffer in due proportion to the sins of which they have been guilty.

2. The miracle of which we are about to speak is one of the most remarkable of all those which our Lord wrought. It is so, partly on account of the large number of evil spirits who had been allowed to take possession of the soul of the poor sufferer

who was delivered, partly on account of the manner in which the circumstances of the story seem to lift the veil which hides from us the unseen world, at least as to certain conditions of the present existence of the evil spirits, and to show us at once their misery, their malice, and their power. We shall have to leave aside a great many thoughts which will occur to us as to these points, in order to dwell more exclusively on that which is to be the subject of this chapter. The miracle is carefully related by the three historical Evangelists, and its circumstances are familiar to us all. After the stilling of the tempest, of which we had to speak in the last chapter, our Lord lands on the coast of the Sea of Galilee opposite to Capharnaum. It was a wild tract, inhabited, as it seems, by a mixed population, in which there was a large proportion of Gentiles. In certain respects it resembled the countries, of which there 'are still so many in the world, in which the Church has hardly set her foot, and in which, in consequence of her absence, the evil spirits are allowed greater licence. Our Lord was met on His landing by two demoniacs, one of whom appears to have been in a worse case than the other, but they were both of them dwelling in the tombs among the rocks, and were so violent and savage that no one could pass along the road which led from the shore to the tombs. St. Mark, speaking of the chief of the two, says that it had often been attempted to bind him with chains, but all had failed, he had broken them all, and that no one could tame him, and he was always in the tombs among the mountains, day and night, crying out and cutting himself with stones. He was possessed, in truth, by a whole " legion " of devils, who forced him to go and throw himself at our Lord's feet, begging Him not to torment them, and then they revealed their numbers at our Lord's command, and also begged Him, first not to drive them out of the country, and then not to cast them out "into the abyss," that is, as it seems, to bid them leave this world altogether. Lastly, they besought Him to allow them to enter into a large herd of swine that were feeding near the place, and when our Lord permitted this, the whole herd was seen to run down the steep side of a hill above the sea, and throw itself over the cliff into the water. The keepers of the swine went into the town, and related what had happened, on which the people of the place came out to beg our Lord to depart from their country. The poor man from whom the devils had been cast out entreated our Lord, on the other hand, to allow him to follow Him and remain under His protection and guidance, but our Lord would not allow this, bidding him instead go home to his family, and tell them of the wonderful deliverance which God had wrought for him.

3. This narrative certainly sets before us, in striking colours, the sufferings which the evil spirits are allowed to inflict, and their own inveterate malice. Their abject fear at the presence of our Lord contrasts with the extreme violence to which they had been able to urge the man who was at last delivered from them. We see their hatred to the human race in their desire not to be forbidden any longer to haunt the earth, which is the home of man. We see their malice and desire to injure any creatures of God which they are allowed to infest, in their craving leave to enter into the swine, and the immediate destruction of the whole herd which ensued when that leave was granted. Power, malice, restlessness, hatred of God and of what belongs

to Him, hatred of man for His sake—such are some of the features of the picture of the devils as drawn in the history of this miracle. We seem to see how they carry their hell with them wherever they go, and it is on this account that we may use this miracle as shedding light on the contrast on which we are engaged. We have a picture which may in some respects remind us of Purgatory, in the poor man who had been delivered from the devils, sitting down at our Lord's feet, clothed, in his right mind, and desirous to be admitted to the blessed company who now followed our Lord whithersoever He went. The difference between this man as he was after his deliverance and as he was before, is not so great as that which we are thinking of—the difference between the sojourners in Purgatory and the miserable dwellers in Hell; but few pictures of the kind in our Lord's life seem to set before us so vividly as this the fierce torments to which those last-named dwellers are subjected.

4. The sufferings which are to be endured in Hell may be divided thus: (1) The pain of loss; (2) the pain of sense, under which head we may include the internal pains of the souls there imprisoned; (3) the place and company; (4) the eternity and consequent hopelessness of relief; (5) the entire aversion of the will from God, for Whom man was created. This last is, in truth, a part of those pains which are included under the former heads, but for our purpose it may be better to consider it separately. Taking this division as embracing, more or less, all that can be affirmed as to the various pains of Hell, we shall not find it difficult to understand the difference which separates Purgatory from Hell. As to the pain of loss, that is in one sense the same in both cases, and in another sense very different. The souls who are

suffering in Hell have lost God for ever, and the souls in Purgatory are banished from the sight of God for a time. In both cases they are debarred from the Beatific Vision, for which they were intended, and which became, as it were, their birthright when they were admitted to the blessings of the Christian Covenant in Holy Baptism. The sense of the eternity and utter irremediableness of this separation must add an immense and inconceivable weight of pain to the loss of the souls in Hell. And the Holy Souls in Purgatory are not separated from our Lord as to grace and charity, though there are certain features in their case which resemble those of the lost souls. For the souls in Purgatory have lost, in many cases, degrees of grace and of glory in Heaven which can never be regained. When their time of purification is over, they will be rewarded eternally in the possession of God, according to what their merits have been, and not according to what those merits might have been if they had been more faithful. If therefore there were degrees of the knowledge and love of God which they have failed to gain when they might have gained them, that is a loss which cannot be in itself repaired, although the perfect union of their wills with that of God and their perfect charity and contentment will prevent any sense of loss in that regard when they are admitted to Heaven. We may find it well to make this part of the pain of loss the subject of a separate chapter hereafter.

5. If, continuing our comparison, we consider, in the second place, the pain of sense, we shall find that it is possible that some souls in Purgatory may suffer pain of that kind for a time to a greater extent and in a greater intensity than some of the lost souls may suffer it for ever. For the pain in each

case is in proportion to the sin, and there may be souls who die in the grace of God, who have committed more sins for which punishment is due than others who die out of the grace of God, and who may have had far shorter lives and far fewer or less powerful temptations. This will hold good of the pains of sense in the strictest meaning of the term. If we go on to include under those words the sufferings which the lost souls have to endure from the torments which afflict their interior faculties, the memory, the fancy, the imagination, the appetites on which the passions work, and the like, it may be said that the difference is immense. In the case of the lost soul, there is the greatest interior disorder and misery, the memory is full of the opportunities of grace lost and the emptiness of the pleasures for which they have been lost, the reason is distorted, the will is perverted, the imagination is haunted by the foulest and most hateful shapes, the whole mind and heart is at war with itself, with its past, with its future, with all around it, and with God. In the case of the Holy Souls, there must have been bitter self-reproval, confusion, and consequently pain and sorrow, when the whole of their lives was presented to them in the light of truth at the moment of their judgment by our Lord. And we cannot doubt that the misuse or disordinate indulgence of any one of the interior faculties of the soul will have its pain corresponding to it. But their present state is one of order, tranquillity, and peace, as we have already seen—they are in their " right mind," like the man in the miracle before us, after he had been set free from the devils, and the only pain that they can suffer is that which is required for the satisfaction due to the justice of God, not that which arises from any present interior imperfection or discord in them.

6. It is hardly necessary to dwell on the obvious difference, as to the next two heads, between Purgatory and Hell. It is true that many writers have placed Purgatory, locally, close to Hell, and have held that there is in each the same kind of fire. This need not be called in question, but if it be not permitted, as we have seen above, that in ordinary cases the devils should be the tormentors of the Holy Souls, the actual juxtaposition of place would still leave a great difference between the two classes of sufferers with whose state we are concerned. As to the company in each, the difference is hardly less than that between Hell and Heaven itself. All the suffering souls in Purgatory love God and love one another, and although they are not allowed that fulness of intercourse and mutual consolation which is the lot of the Blessed in Heaven, still their wills and hearts are all one, the union of peace between them reflecting the internal peace of each soul, as the discord and savage tumult of Hell reflect the internal miseries of the souls there, preying upon themselves, and as it were tearing themselves to pieces. And then, in the next place, we must add to whatever differences we have already considered the circumstance which multiplies the weight of misery in Hell so infinitely—the circumstance of the eternal duration of the pains which are there to be suffered. One single ray of hope that a change or an end might come after an all but endless series of ages would go far towards changing Hell into Purgatory. But that one ray of hope can never shine. And, on the other hand, let the pains of Purgatory be far more intense than they are usually conceived to be, still they would be endurable as long as the certain hope—not less a hope because it is a certainty—remains, that the end will come, and that it

can be hastened on indefinitely by the mercy of God and the prayers of the Church. And when this hope, or rather knowledge, falls like a stream of light upon souls whose condition is already one of peace and resignation under their heavy sufferings, it give an ineffable and heavenly firmness and strength to all the happier elements of their condition in other respects.

7. But that which, after all, is the true essence of the difference which we are considering, lies not so much in any external circumstances of place, or pain, or companionship, or even of duration, as in the radical truth that the souls of those who suffer in Purgatory are united to God and turned to Him with the whole force of nature and of choice, while the poor prisoners in Hell are altogether averse from Him, their only end, and have thus, by their own deliberate and now irreversible choice, rejected the end for which they were made. This aversion from God of the soul which has died in mortal sin, and which, according to the law of its creation, must remain for ever in the state in which it was when the time of its probation closed, is that which makes Hell what it is. This is so true, that the sufferings of Hell, the pain of sense, the pain of banishment from God, the pain of evil companionship, and the like, might conceivably be suffered eternally by a soul that had the love of God and underwent them by His will, and yet that soul could not find Hell in them. The will of God would make all things sweet to such a soul. And, in the same way, if it were possible for a soul which was averse from God, as are the souls of the lost, to be in the midst of Heaven itself, it could not find Heaven there. The mere aversion from God would make Heaven itself a place of torment. This aversion from God is the

root and principle of all the other interior torments of the soul of which we have been speaking—its hatred of itself and all other creatures, the discord and indescribable misery which convulse it for ever. But, when we cast our eyes on Purgatory, we see nothing of this aversion there, but rather the most entire conformity to God's will and the most perfect love of Him, which is the root of all else in the condition of the souls there, which is so happy and peaceful.

8. The comparison between Purgatory and Hell is one of those considerations connected with our general subject which may be used with the greatest possible profit to help us to avoid most carefully even the shadow of deliberate mortal sin. Every such sin, in truth, bridges the abyss between Purgatory and Hell. We all carry about with us, as it were, the seeds of Hell in our souls, because we all bear in our hearts the evil passions and propensities which, if allowed to grow to full maturity, issue in mortal sin. And in our wills, which may consent to the indulgence of such passions or turn away from them, we have the issue of life or death. Indeed, whenever mortal sin has been consented to; the hell of the soul, the essence of all that can be suffered throughout all eternity, has been already kindled, and its flames can never be extinguished but by a turning again of the soul to God by the assistance of His grace, an assistance denied to no one, but made most easy for the children of the Church by means of the life-giving Sacraments. Again, the same consideration brings out into fuller light the truth that the love of God and the union of the will with Him is the essence of Heaven, and of all happiness elsewhere that is the forerunner of Heaven. Through all their intense sufferings,

the love of God keeps the Holy Souls happy and content, as it would keep the souls in Hell, if it could penetrate there, happy and content. This is a lesson of much practical power in every way, and in none more so than in helping us to bear joyously whatever sufferings and afflictions God may send us, far inferior as they must be to those which are so patiently borne in Purgatory. In truth, we might have little satisfaction to pay hereafter, if we bore well here the Purgatory which God sends us in the course of His Providence.

CHAPTER XIX.

The Sense of Shame in Purgatory.

(THE HEALING OF THE WOMAN WITH AN ISSUE
OF BLOOD.)

St. Matt. ix. 19—22; St. Mark v. 24—34; St. Luke viii. 42—48.

1. It happens that we have a fuller narrative than usual of our Lord's movements between the time of His stilling the tempest on the lake and the last of the miracles, of which we shall have to speak in the few following chapters. If we may judge from the manner in which marvellous miracles are crowded into these two or three days, we may fairly suppose that such displays of power and mercy were almost unintermittent with Him, and that the only reason why we do not know of hundreds more than are recorded by the Evangelists is that they were forced to make a not very large selection from the multitude before them. The three Evangelists tell us that on our Lord's return

from the farther side of the lake He found the people thronging to meet Him, and that He was very soon interrupted in His teaching by the appearance of Jairus, the ruler of the Synagogue, who came to beg Him to come and heal his daughter, who was at the point of death. Our Lord at once went with him, and on His way to his house the miracle of which we are now to speak took place. A woman who had suffered for twelve years from an issue of blood, and had " bestowed all her substance on physicians, and could not be healed by any, came behind Him and touched the hem of His garment. For she said, If I shall touch but His garment I shall be whole. And forthwith the fountain of her blood was dried up, and she felt in herself that she was healed of the evil." Our Lord used so very commonly to charge persons on whom His miraculous cures were wrought not to divulge or publish them, that we might have expected that on this occasion He would have allowed the mercy which He had shown this woman to remain a secret between Himself and her. But for many reasons which have been assigned by holy writers, it did not accord with the counsels of His Providence that it should be so. " And immediately Jesus knowing in Himself the virtue which had proceeded from Him, turning to the multitude, said, Who hath touched My garments? And His disciples said to Him, Thou seest the multitude thronging Thee, and sayest Thou, Who hath touched Me? And He looked about to see her who had done this. But the woman fearing and trembling, knowing what was done in her," or as St. Luke puts it, " The woman, seeing that she was not hid, came trembling, and fell down before His feet, and declared before all the people for what cause she had touched Him,

L

and how she was immediately healed. And He said to her, Daughter, thy faith had made thee whole ; go thy way in peace."

2. We must select only one of the lessons which are suggested by this miracle, and which might illustrate more than one point in the doctrine concerning Purgatory. The characteristic which distinguishes this woman among those who were the objects of our Lord's compassionate power is the mixture which we see in her of strong faith and natural shamefacedness. Her strong faith led her to the venturesome step of touching the hem of our Lord's garment, after she had so long tried in vain all the resources of human skill and knowledge. On the other hand, she was too much ashamed of herself and of her disease to come to Him openly when others would know for what she came. So she chose a moment when, as she thought, she could obtain her boon unseen and unknown. No one would notice it if she touched the hem of His garment when He was in the midst of a crowd passing through the street, so she would place herself in His path, win her cure, and go away undetected. But our Lord, for certain wise pur-poses, would not allow this. It is commonly thought that He forced her to confess what had passed, in order to strengthen the faith of Jairus, who was with Him, and who was just at that moment to receive the message from his home, telling him not to trouble our Lord any further, because his child, whom he had left dying, was now dead. But we may well suppose that even if there had not been this reason for the revelation of the miracle, our Lord would not have allowed the woman who had been healed to go away without some acknowledgment of what had passed in her.

There are false shames as well as true shames; there is a reserve in declaring our own miseries and the mercies of God towards us, which is wholesome and wise, and there is also a reserve as to the same which is not so laudable, or which at all events, on certain occasions, must be overcome. So this woman, who appears from her circumstances not to have been of the poorest class, was obliged by our Lord to confess before all the multitude, both her own infirmity and the mercy which had been wrought upon her.

3. The feeling of shame which had kept her back may have been twofold in character. She may have shrunk from divulging her own malady from a sense of its foulness, and she may also have shrunk back, as St. Peter did, after the miraculous draught of fishes, out of a sense of her own unworthiness to be made the object of so extraordinary a mercy. If we turn to the Holy Souls of Purgatory, we may find in them examples of both these kinds of shame. We have often spoken of the new light which is cast at the moment of their judgment upon the whole of their lives, all their actions and words and thoughts, all their opportunities of grace and the like, the whole of God's dealing with them, and of their treatment of God. The great predominant affection which this revelation must cause in them is one of the most intense contrition, but akin to this, and indeed a part of it—for it is founded on the recognition of their unfaithfulness and disloyalty to the ineffable majesty and goodness of God—will be the feeling of shame. This is one of the fruits which we are taught by St. Ignatius to draw from the consideration of sin, which leads us naturally to reflect on the miserable use which we have made of so much grace, our shameful ingratitude, the

petty, shabby, niggardly return which we have made to so much tenderness and generosity, the silly way in which we have managed our lives, the disgraceful and discreditable motives of self-love on which we have often acted, and the like. Again, a great part of that for which, under this head, the souls which stand before the judgment-seat of our Lord will have to feel such intense shame, will be the indulgence of shame itself as a motive of action, which may so often have induced them to be afraid of men, to yield to human respect, to fear not only those who can kill the body but those who could laugh at them, or make them unpopular, or put them to slight inconveniences, or the company in which they found themselves, rather than bear witness to the law or the truth of God in word or in action. Then, again, there are a number of reticences which are the result of self-love as well as of human respect, as when persons have made a mistake and do not like to acknowledge it, or are ignorant of what they have been supposed to know and will not say so, or have done some one wrong or been guilty of some rudeness and will not apologise, or have had credit given them which they do not deserve, and will not disclaim it. This is another class of the pettinesses which are the result of a false shame. Much more dangerous are those which prevent us from being perfectly open in confession, in cases where there may not be an absolute necessity for it, but when it would be much more ingenuous, and gain us much more light and grace from God, to speak, as in the confession of deliberate small sins to which we have an attachment, or again, when to acknowledge the truth about ourselves, our persons, our antecedents, our families, and the like, will bring on us some humiliation in the eyes of men. These are but instances of a very large class of defects and faults which may be represented as in an image by the natural shyness and reluctance of this woman to let people know what had happened to her. Our Lord, Who could have nothing in Himself which was not worthy of the highest honour and of the adoration of all Heaven and earth, hid all that was in Himself which might attract admiration, made Himself the most abject and despised of men as to His outward condition, and courted every kind of external shame and reproach, which He could not deserve, as men court the highest honours. The saints have learnt from Him the love of reproach and shame, and would be willing to make themselves ridiculous in public, in order to indulge their passion for humiliation, if such conduct were consistent with their devotion to the glory of God and the good of souls. The Holy Souls of Purgatory have learnt to look on these things with the eye of our Lord and of His saints, and have seen how much loss they have to regret of opportunities of humiliation out of timidity as to human respect and the subtle power of self-love. And now, if they could choose, they would have all their faults and failings proclaimed to all the world on the housetops, in order that they might gain the merit of due humiliation, and that God might have the glory which belongs to Him for having borne with them and forgiven them.

4. This sense of the shamefulness of their faults and ingratitude towards God will have been one of the afflictions of the Holy Souls at the time of their judgment. It will also blend with that other shame for their own present unfitness for Heaven and the sight of God, of which we have already spoken in the chapter on the Centurion's Servant. Both will

melt away, as causes of any pain or confusion, under the influence of their burning love of God and of the removal of all that has to be cancelled by satisfaction. It is not in accordance with the laws of God's Providence, nor, indeed, would it be well that all these causes of shame should become known to the world. But when the great day of account comes, at which time, among other things bearing on this subject, it will be true to say that no harm can possibly be done to any single soul by the publication of the faults of each and all, however shameful in themselves, then the whole story of each soul will be known to the glory of God, as David says in his penitential Psalm, " that thou mayest be justified in thy words, and overcome when thou art judged."[1] Our Lord will then " bring to light the hidden things of darkness, and make manifest the counsels of the hearts."[2] This will not be to the shame and sorrow of the redeemed children of God, because it will be to His glory, and because also their debt will have been entirely paid, and every lingering stain removed from their souls, so that they will be trophies of His victorious grace and ineffable mercy in regard to every single act which might otherwise cause them shame. But the truth that this is to be so may help to strengthen us against the foolish shame which would hide our sins from the eyes of others, even, if we could, from those of God, and teach us the immense benefit and treasure that is stored up for us in openness as to every defect, and in any humiliation to which that openness may lead.

5. The practice of this simplicity and humility will certainly bring great blessings on our souls, and enable us to advance rapidly in grace. But we must not part from the subject without adding that it may,

[1] Psalm l. 6.   [2] 1 Cor. iv. 5.

in more ways than one, enable us also to help the Holy Souls. It may make our prayers for them more powerful, and it will give us the opportunity of offering to God a considerable number of acts of interior mortification, and sometimes even of exterior humiliation, by way of satisfaction for them, which may be accepted by Him as expiation for the reserve and reticence which He may have been obliged by His justice to punish in the prison of Purgatory.

CHAPTER XX.

The Pain of Sense in Purgatory.

(THE RAISING TO LIFE OF THE DAUGHTER OF JAIRUS.)

St. Matt. ix. 18—26 ; St. Mark v. 22—43 ; St. Luke xiii. 41—56.

1. WHEN our Lord healed the woman with the issue of blood, He was, as has been said, on His way to the house of Jairus, the ruler of the synagogue at Capharnaum, whose daughter had been left by her father at the point of death when, on hearing of our Lord's return from the other side of the lake, he had hurried off to beg Him to come and heal her. The incident of the cure of the woman with the issue of blood, our Lord's pausing on His way, and obliging her to come forth and declare before all what had taken place, must have caused a few moments of delay which were trying to the father. Just as our Lord was sending the woman away with His blessing, some messengers came from the house of Jairus, telling him that all was over and that he need not " trouble the master " any more. Our Lord turned

at once to him, and bade him fear nothing, " only believe, and she shall be saved." They went on together, followed by the multitude, and by the time when they reached the house, the customary mourning had already begun. They found musicians, and a number of people lamenting and weeping, and a confused crowd of weeping friends. Our Lord bade them all cease. " The maiden is not dead but sleepeth." He used these words in His own Divine meaning, for the girl was asleep in the sense in which sleep alone, and not death, admits of an awakening again in this life. They all ridiculed Him, for they knew well enough that, in the common sense of the words, she was truly dead. Then, as the Evangelists tell us, our Lord made them all leave the room, into which He went with the father and mother of the dead girl, and three of His disciples, St. Peter, St. James, and St. John. He took her by the hand as she lay, and said to her, " Damsel, arise! She arose at once and walked." She was about twélve years old, St. Mark tells us, of an age, therefore, at which, in those climates, girls are in the full bloom of youth, and approaching womanhood. Then our Lord earnestly bade the father and mother tell no one what had happened, and also ordered that the girl should take some food.

2. The Evangelists tell us nothing of the character or disposition, or of the after-life, of this girl whom our Lord raised from the dead. The mention of the office of her father as the ruler of the synagogue suggests that he was well known to our Lord, a friend of the centurion whose servant had lately been healed, and also of the nobleman whose son had been cured by our Lord's word spoken at a distance. Our Lord was now about to leave

Capharnaum almost entirely, probably on account of the unbelief of most,of its inhabitants and of the persecution which the emissaries of the priests at Jerusalem were raising against Him: but we find Him once more in the synagogue, where He delivered His great dogmatic discourse about the Holy Eucharist which is related in the sixth chapter of St. John's Gospel, after the first miracle of the multiplication of the loaves. We may conjecture that one reason for the marvellous miracle of which we are speaking in this chapter may have been the kindness of Jairus in admitting our Lord to teach so often in the synagogue. If we turn to the girl herself, it is natural to think rather of the effect which this mercy granted to her may have had on the rest of her life, than of any special reason which may have led our Lord to select her as the subject of that mercy. She was, as has been said, just on the threshold of full womanly life, when all that is naturally enjoyable and delightful was opening to her, the pleasures of the senses, the intoxication of affection, the world, society, position, all that can fascinate the soul and entangle the heart of the thoughtless and the gay. She entered on her new life with the gift of health and strength—for we must suppose that our Lord never worked His cures or His restorations,.as we say, by halves—the idol of her parents, dearer than she had been ever before, and, like some of the children who are now and then favoured with visions of our Blessed Lady or made the instruments by means of which a new devotion or a new shrine is set up in the Church, the object of general interest and curiosity, and even of a kind of veneration. We may well ask how this world appeared to her after she had come back to it with her short experience of the next, and what were the thoughts which she brought with her as to the dependence of the future on the present and the relative importance of the goods and evils here and the good and evils there.

3. All these things are hidden from us by the short narrative of the Evangelists, who concern themselves only with what more immediately relates to our Lord Himself. But the history of the Church contains instances of persons who have in like manner come back, as it were, from the world beyond the grave, who have spoken of its terrors or consolations, and the remainder of whose years has been altogether coloured by the impression made upon them. The daughter of Jairus may have been dead some little time when our Lord arrived at his house, for there must have been some notice required to bring the crowd of mourners and musicians there. But a very few moments indeed after death are enough for the instantaneous judgment which then takes place, and for the assign-ment of the soul which has left the body still warm, to its place in Heaven, in Purgatory, or in the place of punishment. It may have been that in this case the judgment and the sentence may have been delayed by our Lord's intention to raise the maiden to life, but she may nevertheless have been allowed to see the state of things into which she would naturally have been introduced, the peace of the saints in Limbus, the sufferings of the souls in Purgatory or in Hell. Such has been the case with others. That which would strike her most in what she saw would be that part of the sufferings of Purgatory which the senses can most easily grasp. The pain of loss might be made intelligible in many ways, to a visitant who was allowed to stand on the brink of Purgatory, but the pain of

sense is that part of the punishment of the Holy Souls which could not. by any possibility escape her notice. There are many beautiful things in the writings of the saints about the pain of loss; but the relations of those who have seen what Purgatory is in some preternatural manner have dwelt mainly on the pain of sense. This, therefore, we may suppose to have been one great indelible impression made on the mind of the girl of whom we speak, which may have saved her in many a temptation, and urged her on to great efforts in the service of God, even to heroic self-sacrifice, to a life of immense mortification, and also of great and laborious charity for the relief of the Holy Souls. We may use her case, therefore, as the foundation of our considerations on this point.

4. The manner in which the pain of sense affects souls which are separated from their bodies, and how, in particular, the fire of which our Lord speaks when He alludes to Hell acts upon such souls, belong to the class of subjects as to which schoolmen and theologians are full of difficulties and conjectures. All discussion of such questions would be out of place in a volume like the present, and therefore we need only say that it is clear from the language of Scripture, from reason, and from the sense of the Church, which is in full harmony with the general tone of the revelations contained in the lives of the saints, that the pain of sense in Purgatory is something so severe and intense that we can form of it no adequate conception in this life. The revelations in question are not in themselves authoritative. If they are considered simply as expressing the thoughts familiar to the holy persons to whom they are said to have been made, which is the very lowest rank to which they can be reduced, then at

least we have in them, and especially in their uniform tenour, an indication of the mind of the faithful children of the Church as to this matter. If they are considered as generally, or in many cases, representing preternatural communications which have been vouchsafed by God, then their authority rises higher than in the other case. But even then they do not stand by themselves. Reason itself seems to point to the conclusion that the sufferings of souls separated from the body must be very intense indeed, especially when these are inflicted by the special and particular justice of God as the exaction of the satisfaction due for a great number of sins, both venial and mortal. Purgatory has been created to be the place of punishment for those who are not to suffer for ever in Hell. It is not to be thought that God would create a place of this kind but for some strong necessity, or that when it is created it would not fulfil its purpose in the strictest sense. Whatever may be its characteristics, it is certain that they must witness to the wisdom, the mercy, the power, and the justice of God, to His ineffable holiness, and to the manner in which He looks upon sin. " Whatever a man soweth, that also he shall reap," the Apostle tells us. But it is certain that the number of sins which are committed in and through the body is almost infinite, that their guilt is very great, and that very little of sufficient penance is done for them here. If we were to follow the opinion, which can hardly approve itself to a Catholic mind, that the fire of which Holy Scripture speaks is metaphorical, even then we should be obliged to admit that Holy Scripture had used, as an image to represent the sufferings of Purgatory, that one figure of all others which suggests the most excruciating and intolerable of all the pains which can be suffered, and a pain which no one is able to endure for a few moments together, while it is certain that the punishments of Purgatory are continuous, and that, in many cases, their duration is extremely long.

5. It must be remembered that this teaching about the extreme severity of the pain of sense in Purgatory, is found in the writers who have dwelt the most on the happiness which the souls there enjoy, as well as in those who have set before us the more fearful pictures of their condition. St. Catharine of Genoa, who is the Saint to whom the doctrine of the happiness of the Holy Souls may be said to have been entrusted, says, " the soul, understanding that Purgatory has been instituted for the expiation and wiping off of imperfections, willingly enters there in submission to the arrangement of God, and considers itself to be very mercifully dealt with; and yet the bitterness of Purgatory surpasses all human understanding. But the soul, burning with love, thinks its imperfections of more importance than the pain of Purgatory, although that pain is so extremely terrible, that all that in this life we can know, or describe, or experience, or believe, appears to me a falsehood when compared to it. So that although I am obliged to say this, yet I am confounded at the greatness of the matter, which I have explained so much less adequately than I wished." This is very much the same kind of language as that of the Blessed Veronica, of whom the author of her Life writes, after relating some of her visions: " After she returned from that vision to the use of her body and her senses, she gave signs of vehement sadness, terrified sorrow, and great feelings of horror, striking her hands together, shaking her head, and speaking in a woful voice, and saying, ' Alas, alas! what

pains and torments have I seen to-day, inflicted by those same tormentors who are in Hell, and by the same fire, which is there!' And saying this, she fell on the ground, and a violent fever seized her, and her whole body was marked with marks as it were shining with fire, of the size of the palm of a hand." Very much the same is the testimony of the famous St. Christina, who was called back to this world after having seen the sufferings of the next, and who spent the rest of her life in the most severe penances for the relief of the Holy Souls. She stated that immediately on her soul leaving her body, she was taken by the Angels to a dark and horrible place, full of the souls of men ; the torments which she there witnessed were so terrible that no tongue could express them, she saw there the souls of many whom she had known in this life, and was moved to intense compassion for them. She asked what the place was, thinking it must be Hell, but she was told that it was Purgatory, and that the souls whose sufferings moved her compassion so much had been sinners who had repented of their sins, but not done sufficient penance for them. But, in truth, there is but one tone about all these revelations—they uniformly represent the torments of Purgatory as severe in the very utmost degree.

6. Many persons are in the habit of adopting a tone of complaint, and even of indignation, at the manner of speaking of the pains of Purgatory which is, in the main, founded on such revelations as those to which we have been referring. They object, further, to the representations of those pains which are sometimes to be found abroad, pictures of the souls, or rather bodies, representing the souls of Purgatory in burning flames, under excruciating tortures, which are sometimes administered by

demons as the executioners of the justice of God.
Such pictures are frequently used in missions to
the people, or are to be found in popular books of
devotion about Purgatory. The objection to such
representations is not confined to those which depict
the pains of Purgatory alone, but extends itself to
those in which the sufferings of Hell are the subject
which it is sought to bring home to his mind. It
may be worth while to say a few words on the
subject in general. In the first place, then, we
need hardly ask whether any Catholic doubts that
the truth which it is thus desired to represent be
a truth indeed, or whether it is a truth which it is
highly expedient and charitable to enforce in all
lawful ways. It is no doubt a great shock to
modern notions of the dignity of man and his
independence of God, to speak or write as if there
were any future torments at all, or as if these
torments were very severe. In the same way, there
are societies in which it is very improper to mention
or even to allude to death, or to anything else
which interferes with the unruffled sensual enjoyments in which so large a part of what is called
civilised society would so gladly spend, not only
its short span of life here, but an eternity, if it could
command it. It is certain, then, that no Catholic
can see anything to complain of in the constant
teaching about the punishments of sin which has
so much authority in the words of our Lord Himself.
These things are undoubtedly true, and the only
question can be as to the manner of representing
them to the people. In the second place, it may
be said that a vision is of necessity addressed to
the eye of the mind, and the language which it uses
must of necessity be that of sensible objects. If
the pain of sense is to be put before the soul at all,

except by word of mouth, it must be by images which represent the several senses as suffering torments which are intelligible to the mind through the eye. What is true of a vision is true of a picture. There is no difference in this respect between representations of the saints or Angels, of our Blessed Lord or His Sacred Mother, and the representations of Hell or Purgatory. In each case the thing to be set before the mind must be so set before it by means of a picture, rude, it may be, and altogether inadequate to be the full image of celestial beauty or of intense suffering, but still cognate in kind to the thing or person which it has to represent. This is the simple account of so many descriptions of what people have seen of Purgatory, or have endeavoured to depict of Hell. Those who find these things of use, as so many do, had better use them. Those who can represent to themselves the sufferings of our Lord without a crucifix need not use one, and those who can imagine the pains of Purgatory for themselves, may leave the representations of which we speak to others. But it is unreasonable to blame those who use them, or propose them for the use of others, on the ground of the horrible character of any particular picture or sculpture, unless we are prepared to say that the doctrine as to Purgatory or Hell which is there embodied, in the only way in which it can be embodied so as to strike the senses, is exaggerated or untrue.

7. It is here, perhaps, that the real difficulty lies. People are only too glad to persuade themselves that they may forget the severe truths of our faith as to the retributions for sin, whether temporal or eternal, and they turn with anger on whatever reminds them of these truths, rudely and palpably. If

these truths themselves are once mastered by the soul, it is not likely that objections will be made to the manner in which the memory of them is refreshed. It will be better hereafter to have quailed in terror before some picure of Purgatory in which the most fearful torments have been depicted in the grossest way, in which the souls are represented as writhing on spits in the midst of flames, torn to pieces by devils, screaming in agony, and afflicted by some special visible weapon of torture in every limb and every sense, than to have persuaded ourselves that these sufferings of which the saints of God think so much are light and short, and that it can be no such very terrible a thing to fall into the hands of the living God in the day of His Judgment. And if we are to return for a moment to the consideration of the case of the Holy Souls themselves, and their claims on our charity, it can be no kind thing to them, any more than to ourselves, to listen to the teaching or the instincts of self-love and sensuality, as to the supposed exaggerations which the most pious children of the Church may have believed to be truths, with regard to the intensity of sufferings such as theirs.

CHAPTER XXI.

The Eternal Losses of the Holy Souls.

(THE LAST CURES IN CAPHARNAUM.)
St. Matt. ix. 27–34.

1. ONE of the circumstances connected with the miracle of the raising of the daughter of Jairus from the dead, although in itself a common feature in many such incidents of our Lord's life, is still in itself and in its connection very remarkable. This circumstance is the strict injunction to secrecy which our Lord laid on those who witnessed that miracle. It could hardly, under any circumstances, remain long unknown. But it appears to be the case that our Lord was at this time especially anxious to escape observation in Capharnaum. The probable reason to be assigned for this anxiety is the persecution to which He was now exposed, and in a particular way the calumny about His league with Satan, which was one of the features of that persecution. A study of our Lord's life reveals the fact that He was now taking leave, as it were, of Capharnaum. The three miracles which St. Matthew subjoins in the passage cited above were evidently connected in point of time with the miracle on the daughter of Jairus, and the Evangelist is careful to notice this connection between them. They were, as it were, forced upon our Lord, and were not worked

in public.   The last of them, however, gave occasion to a renewed outburst of the calumny already
mentioned.

2. The history of these miracles is very simple.
As our Lord passed away from the house of Jairus,
two blind men followed Him.   They must have
been led to the place by those who had the charge
of them, or they may have been sitting in some
public place or street, and heard of His passing.
They kept crying out to Him, by the popular
name of the "Son of David," to have mercy on
them.   But He did not heal them in public.   He
went to the house where He usually abode, and they
were brought in to Him.   Then He asked them
whether they believed that He could do for them
what they wanted, and on their saying yes, He said,
"According to your faith be it done unto you."
They were at once healed, and though our Lord
severely charged them to be silent about their cure,
they went at once and spread it abroad over all
the country.   Then, after they had gone out, another poor sufferer was brought to Him, whose case
was very like one of which we have already heard.
He was dumb, and had a devil.   Our Lord cast the
devil out, and then the dumb man spoke.   The
multitude, who appear either to have followed our
Lord to the house, or to have been collected by the
cure of the blind men who had received their sight,
"wondered, saying, Never was the like seen in
Israel.   But the Pharisees said, By the prince of
devils He casteth out devils."   Thus our Lord's
precautions against the danger of occasioning a
revival of the calumny were rendered vain.   He
left Capharnaum, and was seldom there after this
time.

3. The circumstance in these miracles to which

our thoughts may be directed, in order to gather from them some illustration of the doctrine concerning Purgatory, may be that which has already been mentioned, that these were the last miraculous cures which are recorded by the Evangelists as having been worked in Capharnaum by our Lord. The time was come when He was forced to withdraw more and more from the city which He had made His own, and in which so many of His dearest friends lived—for this city was the home of some of the first Apostles, of St. Matthew, of the centurion, and the nobleman whose son He had healed, of Jairus, and perhaps of St. Mary Magdalene. Nevertheless, the inhabitants as a community had turned a deaf ear to His teaching—at all events the teachers and priests had turned away from Him themselves, and had led others to reject Him. It may not be certain at what precise time of His Ministry we are to place His famous denunciations of this city, along with others, in which so many mighty works had been done. These denunciations may have been repeated more than once. " Wo to thee, Corozain, wo to thee, Bethsaida; for if in Tyre and Sidon had been wrought the miracles that have been wrought in you, they would long ago have done penance in sackcloth and ashes. But I say to you, it shall be more tolerable for Tyre and Sidon in the Day of Judgment than for you. And thou, Capharnaum, shalt thou be exalted up to Heaven? Thou shalt go down even unto Hell. For if in Sodom had been wrought the miracles which have been wrought in thee, perhaps it would have remained unto this day. But I say unto you, it shall be more tolerable for the land of Sodom in the Day of Judgment, than for thee." [1] These words, and

[1] St. Matt. xi. 21—24.

the departure of our Lord from His usual haunts at Capharnaum, suggest to us the thought of the immense loss which is incurred by the neglect of the opportunities of grace with which our life is filled by the good Providence of God. Loss of this kind is not incurred by those alone from whom grace is altogether withdrawn, and who have in consequence to suffer externally in Hell. Such loss is also incurred in various measures and degrees by all who do not faithfully co-operate with grace, and who thus forfeit higher graces which they might have received, and fall into faults or defects which they might have escaped. We have already mentioned the sorrow which the Holy Souls in Purgatory must have felt when the amount of their own negligences as to grace was made clear to them in the light of their Particular Judgment. We shall make the fuller consideration of this loss the subject of the remainder of this chapter.

4. It is certain that a great number of Christians go out of this world in a state of grace, indeed, and so with the blessed destiny of eternal glory awaiting them, but still, after having lost a great part of the opportunities which was offered them in God's Providence of "laying up treasure in Heaven" by good works, and multiplying the graces vouchsafed to them. The consequence of this is that they have forfeited for ever an immense number of degrees of glory, each of which degrees, as being eternal, is of infinite value, both from the honour which might have accrued from it to God, and also from the blessings which it would have brought to the soul which has forfeited it. St. Paul[2] tells us that "star differeth from star in glory," and, as there are very great distances indeed between the glory of one

[2] 1 Cor. xv. 41.

saint and the glory of another, so also may there be immense differences between the height in Heaven and the nearness to God to which men do attain, and the height and the nearness to which they might have attained. Now the loss which the Holy Souls have thus incurred, and which has been made known to them, we cannot doubt, at their judgment, is a loss which is in itself irreparable. Purgatory can do away with the stains that remain on the soul, cancel the debt of satisfaction which they owe to the Divine justice, but it does not restore to them the time or the graces or the opportunities which have been squandered and have become unfruitful for eternity. This, in truth, amounts to a change, if we may so speak, in the counsels of God towards the souls which are to be eternally glorified in His Presence. According to His first counsel, as we may say, He had intended to give them a certain, it may be a very high, place in His Kingdom, to which they were to rise by their correspondence to the grand chain of graces which He was prepared to bestow upon them. But their own unfaithfulness has made the fulfilment of this counsel impossible according to the law of His justice. In consequence of this unfaithfulness, God has adopted another counsel in their regard: that is, He has determined that they shall gain another, but a far lower, grade of glory, and of all that is involved in that glory. He has withdrawn Himself from them to a certain extent, they have forfeited to a certain extent the fulfilment of the designs of His love, and as to that which they have forfeited, He has turned away from them as our Lord turned away from the cities in which His mighty works were done, and in which, after a time, He would work no more. This loss, as has been said, is eternal. It is made known to the Holy Souls, and a terrible sorrow is inflicted on them in consequence which is one of their most severe punishments. "I think," says Suarez, "that their sorrow, considered as a punishment laid upon them for their purgation, is rather on account of the grades of blessedness which they have lost for ever, or which they have not gained through sloth and venial sins, than on account of the simple deferring of that blessedness which they are, after a time, to gain. In this way, therefore, the souls that are more imperfect, and which have the greater amount of guilt, have to suffer greater sorrow."

5. It seems certainly a hard thing to say, that the sorrow of the Holy Souls for the glory which they have eternally lost, is greater than that which they feel because they are shut out for a time from that which they are destined to enjoy. For this last-named sorrow must be extremely intense, as we may come to see when we consider it separately. Still, what the great theologian above cited has said seems nothing more than what is strictly reasonable and natural. All their love of God, all their knowledge of His beauty, all that they know about the bliss of Heaven, the splendour of grace, the value of time, the power of the sacraments, the all but omnipotence of prayer, the treasures to be accumulated by good works, or penances, or almsdeeds, or satisfaction—everything of this kind must add to the self-reproach which they must entertain, when they consider how ungrateful, how unfaithful, how foolish they have been in their use of the opportunities and aids which God has given to them. It seems, indeed, wonderful that this pain can ever pass away. But it must be remembered that it is inflicted as a punishment only, and there-fore only for what has been wilful in the way of

neglect.   As a punishment, it must come to an end, and then the soul is left with nothing to impede its love of God from rushing forward to its full fruition. The saints who have been most faithful to the graces which God has given them have no regret for other higher graces which have not been offered them, though those other and higher graces would have secured them a higher glory and so a closer knowledge and a more intense love of God.   And so, when the punishment has been exhausted which He has inflicted on the imperfect souls who have been so far less faithful than the saints, they remain absolutely contented with their lot, because they have paid to His justice for the forfeiture of the glory which they might have reached.   It is one of the marvels of the wisdom and love of God that a pain like this can be felt in Purgatory, that the cause of it can remain for ever in its effects, and yet that the pain itself can be entirely assuaged.

6. This consideration is of immense value to us, though it relates to a part of the pains of Purgatory which are connected with an eternal and irreparable loss.   It may be said generally that the class of souls on which these pains will fall most heavily, must be the great number of those called to a certain closeness and intimate service of God who do not aim at the perfection to which God calls them.   If we once admit, as the practical though unavowed rule of our life, that it is enough for us to aim at avoiding mortal sin, and so escaping Hell, then we may be quite certain that, if we do by the mercy of God die in His grace, we shall have a very large share in the forfeiture of glory which is the cause of the pains of which we have been speaking. It seems impossible but that such souls should miss daily a thousand opportunities of advancing in

grace and so gaining higher glory. On the other hand, if we are earnestly and sincerely bent on making the best of our time and of our grace, on abounding in good works in whatever way is open to us, in making the service of God the one great aim of our life, and on using the means of grace in the most perfect manner, then we may have reason to hope that we shall so live and so die as not to have incurred a very severe punishment for very many graces of eternal happiness which we have lost.

7. We know by our faith that the creation and sanctification of a single human soul is a greater and nobler work of God, than the creation and conservation of the whole physical universe. It is a simple truth, that intellectual and spiritual gifts are more beautiful than all the beauties of earth and sea, sky and mountain, trees and flowers and animals, and the whole starry firmament. In both these orders of His magnificence, intellectual and spiritual on the one hand, and the physical and visible on the other hand, God may create kingdom upon kingdom grander and more splendid than any that He has as yet created. But what, if by our own act we had been able to stay His hand, and strike out all that is most glorious and majestic, all that reflects in the highest actual degree His wisdom and beauty and power, and forced Him, as it were, to content Himself with a poorer world, a narrower display of His marvels, something far less honourable and glorious to Him than what we see around us? What if we had been able to stint the profuse multitude of the stars which fill the heavens, to forbid Him to endow the sun with more than a mere millionth part of that light and heat which it now possesses, to limit Him to the peopling of dreary

and unfruitful regions with a few puny forms of life, such as perhaps the tricks of Egyptian musicians aided by evil Angels may have been able to seem to make to live and move? Yet this is but a faint picture of the losses of glory to God which have been caused by the unfaithfulness of His children. The life of each soul is dearer to Him than a thousand worlds, and He has agreed to adorn every moment of it with magnificent gifts, which He wooes His creatures to accept, in order that they may issue, by the working of His grace, in marvellous fruits of glory which are to last for ever. What a thing it is for Him to suffer at the hands of His friends, this sterility of His grace, this niggardly return from the soil which He has watered with His Blood? We may look upon the life of each Christian as intended by God to raise to His honour a stately temple, spacious, lofty, rich in all that can enhance the costliness of its fabric and its adornments with all the beauty that the highest art can bring out of the resources of nature and mind. It has to be finished and made complete in every part within a short space of time, and every day of every year has something to contribute of its own if the pile is to be accomplished. He places in our hands an abundance of materials, He labours Himself with us, He takes care that all that happens to us may work for us, and that all His friends in Heaven and on earth shall stand by to aid us and cheer us on. And the glorious temple which we are to raise for Him to dwell in is our own soul, which is to enjoy the fruit of its own labour through all eternity. Alas! in how many cases is the fabric not begun at all! in how many more does it halt at its very outset, so that the time of judgment comes when hardly the foundations have been laid! Such are the thoughts which rise in the mind when we consider what we have done for God, and compare it with what our work for Him might and ought to have been.

CHAPTER XXII.

Purgatory and Natural Piety.

(THE MIRACLES WROUGHT AT NAZARETH.)
St. Matt. xiii. 54—58; St. Mark vi. 1—6.

1. IT has already been said that the last cures wrought by our Lord at Capharnaum were shrouded by Him in as much secrecy as was possible under the circumstances, probably in order not to provoke the calumnies of His enemies. These calumnies, however, as we have seen, broke out afresh. St. Mark tells us that He now passed from Capharnaum to Nazareth, to pay to that once most blessed town what was to be, as it seems, His last visit. He took refuge, as it were, from Capharnaum in Nazareth, as He had before taken refuge from Nazareth in Capharnaum. The two accounts in St. Matthew and St. Mark, referred to above, evidently refer to the same visit. Our Lord, then, went to Nazareth, and began to teach in the synagogue on the Sabbath. The Evangelists tell us three things concerning this preaching. The first is that the people " were in admiration at His doctrine, saying, How came this Man by all these things ? and what wisdom is this which is given to Him, and such mighty works as are wrought by His hands? "—referring, as it seems, to the great miracles with which the whole country was ringing,

rather than to any which He had wrought at Nazareth itself. In the second place, they went on to speak of our Lord as of one in Whom nothing great could be expected. "Is not this the carpenter?" or "the son of the carpenter? The son of Mary, the brother of James and Joseph and Jude and Simon? are not also His sisters here with us? And they were scandalised in regard of Him." They tell us also of our Lord's famous answer, in which He referred to what He had said in the same synagogue at the very outset of His public Ministry. Then He had said, "No prophet is accepted in his own country."[1] Now He adds, that He is accepted elsewhere. "Jesus said to them, A Prophet is not without honour, but in his own country, and in his own house, and among his own kindred." Then we come to the few miracles which may furnish us with the subject of the present chapter. St. Matthew tells us, "He wrought not many miracles there, because of their unbelief." St. Mark puts it more strongly: "He could not do any miracles there, only that He cured a few that were sick, laying His hands upon them. And He wondered, because of their unbelief."

2. There are many thoughts which rise to the mind at the mention of these few miracles wrought by our Lord in the home of His boyhood and early manhood, the town in which He dwelt by far the greater part of His earthly life, whose streets were more often pressed by His sacred Feet than those of any other place in the world. The incident seems to typify the reception of our Lord by mankind, the race which He chose out of all creation with which to unite Himself, when "He came out unto His own, and His own received Him not."

[1] St. Luke iv. 24.

It seems to represent most forcibly the truth that so few of those who do receive Him allow Him to work in their souls what He desires to work, and that other general truth, of the extent to which the work of God in the world at large is impeded, so that it almost seems as if the fruits of the Incarnation were scanty indeed. But we shall use this motive which may have had some weight with our Lord in bringing about this visit as the ground of our considerations in this chapter. We seem to see that He was led by a holy piety to the place which was so long His home, to His old acquaintances and kinsfolk, in the loving hope that He might do them some little good. Thus we come to a subject which divides itself into two heads. In the first place, it is well to consider the love which, out of natural piety, the Holy Souls may bear to those whom they have left behind them, their own kith and kin, or others with whose lives their own lives have been bound up. In the second place, we may reflect on the duty which presses on us of relieving, to the utmost of our power, those among the souls in Purgatory between whom and us this sacred bond exists. These considerations will be quite enough to occupy us for the present.

3. As to the first point, no one familiar with Catholic doctrine or with Catholic modes of feeling can suppose, that the love of God with which the Holy Souls are so inflamed can, in their case, any more than in that of the Saints and Blessed in Heaven, dull the lawful and natural love which they bear to those who remain behind them on earth, or to those who may be with them in Purgatory, or who have gone before them to Heaven. All natural and human love is transformed and ennobled and purified, but it is also intensified and strengthened,

by the surpassing charity which reigns beyond the grave among the children of God. This is the only reasonable conclusion to which we can come on the grounds of Christian theology, although, perhaps, we feel so much the imperfection and the want of spirituality and unselfishness of our human affections, that we are tempted to think that there can be nothing of the kind in the next world. There can be nothing sensual or selfish or imperfect in kind, but that is all. It would almost seem as if our Lord had vouchsafed to give us a hint as to this in His teaching concerning the Rich Glutton, whether that narrative be considered as a Parable or not. We see that even in that poor soul there were the remains of natural piety and affection, for he desired that Lazarus might be sent to warn his brethren on earth lest they also should come to the same place of punishment with himself. Some writers have thought from this that the soul of the Rich Glutton was placed in Purgatory, as if it were impossible for the souls in Hell to feel any such affection as that which is manifested by his prayer. It may seem that this is an improbable opinion, because it need not be supposed that all natural affection is extinguished in the poor lost souls ; and again, it may be thought that the prayer of the Rich Glutton,[1] which was for something which it was contrary to the disposition of God's Providence to grant, and which was, in fact, not granted, was not the sort of prayer which the Holy Souls of Purgatory would make. But if we suppose the soul of whom we are speaking to have been in Hell, it can only increase the evidence which the case affords, for it is most certain that if there can still be anything like love for those on earth in Hell,

[1] St. Luke xvi. 27.

there must be immensely greater love for the same persons in Purgatory.

4. We may well, therefore, suppose with what tender a love the Holy Souls will yearn for all that is good to those whom they have left on earth: parents for children, or children for parents, husbands and wives, brothers and sisters, friends and spiritual guides or those whom they have guided, one for the other. The love of the Holy Souls must be intense in its purity, and most enlightened as to the true welfare of those for whom they are interested. There seems to be no doubt that they can pray, and their prayer must be very efficacious (though not for themselves) because it has all the conditions which belong to prayer which God will hear. There may be some doubt as to the amount of knowledge which is imparted to them as to the state of the living, but a perfect knowledge as to this is not an element so necessary as to make its absence imply that they cannot pray for us—for those who belong to them most nearly, for their benefactors, those in particular who are helping them towards their perfect deliverance, those whom they may have imperilled by their example or otherwise, and the like. And it is certainly a matter of very frequent experience among those who give themselves to the devotion to Purgatory, or who even occasionally offer spiritual alms to the Holy Souls for the obtaining of some blessing, to find themselves helped in return in some very wonderful manner. But for one favour which is thus consciously obtained by means of the prayers of the holy dead, we may safely assume that there are a hundred others of which we are not conscious. And we may think of Purgatory as a prison indeed, and as a place of banishment, exile, and intense suffering, and yet, because

those who are there detained are princes of the
Kingdom of Heaven and on fire with Divine charity,
it is also a place from which God derives continual
glory and men perpetual and innumerable benefits
by means of the prayers which proceed therefrom.

, 5. As to the second point, a good deal has already
been said which need not be repeated here, both
concerning the general duty of piety to the dead
and as to the special duty which lies on us with
regard to our own near relatives and friends.   It has
been said in a former chapter, that the abandonment
of prayer for the dead may be said to be a mark that
á community calling itself Christian has become
separated from our Lord.   We may also apply here
the words of St. Paul, that, "if a man have not care
of his own, and especially of those of his house, he
hath denied the faith, and is worse than an infidel."
It is most sad to see the practice of good and kind-
hearted people outside the Church, full of natural
affection, and conscientious in the discharge of all
their known duties, in this matter.   No pains are
too great, no sacrifices too severe, no attentions too
laborious for them in the nursing and tending the
sick, and the grief with which they mourn when
death at last comes is most intense.   And yet, while
everything is done for the memory of those whom
they have lost, while their pain remains for months
and years unassuaged, so that they are said never to
forget the dead, or to recover their loss, there is no
thought whatever of praying for them or helping
them.   On the other hand, it is most touching to see
the large space which the holy departed fill in the
religion of a simple Catholic peasantry, as well as
among other classes, in countries which have preserved the faith.   The Masses and Communions and
almsdeeds and prayers and pilgrimages which are

directed to their aid are almost endless. Catholics in a Protestant country may sometimes be chilled by the atmostphere in which they are forced to live with what would seem indifference to their departed when compared to the fervour which is seen elsewhere, and it is therefore well that we should revive our devotion in this respect by considerations such as those which are suggested by the miracle before us. The reflections contained in the next and in some following chapters will help us as to the means by which this devotion may become more fruitful, both to the Holy Souls and to ourselves.

CHAPTER XXIII.

The Holy Souls and the Sacrifice of the Altar.

(THE FEEDING OF THE FIVE THOUSAND.)

St. Matt. xiv. 13—21; St. Mark vi. 30—44; St. Luke ix. 10—17;
St. John vi. 1—13.

1. THE next of our Lord's miracles in order of time is that wonderful display of His power in multiplying the five loaves and two fishes so as to furnish food enough and more for the multitude which had followed Him into a desert place, which consisted of five thousand men besides women and children. This splendid miracle, on account of its great magnificence, and also on account of its great doctrinal importance, is related by all the four Evangelists, and it is the only miracle which is so related. The circumstances are so well known to us that it is hardly necessary to repeat them here. The miracle was wrought at a spot on the shores

N

of the lake of Galilee, to which our Lord had retired with His apostles for the sake of recollection.
But they were followed by the multitude, and
our Lord had compassion on them, as St. Mark
tells us, " for they were as sheep not having a
shepherd, and He began to teach them many things,
and healed their sick." When the evening came
on, the disciples suggested that He should send
them away, but He bade them themselves give
them to eat. They objected the impossibility of
buying food for such a multitude, and then He
inquired how much they had with them, and
St. Andrew answered that there was a lad with five
loaves and two fishes, " but what are they among
so many ? " Then our Lord made the multitude
sit down on the green grass in order, by hundreds
and fifties, and " looking up to Heaven, blessed
them, and brake, and gave to His disciples, and
the disciples gave them to the multitude, and the
two fishes He divided unto all. And they all did
eat, and had their fill, and they took up the leavings,
twelve full baskets of fragments, and of the fishes."

2. The clear relation which this miracle bears to
the Blessed Sacrament of the Altar is enough to
suggest to us to consider in this chapter the importance of the Adorable Sacrifice as a means of relief
to the Holy Souls of Purgatory. The doctrine concerning that Blessed Sacrament is naturally divided
into two heads, considering it both as a Sacrifice and
as a Sacrament in the strict sense of the term. As
this miracle was repeated by our Lord on another
occasion soon after this, we may leave the latter part
of this doctrine till we come to the second multiplication of loaves, and attend at present to the
Sacrifice of the Altar alone. Very few words will
be enough to remind us of the efficacy of this Sacri-

fice for the relief of the Holy Souls. All Catholics know that in that Sacrifice the merits of the Sacrifice of the Cross are offered to the Eternal Father, and that it thus presents to Him a satisfaction in itself infinitely greater than any debt which those souls can owe to His Divine justice. These Holy Souls are a part of the Church, and when her priests are ordained, they receive the power of offering the Sacrifice for the living and the dead. St. Anthony of Padua in his sermon, *In Cœna Domini*, tells us that the division of the Sacred Host into three parts, which is made by the priest before his Communion, signifies the three parts of the Church, the blessed in Heaven, the living on earth, and the dead; and St. Thomas[1] adds that the Mass has a threefold effect, forgiving sins in this world, alleviating pain in Purgatory, and increasing glory in Heaven. Many texts and figures in Holy Scripture are applied in this meaning by the Fathers and Saints. Theologians tell us that the temporal punishment due to sin is directly remitted by the Holy Sacrifice, and that this is the tradition of the Apostles. They tell us that this Sacrifice is the most powerful means of all that we possess for satisfaction, as the Council of Trent lays down that the souls in Purgatory are helped by the suffrages of the faithful, " but chiefly by the acceptable Sacrifice of the Altar." Indeed, the chief fruit of the Holy Sacrifice is said to be that of satisfaction : " for, as sacrifice, especially that of the Cross, has the power given to it of satisfying for the punishment due to our sins, so this unbloody Sacrifice, which is a living image of that Bloody Sacrifice, is properly and directly instituted for the application to us *ex opere operato* of the fruit of satisfaction, so that, as

---

[1] *Opusc. de. Sacramento Altaris* (21 or 58), cap. xxv.

they say in the schools, what is done in that first sacrifice by way of sufficiency, is wrought in this other by way of efficiency."[1] Again, some great theologians hold that the application of the satisfaction which is derived from this Sacrifice benefits the holy dead *ex opere operato*, and by a law of justice, while other things, such as indulgences, and the application of our good works, benefit them by way of suffrage, that is, out of the mercy and liberality of God Who accepts them for that purpose. An argument for this opinion is based on the words of ordination, above mentioned, and on the statements of Councils and Fathers, that the Adorable Sacrifice is to be offered for the dead in the same way as for the living.

3. The lives of the saints are very full of anecdotes which illustrate the efficacy of the Sacrifice of the Altar for the relief of the Holy Souls, but we are obliged in these considerations to omit matter of that kind on account of the great space which it would occupy. But it may be useful here to add some of the reasons which are found in various writers for the Christian custom of celebrating Mass on certain special days for those who are departed. Five Masses may be said to be almost prescribed by that custom, when there is nothing to prevent them, that is, on the day of of burial, on the third, seventh, and thirtieth days after death, and on the anniversary. In many parts of the Church it has been the rule never to let any Christian be buried without the celebration of Mass. The Mass of the third day is mentioned in the Clementine Constitutions,[2] and it is said to represent the Resurrection of our Lord on the third day,

---

[1] Hautin, *Patrocinium Defunctorum*, lib. iii. col. 2, § 1. (n. 934).
[2] Lib. viii. c. 48.

or the restoration in the soul of the image of the
Ever-Blessed Trinity, or the threefold purification
of thoughts, words, and deeds. The Mass of the
seventh day is also significant of the eternal Sabbath
or rest of the holy dead. We find a connection
between seven days and the length of mourning in
the Old Testament, as in the case of Joseph mourning for Jacob.[4] The thirtieth day is said to be
chosen, as that was the number of days during which
the Israelites mourned for Moses, or for the mystical
reason that our Lord was thirty when He was
baptized, or that thirty is the full-grown age of
man, in which, it is said, we are all to rise again.
The institution of anniversaries is traced by some
up to the time of the Apostles, and it is so natural
and universal as to need no explanation.

4. There are many questions which have arisen
as to Masses for the dead, on account of the great
frequency of such Masses, and the various circumstances which may attend their celebration. Thus
although a solemn Mass, with all its ceremonies and
accompaniments, is in itself of no greater intrinsic
merit than a simple Low Mass, still the Church
encourages the practice of celebrating the former,
which may cause greater devotion, and so greater
benefit to the soul for which it is offered. Again,
it is clear that a Mass of *Requiem*, in which all the
prayers have a distinct reference to the relief of
the dead, on that account profits them more than
another Mass, although the intrinsic value of the
Sacrifice is the same in each case. Again, it must
be clear that a Mass celebrated at a privileged altar
is more directly and powerfully beneficial to a soul
in Purgatory than another, and that, if the words
of the concession of the privilege require that it

[4] Gen. l. 10; see Ecclus. xxii. 13.

should be a Mass of *Requiem*, such a Mass alone will gain the indulgence. The thirty continuous Masses which are recommended by St. Gregory the Great to the Abbot of his monastery of St. Andrew in Rome for the soul of one of his monks, seems to have become the foundation of the custom of celebrating thirty Masses for the dead on thirty continuous days, though of course it would not always be possible that such Masses should be of *Requiem.* At one time there was a custom, according to which these thirty Masses were necessarily votive Masses of certain fixed kinds, but this custom appears to have died away since a decree of the Congregation of Rites in 1628. The custom of the thirty Masses still remains, and it would be well if this holy devotion were revived amongst us, as far as is possible, at least as to the number of Masses which those who are able should procure for their own relatives and friends. Some writers would prefer that they should be said at once, and not one by one for thirty days. A kindred question to this would be another, whether it is better to found anniversary Masses for the dead for perpetuity, or to procure a great number of Masses to be said at once. As to this it must be remembered that, although there can be no doubt that many souls in Purgatory are best benefited by procuring them the relief of the Adorable Sacrifice as soon and as plentifully as possible, there are still many circumstances about pious foundations which make them great acts of devotion and charity, by contributing to enhance the splendour of the Church by supporting her ministers, and the like. If the souls for whom such Masses are sung or said are already in Heaven, they may still profit by them in the way of fresh joy or accidental glory. In the last place it is well that we should remember the custom which prevails among the faithful in many countries, of having Masses celebrated or celebrating them for their own souls, the satisfaction of which Masses is to be applied to their deliverance when they come to Purgatory. In some respects this also is a great act of devotion, inasmuch as it costs us much more to do this now, than to arrange that it shall be done after our death by those who represent us.

5. It may also be well to remember that to hear Mass for the holy dead is an act of religion and devotion which is certain to benefit them very much. This is a great incentive to the hearing of as many Masses as possible, and with the special intention of hearing them for the Holy Souls. In this way those who are not priests may in some sort share their power as to helping those in Purgatory, and those who are too poor to be able to procure Masses for them may be able to supply the effect of their poverty by hearing many Masses for them. It is certain that to hear Mass is a very high act of religion, next to that of saying Mass ; and that those who hear Mass do in truth offer it, according to their power, to the Eternal Father, which is the most excellent act of worship that can be performed. The priest in the Mass when he turns to the people at the *Orate, fratres*, calls it "my and your Sacrifice," and the hearers therefore honour God by offering that Holy Sacrifice as well as the priest. Suarez says that as the oblation of this Sacrifice is fruitful in the way of satisfaction and impetration *ex opere operato*, all those who offer it, and therefore those who hear it, receive its benefits in the same way, and not only in proportion to their own devotion. This is not certain, because,

as other theologians say, the satisfactory fruit of
the Adorable Sacrifice *ex opere operato* is received
by the priest alone, who alone offers it in the name
of Christ. But at all events the fruit of impetration,
as it is called, belongs to the hearers also *ex opere
operato*, inasmuch as the priest, in the name of
Christ, offers the Sacrifice for all, and more especially for those who are present. This fruit may
be applied by them for the benefit of the Holy Souls
for whom they may hear Mass. These are more or
less theological considerations, on which Christian
piety may feed itself, and which may be made the
solid foundation of a great amount of practical devotion. A Mass heard every day for the special
intention of relieving the Holy Souls may be in
many cases, not only a daily alms of immense value
to these sufferers who are so dear to our Lord, but
also the source of immense benefits and great protection to ourselves, not only from its own intrinsic
efficacy, but also on account of the numberless
prayers which we may thus win from those for
whom we perform this most blessed act of religion.

CHAPTER XXIV.

Pre-eminence of Charity to the Holy Souls.

(OUR LORD WALKING ON THE WATERS.)

St. Matt. xiv. 22—36; St. Mark vi. 45—56; St. John vi. 14—21.

1. THE Evangelists tell us that immediately after
the miracle of the multiplication of the five loaves,
our Lord made His disciples embark in the boat
in which they had crossed the lake, and pass over
to Capharnaum, He Himself remained alone on the
spot where the miracle had been wrought, and went
up into the mountain to pray. The disciples, fresh
from the fatigue of ministering to so many people
at the end of a long day of teaching, now found
themselves without their Master in the midst of the
sea, with the wind and waves against them. They
laboured at the oars till it was past midnight, when
a strong wind arose against them, and their progress
became more difficult than before. Our Lord's eye
was still upon them, as St. Mark tells us, and seeing
them toiling, about the fourth watch of the night,
as it was near the dawn, He came to them, walking
on the waters, and made as if He would pass them
by. "But they seeing Him walking upon the sea,
thought it was an apparition, and they cried out.
For they all saw Him and were troubled. And
immediately He spoke with them, and said to them,
Have a good heart, it is I, fear ye not. And Peter

made answer, and said, Lord, if it be Thou, bid me come unto Thee upon the waters. And He said, Come. And Peter going down out of the boat, walked upon the water to come to Jesus. But seeing the wind was strong, he was afraid, and when he began to sink, he cried out, Lord save me! And immediately Jesus stretching forth His hand, took hold of him, and said, O thou of little faith, why didst thou doubt? And when they were come up into the boat, the wind ceased. And presently," adds St. John, " the ship was at the land to which they were going."

2. The contrast must have been very great to the disciples, between the magnificent display of power in the miracle of the multiplication of the loaves, and their condition so soon afterwards, toiling by night, without the presence of our Lord to cheer and protect them, over a tossing sea and with an adverse wind, to a shore which seemed hardly nearer to them after many hours of labour. They had had their share, not indeed in the miracle of the loaves itself, but in the distribution of the bread, which seemed to grow in their hands. They had been made the instruments of bringing home to the hungry people the fruits of our Lord's power and mercy, and they had no doubt shared in that holy enthusiasm and exultation with which the multitudes must have been filled. Perhaps they almost took part in the intoxication of the people, who wished to take our Lord and make Him a king. And then, so soon afterwards, they found themselves in the pitiful condition which the Evangelists describe. The miracle which followed, when our Lord walked on the waters, seems to have been wrought out of compassion for them, or certainly, if this was not the only reason for it, it was at least one of the

reasons. We may consider them, in many respects, as representing the condition of the Holy Souls in Purgatory, who are without the consolation of our Lord's presence, and in a state of darkness, solitude, misery, and pain. They are not indeed labouring, for their state is one of reposeful and tranquil, though most intense, suffering. But they are kept back by the justice of God from the shore which they are yearning to reach, and in some respects they are worse off than if they could labour. A part of their suffering is that they cannot do anything that is meritorious or satisfactory for themselves. Thus, putting these two great miracles side by side, we may consider that they afford us an opportunity of making the contrast that has been insisted upon by many writers on this subject—who have made a comparison between works of mercy which are done for the relief of the living, and the similar works which may be done for the dead. This, therefore, may be the subject of the present chapter.

3. The case of the Holy Souls, however, is so clear and their needs so urgent, that it is enough to state positively the good which we have it in our power to do by aiding them, instead of drawing out a strict comparison between this and any other work of spiritual mercy; all the more, as the works of mercy by which we relieve the living, may be applied by a holy intention, as works of satisfaction for the dead. It is well known that the spiritual works of mercy are more excellent than the corporal works, on account of the greater dignity of the soul, which is benefited by them, of the greater good which is conferred, and the higher excellence of the acts of virtue which are exercised, in these spiritual works. In the same way we may find many reasons for esteeming very highly indeed the

opportunity which our Lord allows to us of conferring immense spiritual benefits upon souls very high in dignity and in their nearness to Him, when we distribute our spiritual alms to the sufferers in Purgatory. It is not difficult to draw out in meditation a parallel between the works of mercy, as they are ordinarily enumerated, and this work of spiritual mercy — for it is easy to see an image of the wants of the Holy Souls in the hunger and thirst, the nakedness, the homelessness, the state of confinement and of sickness or languor, which call so loudly upon our compassion in the ordinary subjects of such corporal works. Indeed, no hunger or thirst can be equal to that yearning for God and for the delights of Heaven which consume them. They are naked of that heavenly clothing of which St. Paul speaks in the Second Epistle to the Corinthians, they are without shelter and detained from their home, they are sick and almost plague-stricken, until the effects of their sins are done away, and they are the prisoners of the justice of the King Who is great in all that He does, and thus great also in His punishments. In this way, comparing any earthly miseries with their spiritual sufferings, it is easy to soften our hearts with compassion towards them as afflicted in a degree which has no true parallel upon earth. As has been said, their dignity also surpasses all earthly dignity, and the goods from which they are kept out surpass in excellence any that we can procure for those who are in need upon earth. The work of charity to them is thus in every way most excellent.

4. Thoughts such as these have been the foundation, in many pious persons, of a form of devotion to the Holy Souls which goes far beyond the common bounds of charity. For in charity we are not

ordinarily led to give away that which is of the utmost importance and necessity to ourselves. Such charity is considered heroic, especially when that which is given to others is our own life, or something that is hardly less precious to us. Nevertheless, the impulse of charity which is aroused by the consideration of the very great affliction in which the Holy Souls lie, and of the immense goods which are awaiting them in Heaven, their possession of which may be hastened on by our self-sacrifice, has urged many devout persons to the practice of giving to them all their own satisfactions and indulgences, reserving nothing at all to themselves. This holy practice was at one time questioned, as being inconsistent with the charity we are bound to have to our own souls; but the mind of the Church has been quite sufficiently declared in its favour by the sanction which it has received and the encouragement which has been afforded to it by the special indulgences which have been granted to those who adopt it. This is not the place for any lengthened argument on the subject. It is sufficient to say that the charity which gives away to the Holy Souls all the satisfactions which we gain, or which are applied to us in any way, may at the utmost involve to ourselves what is no doubt a very great and momentous loss—that is, that, when it comes to be our turn to take our places in the holy prison of Purgatory, we shall be detained there far longer than we might otherwise have been detained, in consequence of our want of these satisfactions. We may, therefore, in strictness, make ourselves liable to a great deal of suffering and a very long detention in Purgatory, if we spend, as it were, our satisfactions on others, instead of applying them to ourselves. We may be in the case in which the

prudent virgins in our Lord's parable would have
been, if they had given away their oil to the others,
instead of refusing, "Lest perchance there be not
enough for us and for you."[1] If this parallel were
certainly apt and true in all particulars, then we
might perhaps think that we had even our Lord's
special warning against any such practice as that
of which we are speaking. But it is certain that
our Lord in that parable is not speaking of a temporary exclusion from the Marriage Supper of the
Lamb, but of an eternal banishment from His
Presence, while, on the other hand, the result of
the practice of which we are speaking cannot be
more than a temporary delay in our own entrance
into Heaven. At the utmost then, it would be like
the charity of St. Paul or of Moses, who were ready,
as it appears, to be excluded from the enjoyment of
God, though not, of course, from His grace or His
love, for the sake of their brethren, and it would be
like the charity which is mentioned in the case of
St. Martin, who was willing to remain on earth and
labour longer in order to be more useful to the
Church. The same thing is related of St. Ignatius
of Loyola, and of other saints. And if such are the
actions of saints who are set before us as examples
which we are to imitate, there can be no question
as to the high excellence of charity of this kind.

5. But it must be added that it cannot be certain
that a soul which, while on earth, has made over to
others, in the way here mentioned, all the satisfactions which it may have gained and all the suffrages
which may be made for it after its decease, will in
truth be allowed by God to lose anything by that act
of charity. For, in the first place, it is certain that
it will gain great merit in the sight of God by such

<hr>

[1] St. Matt. xxv. 9.

an act, and that therefore, if it comes to be delayed longer in Purgatory than might otherwise have been the case, it will at least enter Heaven with greater merit, and therefore will enjoy greater glory for all eternity. In the second place, the increase of merit would be accompanied by an increase of grace, by means of which such a soul would become dearer to God and more able to advance rapidly in perfection, and thus have less need of satisfaction when it came to Purgatory, as well as a greater accumulation of virtuous actions. In the third place, it would, in a certain sense, throw itself, not only on the justice of God, but on His special love, and—inasmuch as the application of numberless suffrages which are made in general for the Holy Souls depends upon His will, and is made according to the desires and choices of His Sacred Heart, or of our Lady, or of the Saints —it is very likely that those who have thus exposed themselves to the danger of a very long detention in Purgatory for the sake of others, will share very largely in our Lord's distribution of these general suffrages, and so reach Heaven even sooner than they might if they had retained their satisfactions for their own benefit. Certainly such a soul will have a great number of special friends, both in Purgatory and in Heaven, who will exert themselves both out of justice and out of charity to make its period of purification as short as possible.

6. We may well imagine that our Lord has given us an example which may be used to spur us on to this or any other signal act of charity for the benefit of the Holy Souls, when instead of resting for the night on the mountain, or even of continuing His blessed communion with His Father in prayer, He walked over the water to cheer and relieve the Apostles in their trouble on the lake. His coming

into the ship had the double effect of making the wind cease and bringing the boat, without further effort, to the land. Those who forego the relief which they might enjoy themselves for the sake of helping others to reach the eternal shore more quickly, may hereafter find that they themselves also reach it almost immediately by virtue of that act of charity. But it must be remembered that it may be otherwise, and that an act of this kind, which is by nature heroic, is not to be made without forethought and consultation. People who think very little of venial sins, who do not carefully guard their consciences from stain, who do no penance and take no pains about indulgences, are hardly persons to give away their satisfactions to the Holy Souls. Such an act should be, as it were, the crown of other less perfect kinds of charity, of prayers, of almsdeeds, of mortifications, of Communions, Masses, and the like, offered for the relief of the Holy Souls. If Esau had given away his birthright knowing its value, and at a great cost to himself, it would have been a signal act of charity which God would have rewarded. He gave it away thoughtlessly for a mess of pottage, and he lost the favour of God thereby as well as his birthright. The act of which we are speaking, therefore, should not be lightly done, as if we did not care about our satisfactions and had little fear of Purgatory. The more we know about Purgatory, the more we shall fear it, and the more store we shall set by anything that can deliver us from its pains. The more we fear it, and the more precious we consider our satisfactions, and the suffrages to be made for us to be, the most precious in the sight of God will be the charity that makes them all over to others, and leaves ourselves exposed to the utmost rigour of His justice.

CHAPTER XXV.

Privileges of the Children of God.

(THE HEALING OF THE DAUGHTER OF THE SYROPHŒNICIAN WOMAN.)

St. Matt. xv. 21—28; St. Mark vii. 24—30.

1. IT appears that after our Lord's return to Capharnaum from the place where He had worked the great miracle of the feeding of the five thousand, He did not remain long in that city. The time which He spent there seems to have been chiefly given, as far as the narratives of the Evangelists inform us, to discussions with the Jews in the synagogue and elsewhere on the subject of His teaching or the necessity of the eating and drinking of His Body and Blood, and on the non-observance of certain traditions with which the Pharisees from Jerusalem charged His disciples. Our Lord was, as before, desirous to avoid publicity, which, in the present temper of His enemies, involved persecution and the blackest calumny. So He left the city without, as it seems, working a single miracle, and went into the country of the Gentiles, the parts of Tyre and Sidon. "Entering into a house," says St. Mark, "He would that no man should know it, and He could not be hid. For a woman, as soon as she heard of Him, whose daughter had an unclean spirit, came in and fell down at His feet.

O

For the woman was a Gentile, a Syrophœnician born. And she besought Him that He would cast forth the devil out of her daughter. Who said to her, Suffer first the children to be filled, for it is not good to take the bread of the children, and to cast it to the dogs." St. Matthew mentions one or two circumstances as to this application and our Lord's answer which add to the fulness of the picture. He tells us that the poor woman first applied to our Lord using the name by which, it seems, He was popularly called, " Have mercy on me, O Lord, Thou Son of David, my daughter is grievously troubled by a devil. Who answered her not a word." But she continued her importunities, and " His disciples came and besought Him, saying, Send her away, for she crieth after us. And He answering said, I am not sent but to the sheep that are lost of the house of Israel." Then, it seems, she obtained admittance, or forced her way into the house. "But she came and addressed Him, saying, Lord, help me!" Then our Lord gave her the answer related by St. Mark as well as by St. Matthew, about the bread of the children. "But she said, Yea, Lord, for the whelps also eat of the crumbs which fall from the table of their masters." Such faith could not go unrewarded. " Then Jesus answering her said, O woman, great is thy faith! be it done unto thee as thou wilt. For this saying, go thy way, the devil is gone out of thy daughter. And when she was come into her house, she found the girl lying on the bed, and that the devil was gone out."

2. It is clear that our Lord was highly pleased with the faith of the Gentile woman, as before He had been moved to commend so strongly the faith of the centurion at Capharnaum, but that, as His

special mission was to the Jews, and as the Church was not formally to open its gates to the Gentiles until after the day of Pentecost and by the ministry of St. Peter, the distinction between Jew and Gentile had not as yet been put away, and thus the Syrophœnician woman and her daughter were, strictly speaking, outside the "covenant of Israel" and the range of those to whom our Lord's special and and personal mission applied. But it is clear also that the mercies of God, as well as the tender compassion of the Sacred Heart of our Lord, are ever ready to leap beyond the bounds of the covenant which has been made with men, and that, in particular, our Lord's Heart rejoiced over this woman as over the centurion, because each represented to Him the multitude of the Gentiles who were so soon to be brought within the fold of the Church. Thus we have two principles, as it were, set before us in this incident, and in the words of our Lord to the woman. The first is, that of the exclusiveness of the covenanted mercies of God to man—which means little more than that God exacts certain easy conditions for the reception of His favours, and that if these conditions be not complied with, those favours must not be reckoned on. The second is, that any conditions, which God may lay down as necessary for the special favours which He may promise or impart, do not tie His hands so strictly as that when their exact fulfilment has not taken place without deliberate fault, He is bound not to give His bounties as He may choose, in consideration of the faith or charity of those on whom He would not otherwise bestow them. God is always free to distribute His graces as He chooses, and as a matter of fact He may give them wherever a true faith can exist, as in the case of this woman, who was not, in the strict sense, a child of the house of Israel, but who was, after all, a child of a still earlier covenant than that which was made with Abraham, because she had faith, without which it is impossible to please God. Thus her case shows us that there may be some outside the visible limits of the Body with which God has now made His covenant, who yet, as the Fathers speak, belong to the soul of the Church. It may be well, therefore, to take this miracle as a text which suggests to us to consider the application of these principles to the holy realm of Purgatory, and to remind ourselves who those are who may be admitted into it, and who are therefore the rightful objects of our compassion and charity, and who are those who are excluded from it by the laws of the Kingdom of God.

3. It is clear that, as Purgatory is an intermediate and temporary state, in which those souls are detained who are destined to be in Heaven throughout all eternity, it cannot be the place of sojourn either for those who enter Heaven at once after their death, or for those who are never to enter Heaven at all. In the first class we must place the Saints of God and all the blessed souls who die in the state of grace, either with no debt at all to the justice of God upon them, or having entirely and perfectly cancelled that debt by contrition, penance, and the like. In the same class must be placed the souls of baptized infants, who have been regenerated and made members of Christ and heirs of Heaven, and who have after that incurred no debt whatever to God's justice because they have never attained the use of reason, and so the capacity of deliberate sin. The fundamental reason why these children, and, indeed, all others who enter Heaven, are able to do so, is that they are members

of Jesus Christ, through Whom alone access to
Heaven can be obtained, as the Church says, *Tu
devicto mortis aculeo, aperuisti credentibus regna cælorum.*
And the word "believers" is used here in strict
accordance with Christian theology, which teaches
us that before the institution of Baptism, the removal of original sin, which is the great essential
bar to the entrance of Heaven—inasmuch as no
moral excellence whatever can enter there if original
sin be not removed—was to be obtained by the
exercise of faith, certain truths as to God, and,
implicitly at least, as to the Redemption of man,
being always proposed to mankind as the subject-
matter of faith, according to the character of the
various successive dispensations under which men
have been placed in the course of their history.
We have only a few lines back referred to this prerogative of faith, and to St. Paul's words concerning
it, "without faith it is impossible to please God.
For he that cometh to God must believe that He
is, and is a rewarder to them that seek Him."[1]
These then form the class who cannot enter Purgatory because they are to pass to Heaven at once
—all those who die with no actual sin to suffer
for, and with the stain of original sin removed, the
condition of that removal, under the present law
of God, being Christian Baptism.

4. On the other hand, we must place as the
class of men who cannot be admitted to Purgatory,
because they can never pass to Heaven, all those
who under any dispensation whatever, primitive,
patriarchal, Mosaic, or Christian, have died out of
God's grace in a state of mortal sin, which mortal
sin cannot be committed by any soul except
knowingly and wilfully. Even a single mortal sin

[1] Heb, xi. 6,

unrepented of—in which case the soul departs out of this life in a state of sin—is enough in the justice of God to render that soul guilty of the punishment of Hell. And we must add to this class all those, infants and others, who have died, indeed, without mortal sin on their souls, but who have never in any way been made partakers of the inheritance of the children of God by the removal of original sin. Thus we see who can and who cannot be admitted · to Purgatory. All those can, who belong to the body of Jesus Christ, and who have had the guilt of original sin removed by the application of His merits. All these can be, but not all these are, admitted to Purgatory, because the birthright which is conferred on them when original sin is cancelled may be lost by their own wilful unrepented sin. On the other hand, no one can be admitted to Purgatory in whom original sin remains unremoved, or who is destined to the eternal punishment of Hell on account of his own deliberate sin, that is, by his own unrecalled choice.

5. These statements, it may be said, leave a large part of the human race practically unallotted, and, as it were, unprovided for. That is, it may be said, there may be multitudes of human souls in whom the guilt of original sin has never been removed, and who are therefore incapable of Heaven, and yet they may not have died in the guilt of a deliberate mortal sin, either because they have never had the opportunity, on account of an early death, or because they have been shielded from temptation, or have followed their conscience and what they have known of the law of God faithfully, or because they have had the grace to be truly sorry for sin. These souls, it may be said, belong neither to Hell, nor to Heaven, nor to Purgatory, and yet they may make

up, as has been said, a very large portion of the human race. For, to speak only of one class among those mentioned, as it is probable that of those who attain Heaven a very large proportion will be composed of children who have had the stain of original sin removed through Jesus Christ, without living long enough to attain the age of reason, so it is even more probable that of those in whom the stain of that sin is not removed, a very large proportion is composed of those who have never lived long enough to be guilty of actual sin. For a great part of the human race dies in infancy, and out of this large portion of the race of Adam there are certainly more unbaptized than baptized. For more infants survive in Christian than in heathen countries, in which it is often the custom to expose them to death, or otherwise ill-treat them. It may also be said that the considerations suggested above open many questions as to Purgatory itself. For they suggest that original sin may perhaps have been removed in many cases outside the chosen people of God, by the faith which was the condition from the first, which may also, in the case of many adults, have "worked by love," and have been acceptable to God. They suggest that the earlier conditions of participation in the redemption of Jesus Christ may have remained in force in parts of the world in which the Church has never been set up, long after the first preaching of the Christian religion, and that on this account the entrance to Purgatory may have been open to some who were not Christians. They suggest also that a great number of baptized persons, who have been born outside the fold of the Catholic Church, and who have died in their infancy, or without any deliberate mortal sin upon the soul uncancelled, may find a place hereafter in Heaven, and some of them in Purgatory. The tendency of all these suggestions, if true, is to enlarge very much the range, so to speak, of admittance into this blessed prison—a prison indeed, a place of intense suffering, and yet the necessary ante-chamber, so to speak, of Heaven, to a very large number of the adults who are to find entrance at last into the presence of God.

6. It would be foreign to our purpose here to enter fully into all these questions. But a few remarks may be in place, chiefly in order to guard against any wildness of conjecture, and also to stimulate our exertions for the Holy Souls. For it would be a great stimulus to our charity and our exertions for the sufferers of Purgatory, to know that, in the mercy of God, they are far more numerous and, so to speak, heterogeneous than we had perhaps imagined. But it is well to remember that two of these suggestions must be carefully combined with one another. That is, it is true to say that no one can be doomed to Hell except for deliberate sin, and also that there may be a great many baptized persons outside the Catholic Church who may reach Purgatory on their way to Heaven. But it is equally true, though not always so carefully remembered, that to remain wilfully outside the pale of the Catholic Church is in itself a mortal sin of schism, against charity, and that wilfully to reject any portion whatever of the Catholic Creed is a mortal sin of heresy, against faith. There are positive precepts of God which, when known, are as binding as the precepts which belong to the natural law. Man is as much responsible to God for what he believes as for what he does. And the probation of many a man may be chiefly intellectual —the use which he makes of his will in e accep-tance or rejection of truth, as well as in the obedience

or disobedience which he shows to the moral law. It is also evident, that this kind of probation is very common indeed in the present day, when education is so common, when matters of controversy are made so much matters of discussion everywhere, when every one has the evidence as to the true Church so very much more within his reach than in former generations.

7. But, after due allowance has been made for this and kindred truths, it may still remain probable that the world beyond the grave is very different from our common thoughts concerning it, and that there may be large classes of souls for which we do not ordinarily make provision. Scripture is the record of revelation, of God's dealings with man, and principally and directly of the great Economy of the Incarnation. The Catholic Creed states the great series of truths which sum up this Economy. Both Scripture and the Creed intimate to us that there are large dispositions of God in His Mercy and Justice, of which we have but the slightest glimpses at present. When the Divinely inspired historian of the Creation added to his account of the formation of the sun and moon the simple words, " and the stars also," he passed lightly indeed, in comparison to the magnificence of the work of which he spoke, over the creation of the whole sidereal universe, so far more beautiful and wonderful than the earth with its greater and lesser lights. In the same way the mind is lost in thinking of the countless millions of human souls with whom the Providence of the Father of all has to deal with perfect justice, or rather with justice tempered by immense mercy, in arranging for their eternity according to the manner in which they have met their probation here. It is enough to know that no one

is eternally lost in Hell without his own fault, and that the grace of God is never wanting to any human soul which truly does what it can to make its peace with its Creator and Judge.

8. In our present considerations, however, we have only to deal directly with the subject of Purgatory, and, with the limitation already made, there is every reason why we should continually remind ourselves of the multitudes of souls who may be there, who have been Christians indeed, by virtue of their baptism, but who, for no fault of their own, have lived and died outside the pale of the visible Church. It is no part of our duty to limit the range or power of good faith in excusing men even from inquiring after the Church, as long as they are not obliged to such investigations under the pain of serious sin. Wherever the case of excusable ignorance and good faith exists, there is a soul which has peculiar claims on our compassion. For it has been a child of God deprived of its birth-right on earth, stolen away from its home, brought up in ignorance of so much which would have stirred its heart to love and helped it to the practice of noble and heroic virtues of which it may never have heard. There is a soul which may have learnt the elementary truths of religion, the " beginnings of Christ," of which St. Paul speaks to the Hebrews,[2] but which has been kept in bondage under a hard system, deprived of the food of the children, and knowing little of the Divine charity of which the Catholic Church is the earthly home. It has never been taught to love our Lord in His Sacramental Life, or to know the true sweetness of confession or of communion, or to bask in the smile of Mary, or to exercise its brotherly rights with Saints and

<hr>

[2] Heb. vi. 1.

Angels. The blessings which it has missed are untold, and it may have forfeited great glories in Heaven on account of the cold atmosphere in which it has languished upon earth. In it the counsel of Satan has been defeated to the glory of God, but the glory of God has suffered much loss from the counsel of Satan. It has been already said, such a soul has few to pray for it on earth of those on whom that duty would naturally fall. It is in any case under the bar of a terrible penalty in its almost certain destitution of the aid of prayer and suffrage, and sacrifice after its death. All the more has it special claims on the charity of the faithful. In one of the revelations of St. Gertrude, our Lord is said to have spoken to the Saint of the manner in which He delighted to impart to souls which were dear to Him the suffrages which her community made for those for whom they were under special obligations to pray. Some of the souls of whom we are speaking may be of the class who are so dear to our Lord; those who do " what they can," though it is but little; those " who are faithful in small things ;" those who have had little to give, like the widow in the Gospel, but who have given it all. The Prophet Malachias[8] speaks of those who remain faithful to God in the midst of generations who turn from Him, and His words may apply to the souls of which we speak, " A book of remembrance was written before Him for them that fear the Lord, and think upon His Name. And they shall be My special possession, saith the Lord of hosts, in the day that I do judgment."

[8] Malachias iii. 17.

CHAPTER XXVI.

Particular Punishments in Purgatory.

(CURE OF THE DEAF AND DUMB IN DECAPOLIS.)
St. Mark vii. 31—37.

1. THE miraculous deliverance of the daughter of the Syrophœnician woman was almost immediately followed by another miracle, which is carefully related to us by St. Mark. Our Lord again changed His place of abode, for He returned from the sea coast of the Mediterranean to the remote country at the north-eastern side of the Sea of Galilee, a tract which was known by the name of Decapolis. Here again He was solicited to show mercy to the poor sufferers from disease. "They bring unto Him one deaf and dumb, and they besought Him that He would lay His hand upon him." There seems to have been a multitude present, and our Lord may have been teaching them, but He would not work this miracle in their presence. "And taking him from the multitude apart, He put His fingers into his ears, and spitting, He touched his tongue, and looking up to Heaven, He groaned, and said to him, Ephpheta, which is, Be thou opened, and immediately his ears were opened, and the string of his tongue was loosed, and he spoke right." Our Lord tried in vain to keep the miracle a secret. " And He charged them

that they should tell no man. But the more He charged them, so much the more a great deal did they publish it, and so much the more did they wonder, saying, He hath done all things well, He hath made both the deaf to hear, and the dumb to speak."

2. The circumstances of this miracle, all of which were ordered with the utmost care by the Providence of our Lord, are in some respects peculiar, and it is some of these features which we may fasten on as furnishing us with the special subject of this chapter. There is no mention of any devil possessing the poor sufferer. Our Lord did something by way of application of His own Sacred Humanity to each of the senses which were afflicted, putting His fingers into the ears of the man, and touching His tongue with His spittle. The looking up to Heaven, the groaning, and the use of the word Ephpheta, are also remarkable, as well as the comment of the multitude, that He had done all things well, and made both the deaf to hear and the dumb to speak. Each affliction, therefore, of the poor man had its special remedy. Our Lord did not simply bless him, or touch him, or lay His hands upon him, but healed each sense separately by contact with Himself. This action of our Lord may serve to remind us of the particularity of the pains of Purgatory. In Purgatory, as in Hell itself, each sin has its own punishment, and each sense is afflicted in a marvellous manner for the sins which have been committed through it. As there are sins committed through the eyes, or the ears, or the tongue, or the touch, or the smelling, so there are special afflictions which correspond to each one of these senses, no sin and no class of sin being left without its chastisement in kind. It is

the soul which has sinned through each of these senses, and the presence of which in the body has enabled them to perform their functions, to receive the unlawful pleasure, and so minister to the sin. It is the soul, detached from the body, which has to suffer the punishment of each several sin in Purgatory, or, as it may be, in Hell. Penance must be done for each here, or Purgatory must be suffered in each hereafter, and the satisfactory power of penance or of the suffering in Purgatory comes from the stores of healing which are laid up for us in the Sacred Humanity of our Lord.

3. This truth is of great value to us in our considerations concerning Purgatory, whether we apply them to the subject of the pains of the Holy Souls and of our power in relieving them, or to that of the careful avoidance of sin in ourselves. It is a natural complement to, or even a part of, the doctrine of the pain of sense on which we had to reflect in a former chapter. In that chapter we dwelt more especially on the intensity of the sufferings which are inflicted in Purgatory, and in this we have to consider especially their particularity. Without this last point, we might be inclined to be vague and indefinite in our ideas of the sufferings for sin. Those sufferings are not general, the chastisement of a general unfaithfulness to God in the use of our senses, but most carefully measured and adapted to each several sin of each kind. We had occasion to refer, in that former chapter, to the narratives of the visions which are to be found in the lives of the saints in illustration of Purgatory, and to the pictorial and sensible representations or descriptions by which it is so often sought to bring home to the minds of the faithful the severity of the sufferings there. Now, it is this very circumstance of the particularity of

these descriptions which is so uncomfortable and painful to many who may be unfamiliar to the truth which it is thus attempted to represent. Any account of the suffering of the soul must of necessity be conveyed in language which uses the image of bodily suffering to convey what is intended. But any image of bodily suffering must be particular—it must represent the torment of this sense or that sense, this or that part of the body, and the like. Here again, we may say, let those who can bring home to themselves the truth of which we are speaking without the aid of such representations do so by all means, but let them not find fault with others, who find it useful to aid themselves or those to whom they speak or write by the material means of which we are speaking. The one thing of importance is the truth, and not the manner in which the truth is represented or brought home.

4. The use which we make of our bodily senses is a great trust committed to us, for which, as we see by the truths now suggested to us, we shall have to give in each case a separate account. That is, it is not simply our body for which we are responsible, but for each sense of our body in particular. Each one of these senses opens to us a separate world. The loss of any one shuts us out from a separate world. Each one is a great gift of God, meant to be used for His service and for our delight, or rather, not in all cases for our delight, in the ordinary sense of the word, for the service of God often requires that we should mortify them instead of gratifying them. But each one opens to us a separate field for the practice of virtue, a field in which we may gather day after day fruits which will remain to us for ever among the rewards of Heaven. As to each we have the example of our Blessed Lord to study

to imitate. That is, He has in a true sense touched each one of our senses, and blessed their use, and taught us what that use may be, in order that they may be to us indeed the source of infinite joy here-after. When we receive Him in Holy Communion, we receive the Body Whose senses were used in so perfect a way to the glory of His Father, and if we are faithful and diligent in our imitation of Him in the use of these senses, our contact with His Sacred Humanity in Holy Communion will give us both light and power for the purpose here spoken of. His presence will not only calm and enlighten the mind, and fill the soul with graces and gifts, but it will in particular soothe down the rebellion of the senses, give strength to the ruling power within us which has to control and regulate their use. To get the full fruit of this benefit, we must study to use them modestly and reverently, like precious gifts which may be injured and ruined by carelessness and sensuality, giving thanks for them, keeping them in order as parents keep their children, examining ourselves regarding them, and subjecting them to discipline in order that they may not lead us astray, and to chastisement if they have done so.

5. This would be enough reason of itself for con-stant watchfulness, and continual self-restraint as to each one of our senses. But it may be added, as is so well known to those who study the spiritual life, that the conquest of the senses is an essential means to the gaining of the spirit of prayer, and of the other immense blessings to which prayer intro-duces us. This, however, is a large subject, on which it is not necessary now to enter. And, as we shall soon have to speak of the various means of mortification which can be used for the help of the Holy Souls, it may be enough in the present chapter

to say in general, that we shall have greater power to satisfy for them, by way of prayer and other methods of impetration, if we unite to these some special mortification of the senses; and that such mortification will in itself be a most acceptable satisfaction, which can be directly applied to the relief of the particular sufferings which the Holy Souls may have to endure in the manner here considered.

CHAPTER XXVII.

The Holy Souls relieved by Holy Communion.

(THE FEEDING OF THE FOUR THOUSAND.)
St. Matt. xv. 29—39; St. Mark viii. 1—19.

1. THE circumstances under which our Lord wrought the second miracle of the multiplication of the loaves are in many respects similar to those of the first. The people in the neighbourhood of the Lake of Galilee, from which He was now absenting Himself from time to time, and which He was soon to leave altogether, seem to have been on the watch for Him when He returned and to have flocked to Him with their sick, in hopes of obtaining their cure from His unwearied mercy. This was the case on the occasion of which we are now to speak. St. Matthew tells us that He came nigh the sea of Galilee: "And going up into a mountain, He sat there. And there came to Him great multitudes, having with them the dumb, the blind, the lame, the maimed, and many others, and they cast them down at His feet, and He healed them. So that the multitude marvelled, seeing the

P

dumb speak, the lame walk, the blind see, and they glorified the God of Israel." This, however, was only the beginning of the marvellous mercy which He was now to show them. " And Jesus called together His disciples and said, I have compassion on the multitudes, because they continue with me now three days, and have not what to eat, and I will not send them away fasting, lest they faint in the way." It is not impossible that the Apostles remembered the former miracle, but did not venture openly to suggest its repetition. " And the disciples say to Him, Whence then shall we have so many loaves in the desert, as to fill so great a multitude ? And Jesus said to them, How many loaves have you ? But they said, Seven, and a few little fishes. And He commanded the multitude to sit down upon the ground. And taking the seven loaves and the fishes, and giving thanks, He brake and gave to His disciples, and the disciples gave to the people, and they did all eat and took their fill, and they took up seven baskets full of what remained of the fragments. And they that did eat were four thousand men besides children and women."

2. We have already said that it will be well to consider this miracle, which is the second in which our Lord foreshadowed the great marvel of love which He was to leave behind Him in the Church in the Adorable Sacrament of His precious Body and Blood, as suggesting to us the benefit which we may confer on the Holy Souls of Purgatory by means of Holy Communion—having already spoken of the blessing which remains for them, as well as for ourselves, in the Sacrifice of the Altar. It has been sometimes maintained that the satisfactory power of the act of Communion may be made beneficial to the Holy Souls, like the satisfaction

which is contained in the Holy Mass itself, as theologians speak, *ex opere operato*, and thus independently of the dispositions and devotion of the person who may receive Holy Communion. This, however, does not seem to be the truest doctrine on the matter. The Holy Communion is directly the food of the soul, and not the Sacrifice of our Lord. The office of food is to nourish, and not to satisfy— and it is even uncertain whether Holy Communion, simply and of itself, satisfies for the sins of the recipient, or whether this effect is to be attributed to the devotion and charity, and the like, with which it may be received.

3. Leaving this question to theologians, we may content ourselves with those more general considerations concerning Holy Communion, as an act of the virtue of religion, and as including so many acts of various virtues most dear to our Lord, which may enable us to understand that it may have a very great and almost unparalled power in the way of obtaining pardon and relief for the blessed sufferers with whom we are concerned, by way of impetration, if not by that of direct satisfaction. No act of religion can be imagined more fruitful of benefit to the soul, or of delight and joy to our Lord, than the act of Holy Communion. It is the highest act of faith that we can perform, it expresses and embodies hope in its most perfect aspirations, it is the consummation and crown of charity, of personal devotion and love to our Lord, and to all who belong to Him in Heaven, on earth, and under the earth. The soul who devoutly receives Him in Holy Communion, and gives itself to Him, as it were, in that most intimate act of love and union, rejoices Him as Mary rejoiced Him when she received Him into her pure womb, as Joseph delighted Him when he

carried Him in his arms, as St. John moved His Heart to special love when he lay in His bosom, as St. Martha when she received Him into her house, as St. Magdalene when she anointed Him and washed His feet with her tears, as the holy women when they prepared to honour His body after it had been committed to the Holy Sepulchre. The due reception of Holy Communion implies a thousand holy affections, acts of sorrow for sin, of resolution of amendment, of thanksgiving, of self-oblation, of intercession, and the like. The giving Himself to us in Holy Communion is the last and extreme act of love in our Lord to us, and the receiving Him in Holy Communion is the act by which we show our love to and confidence in Him to the utmost, and by which we take to ourselves in the fullest measure the treasures of grace and the spiritual benefits which are stored for us in His sacred Humanity. In Holy Communion, He becomes the source of that abundant life to the soul of which He spoke to the Apostles; He fills us with light, and opens to us the sweetness and joy which are perfectly to be imparted in Heaven itself, at the same time strengthening the soul with the powers of immortal life. In Holy Communion He wipes away the remains of sins, He forgives in large measure the pains that are due to former transgressions, He fortifies us against our spiritual enemies, and gives us the vigour and resolution which help us to rise again quickly, even if we fall. He increases in us all virtues, especially charity, He confirms all that is good in us already, He imparts to us the capacity of perseverance, a gift altogether foreign to our poor and frail nature, and secures for us the glory to which He destines us, and for the winning of which He has done all that He has done by becoming Man and dying for us on the Cross.

4. It cannot then be imagined, but that this act of Communion, so full of acts on our part which give pleasure to God, and so rich in the spiritual benefits which it brings home to the soul, must be an act which, if offered like any other act of religion, for the Holy Souls of Purgatory, must turn upon them very powerfully the streams of the Divine mercy and compassion. The histories of the saints contain more than a few instances, in which the Holy Souls themselves have made it known that they are helped in a special manner by the devout Communions which are thus offered for them. It may be, that in many cases they are conscious that a part of their detention in the Prison of God's justice is owing to their coldness in receiving Holy Communion, or to their neglect to receive It as often as they might. Those then who help them in this way may use this thought as an additional motive for great fervour in preparation and devotion in reception, as well as for the frequency of the act of Communion itself.

5. Again, we may remember that we have the power of renewing in our own hearts as often as we like the affections and holy acts which prepare for, or accompany, or follow, the actual reception of Communion, making at any time of the day or night, and many times in each, those spiritual communions of which the saints have been so fond. It cannot be doubted that our Lord, on His part, is always ready to crown these tender and secret acts of love with great graces, renewing and confirming in us the effects of His own Sacramental Presence. This is another method of helping the Holy Souls most effectually, as well as ourselves.

6. There is another circumstance about both these great miracles, which we have considered as having

so special a reference to the Blessed Sacrament, whether as a Sacrifice or as a Sacrament strictly so called, which it may be well to dwell upon before we part altogether from the subject. It was a sort of necessity for the splendour of the miracle of the multiplication of the loaves, that there should be a great multitude of persons who should receive the benefits of our Lord's mercy, although the miracle would not have been less a miracle if He had fed only a few scores of persons with the bread that was miraculously increased. If He had fed a hundred persons, for instance, with a single loaf, it would still have been a very great miracle. But on each of these occasions our Lord chose that the persons who were witnesses and recipients of His bounty should be numbered by thousands rather than by hundreds or scores, and we cannot doubt that besides the additional splendour of feeding of so large a body of men, women, and children, there was, in the circumstance of the great multitude itself, something which increased the devotion and kindled the enthusiasm of the disciples and of the crowd. At the same time both these miracles are remarkable also for a certain solemnity and holy order which our Lord insisted on, as in the making the multitude sit down in companies of fifties and hundreds, and in the distribution of the bread by the hands of the Apostles to these companies. The whole scene thus reminds us of some of the most solemn occasions in the Church when there are very large numbers of men present at the celebration of a single Mass, or, still more, of the general Communions which take place at the end of missions, or of the great festivals of the Christian year.

7. No acts of our religion are more naturally accompanied by this circumstance of the union of

large numbers for the purpose of devotion than the celebration of Holy Mass and Holy Communion. The first is the celebration of the One Sacrifice offered on the Cross for the living and the dead. The second is the appointed symbol and testification of our union, through our Lord, with one another, the unity of heart and faith and visible government which is the mark of the Catholic Church, the representation to the world of the charity which unites all the parts of that Church, in Heaven, on earth, and in Purgatory. It seems therefore very right and seemly that the Holy Souls as well as the Angels and Saints, should have their share in these solemnities of charity and unity, Now we find that the Holy See has specially encouraged the devout practice of general Communions for the benefit of the holy departed, by granting indulgences to such Communions, and in other ways. It is the custom in some Catholic countries or cities to celebrate these general Communions once a month for this special intention. It cannot be questioned that a great act of such devotion on the part of large numbers of people is in itself very pleasing and honourable to God, Who delights in seeing His children join together in worship and adoration, in prayer and praise and thanksgiving, that there is a special blessing in the Church on united prayer and public devotion, and that very great graces are often attached to such acts, greater than might have been obtained if each person had performed the same devotions privately. It is on this principle that it is customary to organize pilgrimages to shrines, and other such devotions, and it cannot be doubted that many persons are very much helped in the performance of them by the simple fact of having a great many companions, and that others are led by the popular character of the devotion to join in it, who would not perhaps have the piety or courage required for it if it were to be made by themselves singly. At such times as those of which we speak there seems to be an outpouring of the spirit of prayer, devotion seems to be easier than at other times, and we may hope that the interior graces which correspond to the exterior manifestation of religion are great and large in proportion. It would therefore be a devotion very much to the honour of God and to the consolation of the Holy Souls, as well to the promotion of piety among the faithful on earth, to revive some such holy practices as are here spoken of; as for instance, if the monthly general Communion for the relief of the sufferers in Purgatory were to be made a common practice in all large churches in great towns and elsewhere,

CHAPTER XXVIII.

Degrees of Punishment in Purgatory.

(THE CURE OF THE BLIND MAN AT BETHSAIDA.)
St. Mark viii. 22—26.

1. THE miracle of the feeding of the four thousand was followed, like the other great miracle of the multiplication of the loaves, by our Lord's retirement from the spot in which it had been wrought. This time He bent His steps towards Bethsaida, as it seems, on His road to the extreme north of the Holy Land, under Mount Hermon. Here again He would fain have been unobserved, but He was pursued by those who desired the exercise of His miraculous powers in favour of the sick. " They came to Bethsaida, and they brought to Him a blind man, and they besought Him that He would touch him." Here again our Lord seems to have objected to performing the miraculous cure in public. " And taking the blind man by the hand, He led him out of the town, and spitting upon his eyes, laying His hands upon him, He asked him if he saw anything. And looking up, he said, I see men as it were trees walking. After that again He laid His hands on his eyes, and he began to see, and was restored, so that he saw all things clearly. And He sent him into his house, saying, Go into thy house, and, if thou enter into the town, tell nobody."

2. The characteristic feature of this miracle is the gradual restoration of sight to the blind man. On ordinary occasions, a word or a touch from our Lord was sufficient to work the greatest cure instantaneously, whereas in this case there were stages in the restoration, as our Lord knew was to be the case, for He asked the man, after the first imposition of hands, whether he could yet see. Thus there seems to have been an unusual difficulty about this cure—a difficulty which could not, of course, have been the result of any failure of miraculous power in our Lord, and must therefore have been either a consequence of some slowness of faith on the part of the poor man himself, or caused by some intention of our Lord to set forth or symbolise some truth. With regard to Purgatory, it is not difficult to find a truth which may well be illustrated by this narrative. Just as we have seen that the punishments of Purgatory are particular, and are applied in exact measure and proportion to the various kinds of sin which have to be expiated there, so also is it true that there are some persons whose purgation is far longer and more gradual than that of others. or, what amounts to the same thing, there are some sins the punishment of which is longer and more difficult than the punishment of others. This is a practical truth of great importance, the understanding of which is necessary to a complete intelligence of the Catholic doctrine concerning Purgatory.

3. The truth seems to be that there are immense differences, in the next world, between those who belong to the same great kingdoms, so to speak, of which we know anything at all—the kingdoms of Heaven, of Purgatory, and of Hell. The differences in glory and nearness to our Lord between one saint

and another, one hierarchy of Angels and another, may be so great as to be comparable to those which are known to exist between the various celestial bodies, all of which seem to us so much alike and so near each to the other. So it may also be between the sinners who have to suffer the eternal separation from God which is the punishment of Hell, and so it may be between the various sojourners in the prison of Purgatory—for the difference between the several classes of persons who die in the grace of God are very great indeed. Some are so innocent as on that account to have little punishment, although they may not have served God in any heroic degrees of virtue. Some have laid up very great treasures in heaven by good works of various kinds, and yet they may have a considerable debt to pay in Purgatory on account of the great things which God has intrusted to them as to which they have been unfaithful, or on account of serious faults of character, and the like. Others may have been away from God and His grace for a greater part of their lives, and have been brought home at the last, dying before they had time to do much penance, and saved, perhaps, by His sacramental grace at the last, which has made their sorrow acceptable in God's sight. In a great many different ways these diversities may exist. Thus the purification of some souls may be almost instantaneous, others may remain but a short time in Purgatory, and then pass to thrones in Heaven less glorious than those which await others who have yet a greater debt to pay. Others may have to remain a longer time than the rest in Purgatory, and then may have to occupy some of the lower seats in the Blessed Kingdom of our Lord. Cases such as these may be considered as represented by the slowness with which the miracle on which we are now commenting was wrought.

4. One of the great passages in the New Testament which are used to illustrate the doctrine of Purgatory is to be found in the First Epistle o St. Paul to the Corinthians, where the Apostle is undoubtedly referring to the Purgatorial fire. He is speaking of the various kinds of ministerial work which may be raised by those who have or who assume the office of teachers in the Church. St. Paul says: " The fire (of God's judgment) shall try every man's work of what sort it be. If any man's work abide which he hath built thereupon, he shall receive a reward. If any man's work burn, he shall suffer loss, but he himself shall be saved as by fire." In the verse immediately preceding he gives various figures which represent the different kinds of work which are to be tried. The works are represented by gold, silver, precious stones, wood, hay, stubble. It is common with Christian writers to see in this enumeration an image of various good works and various kinds of lighter sins, all of which are to be tested by the fire of judgment, and some to be consumed in the fire of Purgatory. The gold, silver, and costly stones are good works, of various degrees of value in the sight of God, and for these there can be no suffering in Purgatory, but only various degrees of reward in Heaven. The other three members of the enumeration are supposed to represent three various kinds of sins which have to undergo punishment before the soul can attain its perfect salvation, that is, its admission into the presence of God. The writers to whom we refer say that wood burns slowly, hay quickly, and stubble instantaneously. There are various kinds of venial sins which correspond to this classification ; there

are some venial sins which are in the same order as
mortal sins, but they are saved from being mortal
by want of full intention, advertence, and some
other circumstances. Such sins, for instance, are
evil or uncharitable thoughts not fully consented
to, while full consent would have made them mortal.
Other sins are lighter in substance, even though
there be full consent, such as a deliberate lie or
theft in a small matter. Others, again, are igno-
rances, omissions, distractions, and other defects
which are hardly altogether sinful, because they are
in great part the result of human frailty, and yet
they might have been avoided if we had greater
carefulness, more recollection of God's presence,
more reverence in His service.

5. If we are to give ourselves a complete idea of
the various degrees of the punishments in Purgatory,
we must add to this division of venial sins, founded
on the words of St. Paul, the number of mortal sins
for which many of the Holy Souls may have to
suffer, the guilt of which has been forgiven, but the
punishment of which is, as yet, unpaid. Indeed,
it is the punishment due to the venial sins just now
spoken of with which we have to do, and not with
the guilt. Now, it must be very clear that the
difference between the lighter and the heavier kinds
of sin is in itself very great. It is also clear that
the debt of punishment which may be due for mortal
sin of which the guilt has been forgiven, may be
very great indeed, when their number has been
large, and the affection to them very deeply rooted
in the soul. On the other hand, we cannot think
that God's justice will not deal with, comparatively,
a very light hand in the case of imperfections as
to which there is some little wilfulness, frailties with
which negligence and levity are mixed up, and the

like. It is certain, then, that the gradations of punishment must be very many, and the intervals, so to speak, very considerable. The same may be said as to the cancelling of the debt of punishment which is practically common and easy in this life. It is not very easy to cancel the debt of punishment incurred by a number of mortal sins, which may have become in some cases almost habitual, while, on the other hand, there are a great many ways which Christians ordinarily practise, which have the effect of doing away with the punishment of lighter sins. There is, however, one serious condition for the application of the numberless easier satisfactions which the mercy of God has provided for us, and that condition is that where there has been an evil will in any degree—as in the case mentioned above, of a deliberate falsehood in a light matter—then the sin must be retracted by sorrow before the satisfaction can be applied. The effect of this and the other truths which have now been mentioned is to enhance our ideas of the difficulty which many souls will find in obtaining deliverance from Purgatory, except after a long period of suffering, as also to move our charity towards those who may be in so much need of help. Well also will it be, if the same thoughts lead us to a more careful avoidance of all wilful sin, however light, a greater exactness in retracting any that we may have committed, and a greater value of, and diligence in, all work of satisfaction.

CHAPTER XXIX.

The Holy Souls helped by Prayer and Fasting.

(The Cure of the Lunatic Boy.)

St. Mark ix. 16—28.

1. WE are all familiar with the miracle of the cure
of the lunatic boy, which took place on our Lord's
descent with His three chosen disciples from the
mountain of Transfiguration. We all have remarked
the contrast which the two scenes present as they
are pictured by some great Christian artists, between the heavenly and ecstatic joy of the three
Apostles on the holy mountain, enjoying the vision
of our Lord in His glory with His two great Saints
of the Old Testament, and the struggle, perplexity,
and weakness of their brethren below, with the
crowd pressing around them, the father of the boy
entreating them, and the evil spirit, as it were,
mocking at them on account of their inability to
cast him out. Then the Evangelists tell us in considerable minuteness of detail how our Lord was
met by the crowd, who, as St. Mark tells us, were
" astonished and struck with fear " when they saw
Him, and how the father told Him the pitiful circumstances of the case. " I have brought my son to
Thee, having a dumb spirit, who, wheresoever he
taketh him, dasheth him, and he foameth, and
gnasheth with the teeth and pineth away, and I

spoke. to Thy disciples to cast him out and they could not." Our Lord complained of the unbelief of the generation to which He was sent, and bade the father bring the boy to Him. He questioned the father about the facts of his case, and when with some little confidence the poor man begged Him to help them, " Have compassion on us if Thou canst do anything," our Lord answered, " If thou canst believe, all things are possible to him that believeth." In the end our Lord cast out the spirit, who left him, "crying out and greatly tearing him, and he became as dead, so that many said, He is dead. But Jesus taking him by the hand, lifted him up, and he arose."

2. The description of this possessed boy shows us that his case must have been one of those in which the enemy of God and man is allowed a very great power, and in which he sets up his dominion over the body of his poor victim very firmly. The nine disciples asked our Lord afterwards in private why they had been unable to cast out this devil. He told them, as St. Matthew informs us, that it was on account of their want of faith : but he added also, that that particular kind of evil spirit was only to be cast out by prayer and fasting, that is, that there are certain spiritual powers which are not ordinarily granted, even to the servants and ministers of our Lord in the Church, unless they accompany the exercise of their functions by prayer and fasting. We have here, then, a truth which it is not difficult to apply to our present subject. It may very well be the case, that God, in His inscrutable wisdom and justice, will not allow the deliverance of certain souls from Purgatory, or the cancelling of the debt due to certain sins, on any other condition than that of the offering to Him of a considerable amount

of prayer accompanied by severe mortifications. We have seen in a former chapter that there are some sins the punishment of which is remitted with much greater difficulty than that of others. But this is only one part of the subject before us, because the words of our Lord suggest to us quite as much the positive value of the great spiritual weapons of prayer and fasting, as the comparison between them and other less powerful means. This, then, may be the subject to which our considerations in the present chapter may be addressed.

3. It cannot certainly be denied that the words of our Lord as to prayer and fasting seem to place them, in a certain sense, on a higher level, with regard to the end in view, than other works unaccompanied by them. It seems as if He left us to imply that prayer and fasting, without anything else, might accomplish much, but that there were many things beyond the power of other works to effect without prayer and fasting. It is remarkable that we should have so many instances in this series of our Lord's miracles, in which the casting out of a dumb devil was considered as a work of unusual power, such as to call forth particular enthusiasm on the part of the believing crowd, as well as the special opposition of calumny on the part of His enemies. This, then, was a difficult miracle to perform, beyond the power of an exorcist, even though commissioned by our Lord, unless aided by prayer and mortification. The power of these two great weapons as to the release of the Holy Souls is thus enhanced to us by the comparison suggested by the miracle. As to prayer, we know that it is in general the key to all good graces and favours, and certainly not less than in any other case, the key which opens the doors of His mercy to the sufferers in

Q

Purgatory.   The power of prayer is reckoned by theologians as twofold—the power of impetration, and the power of satisfaction.   Some great and holy writers seem to have hesitated as to the direct power of impetration in regard to the relief of the punishments in Purgatory—just as we have seen the same kind of hesitation with regard to the intercessions of the Saints.   Thus they have allowed to Christian prayer, for the object of which we are speaking, the power to move the intercession of the Saints for the Holy Souls, to obtain from God that the satisfaction offered for those Holy Souls may be applied to them, to obtain the favour that a great number of persons may be inspired to pray for them, and to offer for them works of acceptable satisfaction.   It has also been thought that prayer may win from the mercy of God the boon that the length of the pains which the souls ought to suffer may be diminished, the intensity of those pains being proportionately increased.   And yet they have stopped short of the assertion that prayer may obtain the direct remission of the pains of Purgatory, and this hesitation has been grounded on the reason that justice requires that the punishment of sins should not remain unpaid.[1]   Such teaching shows the very high sense which these holy writers have of the claims of the justice of God, but on the one hand, we have seen so many reasons in the course of these considerations for thinking that His mercy is ever ready to be moved in favour of these holy sufferers, and in the second place, for looking on the prayer of faith as almost omnipotent with Him, that we shall not very easily persuade ourselves that a very large part of the debt of the punishment may not be remitted for faithful and constant prayer,

[1] *Suarez de Purgatorio*, disp. 48, § 5.

even by way of impetration. For we began these reflections by dwelling on the thought that our Lord anticipated His otherwise appointed time for the beginning of His miracles at the prayer of our Blessed Lady. Now He would not have done this, that is, He would not have permitted our Blessed Lady to exert the sweet constraint of her intercession to overrule what was appointed, unless He had meant us to understand that that which we call overruling was, in this instance, and, in principle, in others, exactly that kind of interference which He most of all desired and delighted in, In the same way, in the case of the Syrophœnician woman, we have seen that He allowed Himself to be, as it were, forced to go beyond the letter of His commission from the Father, and we may be certain that this too was a case in which His Sacred Heart very much delighted, and that it would have been a disappointment to Him if that poor woman had gone away without further persistence after He had first rebuffed her. And, with regard to the point before us, we may gather the mind of the Church from the prayers which she suggests and puts into the mouths of her ministers. Now many of these ask directly for the remission of the pain which the Holy souls have to suffer for the claims of God's justice against them. It is true that many of these prayers are offered in connection with the Adorable Sacrifice, which has the power of satisfaction as well as that of impetration. But then all our prayers are offered to the Eternal Father " through Jesus Christ our Lord," and so plead His merits, and the impetration which belongs to those merits.

4. In any case, however, prayer most certainly possesses a power of satisfaction besides that of impetration, and therefore on this ground there

can be no doubt of its immense efficacy for the direct remission of the pains of Purgatory. The power of satisfaction is not necessarily, as it appears, limited to works of piety and devotion which are in themselves in some degree painful, as requiring either bodily suffering or fatigue, or mental strain and exertion. Both these latter qualities are to be found in prayer, which is always to some extent a strain on our poor feeble nature, especially if it be prolonged. This must be the answer to such as complain of the tediousness of the long offices which the Church enjoins as to be said for the departed. They are, indeed, full of beauty and delight to the fervent. They contain the thoughts which have fed the heart of the Church and her saints in all ages. They are the forms of converse with God, so to speak, which our Lord Himself and His Blessed Mother used while on earth—but still, if they tax the attention and fatigue the head, it is not much that we should pay that amount of mortification for the sake of relieving the souls of our brethren from the torments of Purgatory. In this connection we may remind ourselves of the long " Psalters " recited, sometimes daily, sometimes more than once in the day, by the saints and servants of God in old times, of which the history of the Church is so full. It would be easy to fill pages with the accounts that exist of the various long prayers which have been enjoined by particular religious Orders, as intercessions and satisfactions for the departed. St. Peter Damian tells us that the hermits of Fonte Avellino recited the Office of the Dead every day; but that when one of their own number came to die, the remainder were bound to assist him by fasting seven days continuously, by taking seven disciplines each of a thousand stripes, by chanting the Psalter thirty times, by celebrating Mass for his soul thirty days continuously, after which three hundred Masses were said for him, besides seven more by each priest. If any one died besore he had completed these suffrages for the dead, then the remainder was fulfilled for him by the survivors of the community.[1] This is but a single instance of the active charity of Religious Orders for the dead—a charity which shows the mind of the Church as to their needs, and as to the power of prayer to help them.

5. It must be added, that our Lord in the passage upon which we are now commenting, does not speak of prayer alone, but of prayer united to fasting, under which head we may include mortifications of every kind. It would be natural, therefore, to go on in this chapter to the consideration of the efficacy of fasting, and of mortifications in general, in the relief of the sufferings of the Holy Souls. But, in order not to make this chapter too long, the subject of fasting must be put off for the present. Meanwhile, it is well to remember that our Lord is not here speaking of a work which is principally a work of satisfaction, but of a work principally, of impetration. He is speaking of the casting out of a particular class of devils, and He tells us that prayer and fasting together are required for that effect, according to the ordinary laws of God's kingdom. And it is a matter of common experience, that a great many things which we make the subjects of our petitions to God are not granted to us when we simply pray, but are granted to us when we unite fasting and other mortifications to our prayers. Now if this is the case as to other

---

[1] See St. Peter Damian *Opusc.* 14, quoted by Benedict XIII. Triges ii. Serm. 7.

things, when what we desire to obtain is a matter of impetration, it is much more likely to be the case when that which we ask for is mainly a matter of satisfaction, such as is the release of the Holy Souls from the pains of Purgatory. For fasting and mortification have, as has been said, a direct power as to satisfaction which does not always belong to prayer. This may serve to show that there is no case in which it may be more necessary to join mortifications to prayer, in order to obtain our requests, than the particular case to the consideration of which these chapters are devoted.

CHAPTER XXX.

Union between the Holy Souls and our Lord.

(OUR LORD PAYING THE DIDRACHMA.)
St. Matt. xvii. 23—26.

1. ST. MATTHEW relates an incident which occurred on the return of our Lord to Capharnaum, after an absence of several weeks, during which the miracles of which we have lately been speaking had taken place. This incident was the payment of the didrachma, an annual tax which every Jew was bound to furnish for the expenses of the Temple. It seems that the collectors of the tax came to St. Peter, and asked him whether his Master did not pay the tax? St. Peter replied that He did. On his entering the house in which our Lord was —it may have been St. Peter's own—our Lord anticipated any question from him, by asking him whether earthly Kings exacted taxes from their

children or from others? Peter replied from strangers. " Jesus said to him, Then the children are free. But that we may not scandalize them, go to the sea, and cast in a hook, and that fish which shall first come up, take, and when thou hast opened its mouth, thou shalt find a stater, take that, and give it to them for Me and thee."

2. There may have been some reason in the cir-cumstances of the case, as, for instance, if our Lord were at that time the guest of St. Peter, and so his debtor for shelter and food, why he should have told that blessed Apostle that the coin which was to be found in the mouth of the fish was to be paid for both of them, and not for any other. But the whole incident is symbolical as well as simply historical, and forms one link in the chain of acts and sayings of our Lord which set forth the privileges which He intended to bestow on the Prince of the Apostles. We may apply it in another symbolical sense, in order to gather from it a truth concerning the Holy Souls of Purgatory, which is independent of all symbol and figure, but which may be illustrated thereby. The tax which had to be paid for the maintenance of the service of God in the Temple may remind us of the penalties which are exacted from the Holy suffering Souls to fit them for admis-sion into God's presence in Heaven, where they are to praise Him for ever. The poverty of our Lord and the Apostles, and the recourse which He chose on this occasion to have to the Providence of His Father, may remind us of the inability of the Holy Souls to help themselves, and the extent to which God has placed their case in our hands for succour. And the tender affectionate tie, the existence of which is implied in our Lord's words, " for Me and for thee," may remind us of the union of these Holy

Souls with our Lord, so that it is indeed true that what is done for them is done for Him also.

3. We may make this last point the subject of special consideration in the present chapter. For it is of great importance that in all that we do for the Holy Souls we should have our Lord before us as the Person Who is relieved in them, and that this motive for our exertion in their behalf, based upon our love for Him, should be constantly dwelt upon to enhance our zeal and urge us on even to sacrifices and sufferings for their sake. It has been already said, that all the various works of mercy, such as feeding the hungry, clothing the naked, and the like, may be practised towards the Holy Souls in a spiritual sense. When we perform any one of these acts of mercy, it is natural that we should remind ourselves of the words of our Lord concerning them in His description of the Day of Judgment, where He declares that, " I was hungry, and you gave Me to eat, I was thirsty, and you gave Me to drink, I was a stranger, and you took Me in, naked, and you clothed Me, sick, and you visited Me, I was in prison, and you came to Me." [1] And He adds, that when the just ask Him, when have they done all these things, He will reply, " Amen, I say to you, as long as you did it to one of these My least brethren, you did it to Me." In this sense, then, it is certain that charity to the Holy Souls is charity practised to our Lord Himself, for He has no least brethren who are in greater hunger or thirst, who feel so much their separation from their home, who are so truly naked, and sick, and in prison, as these Souls. Indeed, it may be said that they are, in many respects, not the least, but the nearest and the dearest of His brethren.

[1] St. Matt. xxv. 35, seq.

4. Again, we know well that our Lord had a special love for certain classes of persons, as belonging to Himself in a particular way, representing Him bearing His cross, reflecting His character, and the like. He had a great love for the poor, and He has left the poor behind Him in Christian countries, instead of abolishing the holy state of poverty, in order, among other reasons, that they may represent Him to others, and give them the opportunity of being merciful to Him in them. He had a special love for children, because the innocence and simplicity and humility, which are in them only natural shadows, as it were, of great Christian virtues, made them like Him, and in some sort reflections of His character. He had a great love for the afflicted in every way, body and soul, because all such affliction is a certain figure of His Cross, by which He came to heal the world, and He chose to be among us as one whom God had smitten and afflicted. All such affliction bears witness at once to the misery of sin and to the hollowness of the world, and every instance of it which He came across gave Him an occasion, which was most delightful to Him, of mercy and compassion. The poor, the young, the sick, the afflicted in any way, are thus our Lord's own chosen representatives in the world, and it is the secret of perfect Christian charity, not only to relieve them for His sake when occasion offers, but to seek them out and fall on them, as it were, as on a long-sought prey or a most valued treasure, especially because of its love for Him. But in all the characteristics in which they resemble Him and bear His livery, it is not difficult to see that they are even surpassed by the Holy Souls—for they are poor as to spiritual treasures more necessary to them

than what is required by the poor for the sustenance of life, the virtues in which they resemble our Lord are not merely natural images of true virtues, as in the case of children, but virtues seasoned by struggle and well worn by practice, and their afflictions are more like those which He endured on the Cross than any sufferings which strike the eye and the heart in this world. And again, their endurance of their sufferings is more like His ineffable patience, for they are perfect in their resignation, in their love of God, and in their union with His adorable will.

5. Again, although it be true that the Holy Souls are in this manner the most perfect images of our Lord on which we can exercise our compassion and charity, it is also true that they have another pre-eminence as to the point on which we are meditating, because they are so perfectly and inseparably one with Him. The poor, the young, the afflicted, represent our Lord to us, and that representation is enough to justify His own Divine words, "As long as you did it to one of these My least brethren, you did it to Me." We are not to seek in them more than this representation of Jesus Christ, for it is not our business to inquire into the state of the souls of those whom we relieve, except in some particular cases, and then to a certain limited extent. It is enough that they are in the place of our Lord, and that our charity is directed to Him as its motive. But in the case of the Holy Souls there is far more than the representation of our Lord. There is in them perfect and indissoluble union with Him. Holy writers tell us that the pain which our Lord felt in the Garden at the thought of the loss of sinners who had belonged to Him, was far more intense than the agony which might have been caused, if such had been God's will, by the cutting

off of limbs from His Body. But the Holy Souls are members of His Body over which He rejoices, because there is now no more any danger or possibility of their separation. In this sense they are more firmly united to Him than even the Saints while on earth; and this union is a source of intense delight and thankfulness to Him, greater in proportion to the degree of grace to which they have attained, and without anything to alloy or mar it, because there is no internal malice, no admixture of evil with good left in them, but only the debt of punishment to pay, which does not interfere with their absolute love for Him. And their condition of punishment is one which is dear to Him on account of His love for the justice of His Father, while it gives them a special claim on His tenderness, moving His Heart towards them, as the sufferings of an invalid child draw on it all the tenderest affections of a loving parent. Weak and suffering as they are, they are His, they are one with Him for ever, and the air of pain which hangs over them recalls to Him all that He has suffered for them Himself, through which alone their punishments have any healing power, as also the severity of the conflict from which they have emerged. Thus it may be said of their case and of our Lord's care for them that both awaken in Him a special feeling of love, not altogether unlike that joy of which He spoke when He said that, " there shall be joy in Heaven upon one sinner that doth penance, more than ninety and nine just who do not need penance." [a]

6. Such are some of the thoughts which are suggested by the truth of the union which exists between our Lord and the Holy Souls. Of all

[a] St. Luke xv. 7.

those whom we can pray for or benefit by our almsdeeds or other good works, they are the most closely one with Him, so that we may say that what is offered to God for them is like the stater, given for Him and for them at once. Our own union with Him is the condition of our spiritual life. That life is strong and penetrating in us in proportion to the degree of that union. It seems almost impossible to be closely united with our Lord unless we have a most tender love and thoughtful care for all that are one with Him like ourselves, and of all such, the Holy Souls have the highest claims on those exercises of our love to Him which consist in charity and mercy. On the other hand, the exercise of those heavenly virtues is certain to intensify them in the soul, and thus, in this case, as in so many others, the good that we may try to do to others returns upon ourselves in abundant blessings.

CHAPTER XXXI.

The Pain of Loss. I. The Beatific Vision of God.

1. ALTHOUGH the miracles wrought by our Lord in the city and neighbourhood of Jerusalem were very few in number, in comparison to those which made His preaching in Galilee and in the country parts of Judea so famous, yet those which are mentioned are among the most remarkable of all, especially on account of the great effect which they produced on the minds of His enemies, who, in every recorded case, seem to have been driven to great fury against Him thereby. We have now to speak of one of these remarkable miracles, which took place within a few months of the Passion, and which provoked the ecclesiastical rulers to such an extent as to make them excommunicate the man on whom the miracle was wrought. Our Lord was at Jerusalem when "passing by, He saw a man who was blind from his birth. And His disciples asked Him, Rabbi, who hath sinned, this man or his parents, that he should be born blind? Jesus answered, Neither hath this man sinned, nor his parents, but that the works of God should be made manifest in him." That is, the reason why this man has been born blind is not any sin of his own or of his parents,

but he has been afflicted in this way in order that
the works of God may be made manifest in him by
his cure. " I must work the works of him that
sent Me, whilst it is day; the night cometh when
no man can work. As long as I am in the world, I
am the Light of the world." Then He proceeded,
as in the case of the man whom He had cured at
the Probatic Pool, to work the miracle unasked,
in order that His Father might be glorified by this
great manifestation of the power of His Incarnate
Son. " When He had said these things, He spat
on the ground, and made clay of the spittle, and
spread the clay upon his eyes, and said to him, Go,
and wash in the pool of Siloe (which is interpreted
Sent). He went, therefore, and washed, and he
came seeing."

2. This miracle is related by St. John, as is his
wont, chiefly for the purpose of dwelling upon the
results to which it led. It was in itself a very remarkable instance of power, and the enemies of
our Lord had no resource but to endeavour to
intimidate the poor man to whom the wonderful
world of sight was thus miraculously opened, and
when they found they could not succeed in this,
they excommunicated him. We need not dwell on
these results, nor on the long conversations related
by St. John as following on this miracle. But it
enables us to consider that which is the chief among
all the pains of Purgatory, and of which we have
as yet hardly spoken. This is the pain of loss,
which consists in the sufferings of the holy dead
because they are debarred from the Beatific Vision
of God during their detention in Purgatory. This
pain is also the chief pain which the poor sufferers
in Hell have to endure, but it differs in them from
that pain which the Holy Souls suffer, because in

these it is only for a time, while the lost souls know that in their case the loss is eternal. The Catholic doctrine on the subject amounts to this. The essence of beatitude consists in the vision and possession of God, the possession or fruition of God being inseparably connected with the vision and knowledge of Him. According to the great school of St. Thomas, this alone constitutes the essence of beatitude. According to the other school, the greatest name of which is that of the Seraphic Doctor, St. Bonaventure, the love and joy which result from the knowledge and possession of God also belong to the essence of beatitude. That is, the good of goods, which is God, is not perfectly and absolutely possessed unless it be, as it were, joyously embraced as well as seen and known, and unless the soul satisfy all its affections in this knowledge and love. This is the good of which the lost souls are deprived for ever, and of which they know that they are deprived by their own fault. This is the good of which the Holy Souls are deprived for a time, and of which they know that they are deprived by their own negligence. As it would be difficult to compress all that may be said on this great subject into a single chapter, we may treat at present of the knowledge and fruition of God alone.

3. We can imagine few surprises more great than that of this poor man, mentioned by St. John, when for the first time the beautiful world in which our lot is now cast was, as it were, revealed to him after he had spent so many years in darkness, without the slightest memory to aid him in picturing to his mind the scenes in the midst of which he was moving. We may be quite sure that if he had formed any conceptions of light and colour and form, of the sunshine, and of the various beauties of earth and

sky, tree and flower, the human form and face, and the works of the mind and hand of man, such as the magnificent Temple at Jerusalem, and the like, those conceptions would have seemed to him as meagre and miserable indeed when compared with the sights now opened to him by the gift of his new sense.　But no marvels of nature or of art can bear the slightest comparison with the beauty of God as He is to be seen by the Blessed in Heaven, nor can we now form of that beauty any conception at all, however poor and unequal to the original, because the knowledge and possession of God constitute a good altogether above our nature, and are concerned with a range of being of which He is Himself the one single instance.　It follows from this that we shall weary ourselves in vain, if we endeavour to frame any description at all of what it is that is known and possessed in God.　The fullest sight and knowledge of material things does not make them ours, does not make them present to us or enable us to enjoy them, but it is otherwise with the spiritual sight of God which is imparted in the Beatific Vision.　To see God is to possess His Eternity, Wisdom, Love, Mercy, Power, Holiness, Truth, Sovereignty, Justice, and Infinite Happiness.　"So great," says Suarez, "is the beauty and sweetness of this Eternal Light, that even if it were not allowed us to remain therein longer than a single day, yet, for this alone, we might well and rightly despise innumerable years of this present life, full of delights and abundance of all temporal goods.　For that has not been falsely or wrongly said, ' Better is one day in Thy courts than a thousand years.' " [1]　For what is seen in God, even although He can only be fully comprehended by Himself, is more truly beautiful and noble than all

[1] Suarez, tom. i. *De Lib. Arbitrio*, lib. iii. chap. 23.

that can be enjoyed in this world, and it is seen and enjoyed in a truer and more noble way. This sight of God is so great a good, that its possession even for a moment would be an abundant reward for all the toils and sufferings of this life. If God were to exact that we should suffer all the torments of the martyrs, or the pains of sense in Hell itself for a time, as the condition of enjoying the sight of Himself, it would not be too much to pay as a price for such a blessing, even though it were to be enjoyed only for a time. Indeed, it is so great a good that nothing but the infinite merits of our Lord can earn such a prize—not even the most difficult works of heroic virtue, or the most terrible sufferings faithfully borne. St. John, speaking of this vision, says that it will make us like God : " We shall be like to Him, for we shall see Him as He is." [a]

4. The possession of God being so great, and, in a certain sense, infinite a good, it follows that to be deprived of it for any time is in itself a proportionate loss, a loss greater than can be calculated by the mind of man or Angel. The eternal loss of God is, as has been said, the greatest of the pains of Hell, and the temporary loss of God the greatest of the pains of Purgatory. This loss is not less a loss to them for the time that it lasts, because that time is to come to an end. For it is not a simple loss, or rather, absence of possession, of a thing which they know nothing of and could not in any case gain. The want of the possession of God is thought by some theologians not to have been felt, at least as a great pain, by the Fathers in Limbus, and it is commonly thought that it is no pain at all to children who have died without baptism, and brings them no sorrow, because they never could have obtained it.

[a] 1 St. John iii. 2.

R

For no wise person can afflict himself because he is not in possession of a good which he has not lost by his own fault, and which it was never in his power to gain. In order that there may be true sorrow in such a case, there must have been a power of enjoying the good which is absent, there must have been some fault which has been the cause why it has been lost, and there must be a longing desire for its possession. If we apply this to the case of the Holy Souls with regard to their privation of· the Beatific Vision, we find all these elements of intense sorrow. They are capable of that Beatific Vision, they have lost it through their own fault, which· bars against them, for a time at least, the gates of Heaven. There is no longer any low or bad affection in their will, or any error or ignorance in their mind. St. Thomas[8] tells us that the affection with which the Holy Souls desire the chief good after this life is most intense, because it is no longer hindered by the weight of the body, and because their time for enjoying that good would already have come if there had not been an impediment. The reason of this intense longing is simply their love for God and their inability to enjoy Him.

5. Their love of God is measured by their knowledge of Him; a knowledge which may be greater or less in various souls, but which in all that die in grace is very great. In the first place they have the gift of faith, and although nothing new in kind may be added to this on their entrance into the world beyond the grave, yet still the soul separated from the body is able to grasp far more firmly than before the truths of faith. It is no longer troubled by the clouds raised by fancy, imagination, evil affections, and the like, and so it can see what is

[8] St. Thomas *in Sent.* lib. iv. dist. 21, qu. 1, art. 1.

before it, and especially God, far more clearly and in a purer light than before. Thus it understands and loves the Goodness, the Mercy, the Wisdom, the Truth, the Justice, the Holiness of God, and all His other attributes, which are natural causes of love and desire. There is nothing in the new state, in which the soul finds itself, to prevent it from reaching forward to such objects and working upon them with all the intensity of an unbroken energy. There is no languor, or interruption, or weariness, or feebleness about the operations of the soul in the next world, and thus the same faith which has been, as it were, drowsy or half dead in this life, is there full of vigour and keenness, and gives birth to a love of God which is proportionate to the full intensity of its powers. Moreover, no thought can conceive the immense effect, on the soul which dies in grace, of that vision of our Lord as Judge in the Particular Judgment, which it takes so few words to speak of. That vision has opened to them an entirely new sense of the wisdom, the justice, the love of God, and we may say the same of the keen insight which is imparted to them at the same moment as to the whole of their past life, with its boundless accompaniment of graces and blessings and mercies, what God has been to them, and what they have been to Him, and also as to their future, the rewards which the faithfulness of God has in store for them after their faults have been expiated in Purgatory. All this, as we have said, is grasped by the soul with the utmost firmness and understood with the utmost clearness, and it rivets the attention and engrosses the affections without any intermission or relaxation. They see the Truth Itself, and they are drawn to its embrace by an attraction abso- lutely irresistible, and urging them with its whole

force at every moment, the power of which is but
faintly pictured by any physical attraction which
the world knows. Their love, like their faith, is set
free from all impediment, and is secured in one
strong unchanging and most intense act of desire
to its true and only object.

6. These thoughts may enable us to understand
the intensity of the longing which the Holy Souls
feel for the assistance of the suffrages of the Church,
and the immense claims which they have upon our
charity. We may conclude this chapter by repeat-
ing the often-quoted image in which St. Catharine
of Genoa has endeavoured to express the longing
of the Holy Souls for God. " If there were in the
whole world but a single loaf of bread, the mere
sight of which was destined to appease the hunger
of all creatures, and if a man who had that desire
to eat which is natural to all of us in a normal state
of health, yet could not satisfy it, and yet, though
deprived of all food, could neither die nor fall sick,
is it not clear that he would suffer a hunger that
was always increasing ? Suppose this man to know
that the single loaf in question could alone, by his
seeing it, satisfy him, and that, without it, he would
remain in his hunger in a state of intolerable torture,
is it not evident that the nearer he came to that loaf
without being able to look upon it, the more would
his hunger be provoked, and that his torments
would be all the more cruel in proportion as his
appetite yearned with greater force for the sight of
this loaf, the single object of his desire ? And again,
if in the midst of this torture of hunger devouring
him always more and more as time went on, this
man were to acquire the dreadful certainty that he
was never again to see that loaf, what would take
place ? He would at once feel the beginning of

Hell within himself: he would from that moment be as are the souls of the damned who have lost all hope of seeing the Bread of Life, God, their Saviour. Well, then, the hunger which this man would feel is precisely that which the Souls of Purgatory experience, with the exception of the despair —for they have the hope that they shall one day see that loaf, and satisfy themselves with it as they will. But the hunger and martyrdom which they suffer are something which cannot be described, as long as it is not given them to fill themselves with the Bread of Life, which is Jesus Christ, the true God, our Saviour and our Love."[4]

[4] St. Catharine, *Treatise on Purgatory*, c. 6.

CHAPTER XXXII.

The Pain of Loss.   II. Exercise of the Love of God.

(THE CURE OF THE MUTE DEMONIAC.)
St. Luke xi. 14—26.

1. THE miracle which comes next in order of time to that of the giving sight to the man who had been blind from birth, is the casting out of the dumb devil, mentioned by St. Luke in the place cited above. This miracle is very like a former miracle on which we have already commented,[1] except that in that case the demoniac was blind as well as dumb. That miracle was worked in Galilee, and this in the country of Judæa, and it is possible that each of them has been selected by the Evangelists— this by St. Luke alone—on account of the calumny

[1] See Chap. xvi.

to which it gave occasion from the malignant enemies of our Lord. For it seems, as has already been said, that the casting out of a devil who had the power of inflicting dumbness on his victim was considered a work of very singular power, and thus, whenever our Lord performed this work, His adversaries were driven, either to acknowledge His Divine mission, or to impute the power which He exercised to a league with Satan. When it was our business to speak of the former miracle of this class, it was used as an occasion which suggested the consideration of the longing desire which the Holy Souls feel for the society to which they are destined in Heaven, and the enjoyment of that blessed communion and intercourse with the Angels and Saints which is to form so great a part of the blessedness there, from which they are, for the time, detained. We may use the present miracle in the same way, as illustrating that part of the pain of the loss in Purgatory, which consists in the inability of the Holy Souls to converse, not with the Saints and Angels alone, but with God Himself, in acts and exercises of love. It has been already said that the Beatitude of Heaven consists in the knowledge and possession of God, but that these cannot be separated from the exercises of love and joy which spring from them. Inasmuch as love on earth finds its chief vent in language, the gift of which enables us to communicate the feelings and thoughts of our hearts to each other, the restoration of the gift of speech to the poor man on whom the miracle was wrought may be used as an illustration of that admittance to the love of God which the Holy Souls are for the present forbidden to enjoy.

2. It must be remembered that the vision of God, which is the foundation of that love for Him which

reigns in the hearts of the blessed dwellers in Heaven, shows Him to them in a manner which is far higher than that in which faith represents Him. The vision of faith is certain, but it is not clear and distinct—for now we see, as St. Paul says, " through a glass in a dark manner, but then face to face." [1] Thus the intuitive vision of God represents Him to us, if we may so say, almost as a new God—as if we had never before heard anything about His Goodness, His Wisdom, His Charity, His Justice, and the rest. And the novelty of the effect on the will is the same as that of the effect on the mind, and thus an entirely new kind of love is kindled, so that it seems as if they had neither known nor loved God at all before. The difference may be compared to that between the delight which is produced by exquisite and scientific music on persons who have no ear and no knowledge of the science, and that which the same music produces on persons who are by nature endowed with a marvellous perception of its beauties, and who are able to understand the skill and genius with which the whole of a great piece is arranged and combined. Or we may use the sense of sight to furnish us with a comparison, and say that the difference is that between the pleasure caused by a most beautiful landscape on a person whose eyes are so dim that he can only see the principal objects vaguely, and this while a mist hangs between him and it, and the rapture occasioned by the same landscape glowing in the rich sunshine, and flecked with the varieties of light and shade, on the eyes of men who are fully able to take in all that lies before them. Some writers speak more strongly than this, and say that our knowledge of God now is like that which a

[1] 1 Cor. xiii. 12.

blind man has of the sunshine. But it is probable that no difference of this sort that we can imagine can span the distance between the two kinds of knowledge and the two kinds of love respectively, while those which are here suggested are enough to let us see, at least, how immense that distance is.

3. That, however, which it is difficult for us to find images adequately to express, is clear and well known to the Holy Souls, or at least, if they do not yet know the Beatific Vision in itself and its effects on the heart, they know how immeasurably it surpasses the knowledge of God and the love of God which they now possess, and that it is their own fault which shuts them out from the experience of what they thus know. In their prison of Purgatory they love God most ardently, but as they are still limited to the darker perceptions of faith, and as they know how far more intense is the love of Heaven, with which they would now be burning if it were not for their own negligence, the comparative coldness of their present love is a source of regret and self-reproach. Their hope reaches forward to the possession of God, but all the love which they now have is absorbed in an intense longing for that more perfect love for which they are destined, the very least delay of which is the cause of a pain which is almost intolerable. We see something of this in the longing for death which has consumed so many of the saints, the cause of which has been their unquenchable desire to see God as He is, in order that they may love Him with the love of the celestial home. In that immense longing of theirs we see some image of what is common in Purgatory.

4. The effects of the love of God, as they are described to us by spiritual writers, must not be

passed over here, although it is difficult to speak of them and still more difficult to understand them where there has been no practical familiarity with them. But we are not at liberty to treat the experiences or the descriptions of the saints as if they did not embody the most substantial and real of truths, merely because they are truths of which ordinary Christians have no practical perception. We read, for instance, in the lives of the saints, of their frequent ecstasies, in which they are drawn so forcibly to God by their love that the powers of the body fail, and the usual operations of vitality appear to cease. This is the consequence of the great weakness of the body, and there can be no effect of this kind in the state of glory, and we do not find it in our Lord or in the greatest of His saints. But, putting this accidental accompaniment of the state of ecstasy apart, the state itself, which consists in a most close and inseparable clinging of the soul to God, is one of the conditions of the state of glory, and one of the effects of the love with which the Blessed in Heaven are drawn to Him. This does not prevent their seeing and knowing and caring for all other things in Him, any more than it prevents their conscious and perfect adhesion to Him and to His will in everything, even when, if so it be, those whom they have loved dearly on earth have to be separated from Him and them for ever. But this perfect rapture of the soul in God is not as yet the possession of the Holy Souls, and their love has not as yet mounted up to this high perfection. Another effect of the love of God on the Blessed in Heaven is that which spiritual writers speak of as union. The minds and hearts of the Blessed in Heaven, cannot divert themselves from God. It is part of their immense happiness to be most perfectly united to Him Whom they so love, as a willing instrument to its mover and end, for all that belongs to His will or greater glory. It is the part of love to wish well to the person who is loved. The highest good that can be wished to God is His own glory, whether His intrinsic glory, which embraces all His Divine perfections, or His extrinsic glory, which consists in His being known and praised. This glory they desire to be rendered to Him by all, but they themselves give it to Him in the most excellent way, by knowing Him and loving Him most perfectly. All this is understood by the Holy Souls, and yet they know that they have shut themselves out for a time from the exercise of love, and the delay which is to be their punishment for this negligence is felt by them as a cause of the most intense pain.

5. Spiritual writers tell us of two other effects of the love of the Blessed for God, with which we may conclude this chapter. The first is a kind of absorption of the blessed soul in God, by means of which it is said, as it were, to melt away and lose itself in Him. " He who does not intuitively see God," says Lessius, [*] " stands without, and is even far distant from Him, because God is to Him as One Who is far distant. But he who sees Him in clear vision is present to Him, and he does not remain as it were outside on the surface, but enters into Him, and plunges himself, as far as may be, into that great depth. For love desires to abide within the Beloved, for there is its place, and home, and rest, and security, and all. But each one penetrates more or less into that depth, and is more or less deeply merged therein, as he has more or less of the light of glory, or of charity." This is the

[*] *De Summo Bono*, ii. 12.

" circle " of which St. Dionysus speaks—the Divine
Light shedding forth the light of glory on the soul,
love proceeding from that light, which in turn draws
the mind to God and plunges into Him. The
Blessed in Heaven see that they proceed from God
as from a principle of the most marvellous fecundity,
and they endeavour with all their might to return
to Him wholly by contemplation and love. Again,
the Holy Souls know all this, while they themselves,
instead of plunging into that great abyss of the
Deity, are detained in another abyss of misery,
because, when on earth, they turned away from
God, and spent themselves on created goods, which
are not true goods, but only shadows of good,
vanities of vanities. God is their home, and yet
they are shut out from Him. " How lovely are Thy
tabernacles, O Thou Lord of Hosts ! my soul
longeth and fainteth for the courts of the Lord .
. . for the sparrow hath found herself a house,
and the turtle a nest for herself where she may lay
her young ones, Thine Altars, O Lord of Hosts, my
King and my God. Blessed are they that dwell in
Thy House, O Lord, they shall praise Thee for ever
and ever."[4]

6. These words lead us to the fourth effect of the
love of God in the Blessed in Heaven, which is that
they are for ever praising Him. " And all the
Angels stood round about the throne, and the
ancients, and the four living creatures, and they
fell down before the throne on their faces, and
adored God saying, Amen, Benediction, and glory,
and wisdom, and thanksgiving, honour, and power,
and strength, to our God for ever and ever."[5] The
Holy Souls in Purgatory do indeed sing the Divine
praises. They break out into constant thanks-

[4] Psalm lxxxiii. 1—5.   [5] Apoc. vii. 11, 12.

givings for the certainty of their salvation, and for the suffrages which are made for them. But they know that these praises of God are cold indeed, in comparison to the praise which they might be rendering to Him in Heaven. They know, if they do not hear, as some have thought, the curses and blasphemies which assail the majesty of God from Hell. They know that they themselves cannot make Him as yet the compensation of that praise which springs from beatific love. They cannot sing the Lord's song in a strange land. The loss of these great privileges and effects of the love of which we speak is to them a reality, since it is from their own fault, tormenting them with a pain which no human words can describe. Their suffering is indeed a lesson to us to advance as far as possible in the love of God which is open to us while we are yet alive, and, by our suffrages for them, to set them free as soon as may be to love God for us with that beatific love of which we have been trying to speak,

CHAHTER XXXIII.

The Pain of Loss.   III. The Loss of the Joy of Heaven.

1. THE holy writers whom we have been following on the subject of the pain of loss add a third element to the sorrow which that pain produces in the souls of the prisoners of Purgatory. This third element is the result of their forfeiture, though only for a time, of the ineffable joy which results from that knowledge and love of God which reign in Heaven. The present chapter, therefore, must be devoted to some thoughts on this subject, and we shall find that they may very well be connected with the next miracle of our Lord, as related by the Evangelist St. Luke. It is one of the miracles wrought on the Sabbath-day by our Lord, in that latter period of His preaching in Judæa of which the third Evangelist has made himself specially the historian. In its main circumstances it is very like other miracles of the same sort wrought in Galilee. That is, the miracle was wrought without any application first made to our Lord to work it, and it aroused the indignation of our Lord's adversaries, an indignation which found a mouthpiece in the ruler

of the synagogue. Our Lord answered His enemies
in the same way as in earlier instances in which
the same objection was made against works of
Divine mercy on the Sabbath, His adversaries
were silenced and the people, on the other hand,
rejoiced.

2, St, Luke then tells us that our Lord "was
teaching in their synagogue on the Sabbath." It
is not the wont of this Evangelist, writing for
persons who did not know the Holy Land, to
specify the places in which such miracles were
wrought, but there need be no doubt that it was
in the country parts of Judæa that almost everything that is mentioned in this part of his Gospel
took place. "And behold, there was a woman
who had a spirit of infirmity eighteen years, and
she was bowed together, neither could she look
upwards at all." This woman may well represent
to us the state of the Holy Souls detained in many
cases from the vision of God for a term quite as
long as that here mentioned,—a state of joylessness,
their hearts bowed down with grief, on account of
the punishment of loss, "Whom when Jesus saw
He called her unto Him, and said, Woman thou
art delivered from thy infirmity. And He laid His
hands upon her, and immediately she was made
straight, and glorified God." We need not dwell
at any length upon that part of the narrative which
relates to the hostility which this miracle aroused.
Our Lord answered the objection in His usual way.
"Ye hypocrites, doth not every one of you on the
Sabbath-day loose his ox or his ass from the
manger, and lead them to water? And ought not
this daughter of Abraham, whom Satan hath bound
lo, these eighteen years, be loosed from this bond
on the Sabbath-day? And when He had said

these things, all His adversaries were ashamed, and all the people rejoiced for all the things that were gloriously done by Him."

3. This rejoicing of the people at the glorious things which were done by our Lord may serve as a sort of image of the joy of the Blessed in Heaven, which, as we shall see, is founded on God and on His glorious works. Joy, we are told, is the necessary complement and filling up of beatitude: so that, if we can separate in idea the three elements of beatitude of which we have spoken, the knowledge of God, the love of God, and the joy which results from these two, it may be said that beatitude itself would be incomplete without the last of the three. Joy is the very quintessence and crown and flower of happiness. Innocent joy, even on earth, is the most beautiful thing that can be seen in this valley of tears, and the supernatural joy of the Blessed is, in like manner, the most beautiful thing in their state in Heaven. Joy has three causes, each of which must be present if it. is to exist. There must be the possession of a great good, there must be the apprehension of this good and of its possession by a high and excellent faculty, and there must be a great love for the thing which is thus possessed and apprehended. In the case of the joy of which we are speaking, the good thing which is possessed is nothing else than God Himself, the highest and most ineffable of goods, the only True Good, the good perfect in every degree of goodness and of perfection. The organ or faculty which, as it were, appropriates this immense Good, containing infinite beauty, sweetness, and perfection, is the beatified mind, the noblest faculty of man, raised far above its natural powers by the light of glory, and strengthened thereby for the participation and

possession of that supreme essence of the Divinity. The love with which the soul clings to its object is, again, the most sublime and intense that can be conceived. These, then, are the causes of the intense joy in which the Blessed in Heaven live— a joy to which no delights of the senses can be compared without degrading it, which rises as far above even the joy in God of the saints on earth, St. Paul, St. Francis, and others, as the light of the sun above that of a poor candle. All the joys that can be felt on earth, even of the highest kind, if they were gathered into one soul, multiplied a thousand-fold, and made eternal, would not yet come up to the joy which the soul of one single beatified infant tastes in Heaven in the space of a short hour, for the simple reason that the knowledge and love on which those joys are founded are altogether of a lower order than the knowledge and love which give birth to the joy of which we are speaking.

4. It is but little that we can say by way of an attempt at describing the subject-matter of the joys of Heaven, and yet it is well, as a help to meditation, to set down the chief heads under which that subject-matter can be ranged. In the first place, as the Blessed know and possess God, their joy is founded on the goods which belong to God. The intrinsic goods, so to speak, of God, are His Own Ineffably Perfect Essence and Attributes, which have more than once been spoken of in these chapters. There is a second class of goods external to His Divine Essence—the glory which accrues to God from the Sacred Humanity of our Lord, the Hypostatic Union, the grace of Jesus Christ, His Virtues and Works in the world, the Blessed Sacrament, and the like, and again, from the Immaculate Mother of God, the Saints and Angels, and their

incessant praises before His throne, the wonderful kingdom of the Militant Church on earth, its struc- ture, mission, powers, government, the Providence which guides it, and the " healing of the nations" by its means. And among these goods of God must be reckoned also the Kingdom of His Justice, in which His enemies suffer for their rebellion against Him, or those who are to live for ever in His Pre- sence are prepared for it. Then again, the Blessed in Heaven rejoice over another class of good, which may be said to be their own. The Beatific Vision of God begets in them a sort of participation in the glory and felicity of God Himself, as if, according to the words of the Psalmist, as quoted by our Lord,[1] they became, in a manner gods. Again, the joy which the Beatific Vision creates in them would be ineffable, if it lasted but for a moment, but it is much increased and perfected. by the fixity and eternity of that vision. The Blessed rejoice, more- over, in the extreme splendour of virtue .in which they are, as it were, clothed, when they enter Heaven, in the clear knowledge of all things which they possess, and the delight with which the beauty and sweetness of all the works of God fill them. Even the past is full of delight to them, because they see all the dangers from which they have been guarded, and the eternal pains from which the mercy of God has saved them. And, if each one of those blessed citizens of Heaven is flooded with delight for the goods which are thus his own, not less is it true that this delight is reflected on all and multiplied in each soul, as it were, by the joy with which they rejoice in the goods which others possess, for they know each other perfectly, and all that God has done for and given to each,

[1] St. John x. 34 ; Psalm lxxxi. 6.

S

and each one rejoices in this as if it were his own.

5. And now, it must be added that all these causes of joy in the Blessed in Heaven are known to and understood by the Holy Souls in Purgatory, not indeed with that clearness and intensity which are to be found only in Heaven, but still with a clearness and intensity which far surpass any that we can have on earth. They know that they ought to be enjoying all these ineffable delights, and thanking God with the gratitude which corresponds to His mercies and gifts in their regard, and that they are unable to do this on account of their own fault. They are like guests bidden to a most exquisite banquet, for which they yearn with an ineffable hunger, who are yet, for their disrespect to the King Who has invited them, made to sit by it with their hands tied behind them, unable to taste it except in desire—a desire which is stimulated but never satisfied by their having to gaze upon it. How gladly would they turn to us and pray us to help them to their release! How gladly would they warn us to practise ourselves in thoughts concerning the eternal goods of Heaven, and in holy desires and aspirations of longing for them—knowing that, in many cases, their detention from the possession of this ineffable joy of which we have been speaking is the punishment of nothing more than a neglect to think of God, and to desire and long for the eternal possession of Himself which He has prepared for His children!

CHAPTER XXXIV.

The Pain of Loss.   IV. Causes of Sorrow to the Holy Souls.

(THE CURE OF THE MAN WITH THE DROPSY.)

St. Luke xiv, 1—6.

1. IN the last chapter the Holy Souls of Purgatory were spoken of as guests at a most excellent banquet, who were forced to sit and gaze upon it with their hands fastened behind their backs, and altogether unable to satisfy their hunger upon it.   We may conclude the subject of the pain of loss which these Holy Souls suffer, by some other considerations concerning it which may be connected with the next miracle of our Lord, which, like the last, is related by St. Luke alone.   It is another of the miracles wrought on the Sabbath-day; but it was not in the synagogue, but at one of the feasts which it was customary, as it seems, to connect with the Sabbath.   " And it came to pass, when Jesus went into the house of one of the chief of the Pharisees on the Sabbath-day to eat bread, that they watched Him.   And behold, there was a certain man before Him who had the dropsy.   And Jesus answering, spoke to the lawyers and Pharisees, saying, Is it lawful to heal on the Sabbath-day ?   But they held their peace.   But He taking him, healed him, and sent Him away, and answering them, said, Which

of you shall have an ass or an ox fall into a pit, and will not immediately draw him out on the Sabbath-day? But they could not answer Him to these things."

2. The Holy Souls in Purgatory, in regard to the blessings of Heaven to which they are heirs, are very like this poor man, who was healed by our Lord and then sent away from the banquet. His dismissal, however, did not imply any reproach or blame, for he was not among the invited guests, and had no right to be admitted to their company. The Holy Souls, on the other hand, are excluded from it through their own fault, like the foolish virgins, as has been said, though only for a time. The last chapters have shown us, in some measure, the outlines of the good of which they have deprived themselves, and it seems natural to follow these with a few considerations as to the method in which the forfeiture has been incurred. This is a subject supplementary to that of the pain of loss in itself. And we cannot doubt that this is a subject constantly present to the minds of the holy sufferers of whom we speak, inasmuch as it is directly connected with the pain of loss as a cause with its effect, although the fault which may have been involved in it has been already forgiven.

3. The chief heads of the sorrow of which we are now speaking are referred to, more or less, in various chapters of this work, so that we are not under any necessity of dwelling on them here at any great length. We may imagine that a holy Soul, in the midst of its pain at its banishment from the sight of God, and the consequent delay of its entering on that life of love and joy which belongs to those who are in His presence, might ask itself, how it had come about that it had

incurred this banishment ? It would remember in
the first place, how often it had rejected or turned
away from the grace of God, the holy inspirations,
suggestions, promptings, warnings, with which its
most loving Father had so frequently, as it were,
wooed it to greater carefulness and exactness in
His service. The light in which it is now able to
see the character of God, His immense dignity, the
wonderful condescension and love which are implied in every suggestion of grace addressed to
His poor creatures, will make its grief for the
rejection of any single such suggestion very poignant
indeed, especially when it adds to such considerations those of the relationship to God to which it
had undeservedly been raised, and the immense
debt of gratitude which binds it to Him. In the
same way the consideration of the truth as to the
beauty and worth of sanctifying grace, of which it
has made so little, will produce the same effect on
the mind. Sanctifying grace is called by theologians,
following the language of Scripture, a " partaking
of the Divine Nature ;" it is the infusion and
presence of the Holy Ghost in the soul, making
us act and live as the children of God, His friends,
His Spouses. The more clearly the Divine character
of sanctifying grace is allowed to dawn upon the
soul, the more miserable, sorrowful, and shameful
does the neglect of it appear. That neglect is a
sort of contempt of God, as our Father, our Lover,
our Friend, and this it is which has brought about
the exclusion of so many thousands of souls from
His sight for ever, and of so many thousands
more from His sight for a time.

4. The same considerations may easily be formed
in regard of sin, in the light in which the Holy
Souls now regard it. All their sins are perfectly

forgiven as to their guilt; but this does not prevent the memory of the causes of their exclusion from Heaven from abiding in the minds of these blessed prisoners as a part of their pain. They know now what sin is, or rather they knew it before, and there is nothing to intervene to prevent them from attentively contemplating and comprehending it, and they love God intensely, Who is injured by sin. Sin is a wrong and a harm done to God, and the more His Majesty is understood and His Love esteemed, the greater must be the sorrow that He has been offended. There is nothing on earth that is loathsome and disgraceful and monstrous, which is so loathsome and so disgraceful and so monstrous as sin is seen to be by the Holy Souls. They see that they have lifted their hands against God, in a manner which, in mortal sin, implies a readiness to kill and destroy Him, if such a thing were possible, to crucify our Lord over again, and drive away the Holy Ghost. They understand how far they have gone towards depriving themselves of the dignity of sons of God, towards renouncing their Heavenly inheritance, and even towards incurring, at the hands of God's justice, the extreme degradation and misery of eternal damnation. This sentence has been actually incurred in the case of every single mortal sin, and an approach towards deserving it has been made by every wilful sin of a lighter kind. Other heads of sorrow may be added to these, which may help us to estimate as it ought to be estimated this pain of loss. One is that of the grief with which the Holy Souls regard their own neglect to make satisfaction for their faults, while satisfaction was as yet so easy, by almsdeeds, by prayer, by fasting, and other works of penance; or again, to obtain the benefit of that satisfaction

which is to be had by means of the sacraments,
especially the Sacrament of Penance, by hearing
Mass, by gaining Indulgences, and the like.

5. If these thoughts be added to the other considerations which have been suggested in the three
preceding chapters concerning the pain of loss, we
shall find it easier to set before our minds some
kind of image of what that pain is. We may add
to them, however, a few more reflections concerning
points as to the detention of the Holy Souls which
have been left unnoticed in other parts of this
work. Such is the thought, that Purgatory is
uniformly represented to us as a prison, not merely
an abode or resting-place, but a place of detention
and confinement. This element in their condition
is all the more felt by these Holy Souls, not only
because they would so gladly fly at once to their
home in the presence of God, but because of the
natural activity of spiritual existence, and the intense vitality and energy which belong to it in such
a state as theirs. It is useful to remind ourselves
of what holy writers have told us of the place of
Purgatory, lest we should get unconsciously to think
of it as something less real and true than it is. It
is well to remember that it is a place of pain and
punishment and torment, even if it be not, as many
writers think, close to Hell itself, and within reach of
the sights and sounds and company which are there.
It is well to remember that to this sad and penal
abode the Holy Souls are bound by chains far more
stringent than any material fetters. These circumstances all belong to the subject on which we have
been engaged, as well as the privation of the Beatific
Vision, the delay of the time when their love for God
and their joy are to be made perfect, and their grief
for the causes which have led to their detention there.

CHAPTER XXXV.

Visits to the Blessed Sacrament for the Holy Souls.

1. ST. LUKE tells us that in one of our Lord's journeys at this time of His Ministry, He passed along the confines of Galilee and Samaria, and that at the entrance of a certain town He was accosted by a company of lepers, who "stood afar off, and lifted up their voices, saying, Jesus, Master, have mercy on us." These poor sufferers were banished from their homes on account of their dreadful disease, and so were fain to consort together. They were afraid to approach our Lord and His little band of followers, and so called to Him from a distance. "Whom when He saw, He said, Go show yourselves to the priests. And it came to pass, as they went, they were made clean. And one of them, when he saw that he was made clean, went back, with a loud voice glorifying God. And he fell on his face before His feet, giving thanks, and this was a Samaritan." It may be that, as a Samaritan, he would not have been received and examined by the Jewish priests; but he found his way to the one true Priest, and, at all events, he did not fail in the fulfilment of the great paramount duty of thanksgiving. "And Jesus answering, said,

Were not ten made clean, and where are the nine ? There is no one found to return and give glory to God but this stranger. And He said to him, Arise, go thy way, for thy faith hath made thee whole."

2. It is easy to see that the point in this miracle which gives to it a particular character, is the incident of the thanksgiving of the restored leper, and of our Lord's remarks on the absence of such thanksgiving in the others, from whom it might, perhaps, have been expected rather than from him. Our Lord speaks, as if He were pained and hurt at their ingratitude. This point may serve us as a guide in our application of this miracle to the state of the Holy Souls in Purgatory. The reflections which we have lately been making on the subject of the pain of loss, and all that is contained in it and connected therewith, naturally suggest the further thought of the immense and burning devotion which they must feel to the Sacred Humanity of our Blessed Lord. It is by means of that Sacred Humanity alone that they have had the prospect of the Beatific Vision opened to them, that it has become possible for them ever to glow with the ecstatic love of Heaven and to lose themselves in its joys. It is by means of that Humanity alone that. the treasures of sanctifying grace have been laid open to them, that they have had the capacity of propitiating God for their offences and shortcomings by prayer, fasting, and almsdeeds, and that the satisfactions stored up in the Sacraments, and in such means of grace as Indulgences, have been placed within their reach. Every thought of grief or self-reproach which has arisen within them on account of the losses, temporal or eternal, which they have incurred, on account of the sins, mortal or venial, with which they have

been stained, is a thought which brings our Lord Jesus Christ home to them, as their Master, Friend, Ransomer Lover, and Eternal Reward. Everything reminds them of their ingratitude to Him, and of the wounds which they have inflicted on His loving Heart. Closely as they are united with Him, they are detained from His Personal Presence; they cannot see His face, though it has shone upon them at the moment of their judgment with a light of love, but still of displeasure, nor have they now that Sacramental Presence of His to be their consolation and resource, which they had the opportunity of enjoying while they were still members of the Militant Church. It may be that they have to reproach themselves with this among other things —that they have been wanting in gratitude to our Lord in His sacramental love. This may be a special cause of sorrow to them, now that they are deprived of the opportunities of which they have thought too little.

3. We have already spoken of the marvellous blessings which we possess in the Sacrifice of the Altar and in Holy Communion. It seems natural, therefore, that we should find a place in this work to speak of the third great display of our Lord's love to us in the Blessed Sacrament, which consists in His continual residence among us in the sacred Tabernacle. We have in that Presence of His a blessing which turns earth into Heaven, if we would but know it. The perpetuity of His abiding there, and the circumstances and manner of that abiding, the silence, the confinement, the solitude, the neglect, often the irreverence and ill-treatment to which they expose Him, are all so many proofs of His immense love as shown in this mystery, because it must be thought that He could not submit to so

much, except for the purpose of gaining a very great good indeed—a very great good, not to Himself, certainly, but to our poor souls, for whom all this is endured. In nothing is our Lord exposed to so much negligence or ingratitude—His Church, His Priests, His Truth, His Grace, are all His, but they are not Himself, as is the Blessed Sacrament. Holy Mass passes away in half an hour, Holy Communion is over in a few minutes, but the dwelling of our Lord in the Tabernacle goes on hour after hour, day after day, week after week. Here we have His Presence, which the Blessed in Heaven have in another way, but which the Holy Souls in Purgatory have not. It is a Presence, the condescension of which it would over-task the tongues of all the saints and Angels to declare, and in order to secure which for us He has to work more stupendous miracles than we can give an account of. It is a Presence which imparts blessings to the Church, to the world, and to His faithful worshippers in particular, as many as the sands on the sea-shore and more glorious in their effects than the stars of the heavens. And this may be said to be the very chief of all the uncomprehended and most disregarded mercies of God to us in our present state: more so, when the immensity of the graces which might be won by it is considered, than the guardianship of the Angels, of which we think so little, or the practical benefits which flow from our membership of the Church, or from the prayers and and protection of the Saints, or even from the mightiness and power and vigilant tenderness of the motherly care of Mary herself. Each one of these indicates a great ocean of blessings, in which we float, as in the air which we breathe, with scarcely the consciousness of its existence and of what we owe to it. But all taken together are as little when compared to the Personal Presence of our Lord in the sacred Tabernacle.

4. As the Holy Souls are now deprived of this ineffable blessing, it would certainly be a thing very highly consoling and refreshing to them in their indigence if we connect our prayers for them, as far as possible, with some special honour done to our Lord by way of gratitude for His sacramental love. As we hear or say Mass for them, or endeavour to refresh or aid them by receiving Holy Communion, we may add to these devout practices that of frequently visiting the Blessed Sacrament for their intention, or to perform an act of religion which may help to their deliverance. The time which we spend in thus honouring our Lord may be used for any holy purpose whatever, for meditation, examination of conscience, imploring pardon for sin or strength against temptation or increase in virtue, or in any other such way. But it seems very natural indeed that it should be in part spent in special exercises of adoration, praise, thanksgiving, and intercession, and these, both on our part and on the part of the whole Church, and on the part of the Holy Souls. If we give ourselves earnestly and thoroughly to the devotion to Purgatory of which this little volume treats, we shall be able to say to ourselves after a time, that though we cannot ourselves worship and thank and praise God as the Saints and Angels worship and praise and thank Him in Heaven, still we have contributed something towards sending into His Adorable Presence at least some souls, who might otherwise have not been so soon delivered from Purgatory, who may praise and thank Him in our stead. And, in the same way, when we kneel before the Taber-

nacle, and take with us, as far as is in our power, the Holy Souls to be the companions of our adoration, we can give them the satisfaction that, if they cannot worship the Blessed Sacrament themselves, they are at all events not unrepresented before the throne of His infinite condescension.

CHAPTER XXXVI.

Purgatory and the Glory of God.

(THE RAISING OF LAZARUS.)
St. John xi. 1—44.

1. WE are now drawing near to the one of the glorious cycle of the miracles of our Lord, and it will be necessary to adapt the few remaining subjects which are usually handled in treatises about Purgatory to the narratives which have yet to be considered. The next miracle in point of time is that most stupendous work of the raising from the dead of our Lord's intimate friend Lazarus, after he had been laid in the grave for more than four full days. The incidents of the history are so familiar to all, that it will not be necessary to repeat them. Our Lord, at the time of the dangerous illness of Lazarus, was at some distance from Bethany, but not too far for the holy sisters, Martha and Mary, to send to Him, and, by telling Him, to implore Him to come to the relief of their brother. Our Lord remained in the place where He was for two days, after answering the message of the sisters by the implicit promise, "This sickness is not unto death, but for the glory

of God, that the Son of God may be glorified by it." He afterwards, as St. John mentions, referred to this message, as containing an assurance from Him that the sisters were not to be deprived of their brother. Our Lord, after the lapse of the two days already spoken of, proposed to His disciples to return into the land of Judæa, the neighbourhood of Jerusalem, from which He had lately withdrawn on account of the attempts made by the ecclesiastical rulers to put Him to death. This proposal was objected to by the Apostles, and when our Lord persisted in His intention, St. Thomas uttered those memorable words of affectionate devotion, "Let us also go, that we may die with Him." When He came near to Bethany, His coming became known first to Martha and then to Mary Magdalene her sister, each of whom went forth to meet our Lord. Mary's movement to meet Him was mistaken by the Jews who had come to mourn with and comfort the sisters, who thought she was going to indulge her feelings of grief by weeping at the grave, and thus they followed her. Each of the sisters addressed our Lord in the loving words, "Lord, if Thou hadst been here, my brother had not died." Martha was led on by our Lord to a formal professson of faith in Him, very like to that which was so much commended by Him in St. Peter: "I have believed that Thou art the Christ, the Son of the living God, Who art come into this world." But this did not prevent her, when they had come to the sepulchre, and our Lord bade the bystanders take away the stone, from remonstrating, on account of the length of time during which the corpse had laid in the grave. Our Lord answered her, "Did I not say to thee, that if thou believe, thou shalt see the glory of God?" And when the stone had been removed, He lifted up His eyes, and gave thanks before them all to His Father for hearing Him, before He called Lazarus forth. Thus, all through the narrative of the Evangelist, we have the thought of the glory of God constantly recurring, as the end and object of our Lord in working this great miracle.

2. The sequel of the history shows how true and how prophetic were these words of our Blessed Lord. The glory of God and of His Son was greatly advanced by the death of Lazarus, inasmuch as that death gave our Lord the occasion of raising His friend from the dead. And although the immediate consequence of the miracle was the determination of the Jewish rulers to take away our Lord's life, a resolution which was carried out in His Passion a few weeks later, still that also conduced in the most wonderful manner to the glory of God and of our Lord, because the redemption of the world and the foundation of His eternal Kingdom came about as the fruit of the Passion. Thus God permitted a calamity to befall the household which was so dear to our Lord, in order that their sufferings and faith might give an opportunity for the exercise of His miraculous power in the most stupendous instance which is recorded for us in the Gospels. And He also allowed the enormous sin of the judicial murder of our Lord, in order that, by means of that sin, He might be glorified as the Redeemer of mankind. We have here, then, set before us the principle of God's government which is exemplified whenever He does or allows anything which may be, on certain grounds, undesirable or strange, apparently contrary to His mercy or love or to some other of His attributes, but which is not so in truth, or which illustrates other parts of His

all-perfect character, such as His justice or His love of purity. This thought will be enough to occupy us profitably with regard to His permission that the Souls whom He loves so tenderly should suffer in the flames of Purgatory.

3. It is most true, as we shall see, that the existence of Purgatory is a great witness to the glory of God in many different ways, so that, if there were no Purgatory, the glory of God would be less than we know it to be. So that, putting aside any direct decree of God, by which He might provide for His glory in the same degree in some other manner, it may be said that souls in love with the glory of God might wish that, if Purgatory did not exist, it might be created. Let us consider a few of the reasons which may be given for this truth. In the first place, it may be said that as God is glorified by anything in His kingdom and the arrangements of His government, which displays either His Wisdom or His Mercy, so also He is glorified by anything therein that displays in a striking way His Justice and Holiness. So there is perhaps nothing in the whole range of the kingdom of God which more clearly displays His justice, than the punishments which are inflicted in Purgatory. For this reason God desires and allows those punishments, because they are due to His justice. The souls who are there imprisoned are very dear to Him and confirmed in His grace, but they are not sufficiently purified to stand in the presence of His infinite holiness. God does not inflict the sufferings of Purgatory because they torment and afflict the souls that suffer there, nor does He take delight in their sufferings, as such, but because they are just and conduce to His honour in the first place, and because they are of

immense profit to the souls in the second place. His ineffable goodness cannot allow any good work or service done to Him, however trifling it may seem, to go without its reward. And in the same way, His ineffable justice cannot allow any fault to go without its punishment. But if there were no Purgatory, many evils would remain unpunished, unless, indeed, as some of His enemies have imagined, He were to punish all sins alike by the eternal pains of Hell. The perfect equity of His rule requires that the soul that has despised Him, the highest good, and postponed Him to the lowest kind of good, or rather, to the false good, of pleasure and sin, should in its turn be placed in subjection and captivity, as it were, under the dominion of pain. Every sin contains in itself three things, for it is an offence against His Divine Majesty, it is an injury to the Holy Church, and it defaces and deforms the Divine Image in the soul itself. The offence requires punishment, the loss to the Church requires satisfaction, and the defacement of the soul requires purification. These three things may be wrought out here on earth and during this life. But if they are not, they remain to be accomplished hereafter, and the place in which they are accomplished is Purgatory. It is there then, that the honour of God is avenged, the injury to the Church repaired, and deformity of the soul done away. That so it should be, is a great triumph due to the most pure and holy justice of God.

4. And again, it is a great triumph to the mercy of God that He should have made a place where His justice can be satisfied, and yet, after all, His mercy have its way. No doubt, the great feeling which dominates the souls of these holy sufferers, is that they are very leniently dealt with, even

T

though they are in the hands of God's justice. After all the opportunities of grace and penance and satisfaction which they have neglected, it is a great mark of mercy that God should take into His own hands the purification of their souls as far as the punishment of sin is concerned, the inflicting of which on themselves is the most difficult task, it may be said, which their poor nature had to undertake. Moreover, the realm of Purgatory is full of alleviations, all of which are granted by God in His mercy, as when the prayers of the saints and Angels and of Christians on earth are heard for the Holy Souls.

5. We know that God is His own end, and that He can do nothing at all for anything less worthy of Him than His own honour. The Psalmist says: "Mercy and judgment will I sing to Thee, O Lord."[1] And in another place, "Holiness becometh Thy house, O Lord, for length of days." This idea of what is becoming and worthy of God is used by St. Paul as an argument about the Passion, where he says that it "became Him for Whom are all things, and by Whom are all things, Who was bringing many children to glory, to make perfect the Author of their salvation by His Passion."[2] Thus we may say that it became God, in the great work of calling millions of spirits whom He had created free for that purpose, to share His own eternal glory and blessedness in Heaven, to show Himself bountiful as well as wise, and just as well as merciful. It is becoming to Him Who has redeemed the world by the Incarnation and Death of His Son, to give the free gift of eternal life for His sake to an immense number of souls who have never themselves toiled and struggled for it. Such as are the souls of Christian children saved by their

[1] Psalm ci. 1.   [2] Heb. ii. 10.

baptism, and who have never lived to the age of reason. It is also becoming to Him that, in the case of millions of others, the crown which is awarded them, through the merits of our Lord, should be, as St. Paul calls it, a crown of justice, won by their own 'faithfulness and exertion, by their successful struggle, in their weak human flesh, against all the snares and dangers by which they were surrounded in the world, against the malice of their invisible foes and against the traitorous suggestions of their fallen nature. It became Him also that there should be in His kingdom another class of redeemed souls, which have not passed through the battle of life unscathed, and who have yet, by means of His abundant provisions of grace been able to reach the shore of Heaven in all the holiness and purity which that abode of bliss requires in its inmates, and who have yet not left one farthing of their debt to the ineffable justice of God unpaid. It is becoming that nothing in the slightest degree impure or imperfect should approach the realm of the Divine light, and present itself before the all-searching eyes of the Holiest of Holies. And as so great a number of the souls for whom our Lord died would pass out of this world not perfectly pure enough for His sight for ever, it became Him to provide at once for the dignity of His dwelling and for the purposes of His loving condescension, to satisfy alike the claims of His justice and the demands of His mercy, to fill His banquet with guests, according to the parable of our Lord, and yet to see that no one entered there without a wedding garment. And this He has done most perfectly and beautifully by the institution of the sacred prison of Purgatory, without which these things could not be brought about.

6. Again, Purgatory, and the sufferings which are there endured, add not a little to the glory of God in His character of our Redeemer as well as in that of our Sovereign and our Judge. Just as it adds to the honour of our Lord that there should be so many souls in Heaven who are there through His merits alone, and without any working of their own by way of correspondence—for they have never, as has been said, reached the age of reason so as to be capable of sin or merit—so it is greatly to His glory that there should be many saved by means of His sacramental grace alone, after they have lived to offend Him. And this is the case with those who have received the Sacrament of Penance duly at the point of death, without having that full and perfect contrition which would have reconciled them to Him even without that Sacrament, if it had not been in their power to receive it. Such persons are often burthened with a large debt to the justice of God, which can only be paid in Purgatory, but, being reconciled to God at the last, they are confirmed in grace at the moment of death, and so are made capable of the salutary sufferings of Purgatory. Their number may be very great, and thus a large portion of the Holy Souls may witness in this special manner to the efficacy of the grace which He has left behind Him in the Church.

7. Again, God is glorified not only in the institutions and arrangements of His wisdom and mercy, but in the manner in which they call forth from those who belong to Him the exercise of the virtues which reflect His own perfect character. In this way our Lord is glorified by the patience, and resignation, and zeal for His honour, which make the Holy Souls willing sufferers, desirous rather to see His justice vindicated in their regard than to ap-

pear before Him unfit for His Presence. They
love His justice, though it has to be wreaked upon
themselves, and the knowledge that it is His will
that they should suffer as they do, is enough to
stifle in them all murmuring and repining. Their
state also calls forth great and intense compassion
and sympathy in the Saints, whose charity is kindled
by the sight of so many souls who are destined to
share their own glories and blessedness, and whom
they know to be left by the Providence of· God to
their intercessions and to those of the Church upon
earth for the shortening of their period of banishment.   In the same way is the charity of the
Church Militant excited, and aroused to activity
and exertion, by the state of the Holy Souls, and in
in this way also God's glory is advanced. He is
honoured by the urgency of prayer, which has its
efficacy through the Incarnation and the Communion of Saints; He is honoured by the labours
of charity, which afflicts and puts itself to pain out
of love for Him and those who belong to Him; He
is honoured by the offering of the Holy Sacrifice
and of the works of satisfaction or mercy for the
Holy Souls. He is honoured again by the tenderness with which the Holy Angels, as we shall see,
pray for or relieve, according to what is permitted
to them, the sufferers on whom the hand of His
justice is heavy for a time, but whom He intends
throughout all eternity to praise and adore Him
along with those Holy Angels, and to thank them
also for their charity, and to give thanks to Him for
His mercy and love ·towards them. In these and
in other similar ways we may see how true it is that
the holy prison of Purgatory gives glory to God for
His mercy and wisdom, as well as for His justice.

CHAPTER XXXVII.

Diligence in Relieving the Holy Souls.

(THE CURE OF THE BLIND MEN AT JERICHO.)

St. Matt. xx. 29—34; St. Mark x. 46—52; St. Luke
xviii. 35; xix. 1.

1. THE miracles of which we are now to speak are
almost the very last which our Lord wrought before
His Passion of which we have any detailed
account, and it is perhaps for some reason connected
with this that they are related by the Evangelists.
St. Matthew, in his summary manner, puts them
together, but St. Luke and St. Mark seem carefully
to distinguish two several cases, and the lesson
which we may learn from them is much enhanced
in its importance and force if we take the whole
narrative together. Our Lord was on His way to
Jerusalem from Peræa, that part of the Holy Land
on the farther side of the Jordan, and He was
accompanied in His progress by a large multitude
partly from Peræa, and partly, as it seems, made
up of the crowds of devout Galilæans who were
going up to the feast at Jerusalem, and whose
ordinary route lay along the farther side of the
Jordan valley, in order that they might avoid
passing through the schismatic and hostile country
of the Samaritans. Jericho was the great town
between the ford of the Jordan and Jerusalem

through which the line of march lay; and the two
miracles before us took place, one at the entrance
of the city towards the Jordan, the other just
outside the gate which led towards Jerusalem.   It
was naturally at the gates of the city that beggars
and suppliants of all sorts took their posts on such
occasions as the passing of the great caravans of
pilgrims towards the holy city.   Thus it was that
on this occasion our Lord's progress was twice
stopped, once at each side of the city.   At the gate
on the Jordan side a blind man was sitting begging,
and hearing the footsteps of the large multitude he
asked the bystanders what it was, and was told
that Jesus of Nazareth was passing by.   He began
immediately to call on our Lord as the Son of
David to have mercy on him.   The leaders of the
caravan, anxious that there should be no stoppage
on the way, especially as they were about to pass
through the narrow street of the city, rebuked him,
and bade him hold his peace.   " But he cried out
much more, Son of David, have mercy on me !   And
Jesus, standing, commanded him to be brought to
Him.   And when he was come near, He asked him,
saying, What wilt thou that I do for thee ?   And
he said, Lord, that I may see.   And Jesus said to
him, Receive thy sight, thy faith hath hath made
thee whole.   And immediately he saw, and followed
Him, glorifying God.   And all the people when
they saw it gave praise to God."   Our Lord then
went on and passed through the city.   At the
farther gate there was another collection of beggars,
and a very similar scene was repeated.   Here there
was a blind man, who seems afterwards to have
been known in the Church, as St. Mark mentions
his name, Bartimæus.   He too, when he heard
Who was passing by, called on Him as the Son of

David, and insisted all the more the more he was rebuked. Our Lord again stopped on His way, and bade them bring the blind man to Him. " And they call the blind man, saying to him, Be of better comfort, arise, He calleth thee. Who, casting off his garment, leaped up and came to Him." Our Lord asked him the same questions as in the former case, and received the same answer. " And Jesus saith to him, Go thy way, thy faith hath made thee whole."

2. The most prominent point in this beautiful narrative is the manner in which our Blessed Lord makes everything, as it were, give way to the interest of these blind men. It was, no doubt, a great inconvenience to stop the march of so large a procession of people, for those who were behind would naturally crowd on those in front, up to the point where our Lord was, and those who went before Him would press on unconscious that they were leaving their companions behind. But nothing of this sort had any weight with our Lord, and He seemed determined to listen, with the utmost patience, to the prayer of each suppliant, and to miss no opportunity of relieving misery such as theirs. He knew how short His time now was, and that He would never again pass along that road to the feast. He seems to teach us in this way the great lesson concerning works of mercy, something like the lesson as to the forgiveness of injuries which is conveyed in His injunction to go on forgiving, not until seven times, but until seventy times seven.[1] The lesson which is here taught us is that we are never to weary in doing mercy and charity, never to let the trouble which they may cause us hinder us from them, never to let the fact

[1] St. Matt. xviii. 22.

that we have done one act of kindness make us think ourselves dispensed from doing another. In hearts full of charity this lesson is not so much needed. But charity and mercy, beautiful as they are in themselves, and full of comfort and joy to those who practise them, are yet directly against the current of our self-interest and natural indolence, and so they require a fresh impulse of grace and a fresh exertion each time that occasion presents itself. It is very often a slight trouble or fatigue which makes us put off doing a good work ; and we very often say to ourselves that we have done enough, and now may rest, whereas it is God's way constantly to send us another call on our charity just after we have put ourselves out for the same purpose. Such calls are in truth rewards for what we have already done, but our foolish nature does not always recognise the hand and intention of God.

3. The lesson which we thus learn in regard to the assistance which we try to render to the Holy Souls in Purgatory is very obvious and simple. We have already had occasion to speak of the virtue of promptitude in this respect,[2] and we must now add the perfect diligence and care to miss no opportunity which comes to us for the practice of this great charity, greater than that of giving sight to the blind, inasmuch as the vision of God in Heaven is infinitely more precious than the light of this world. We shall not be thoroughly penetrated with the truths about Purgatory, and about our duties to the Holy Souls, we shall not be altogether filled with the devotion to which those truths lead, or with understanding as to what is God's desire, and our own great interest in the matter, till we come to see that the law of charity

<hr>

[2] See Chap. vii.

binds us, not only to occasional and intermittent exertions on their behalf, but to a perpetual and ever-vigilant service, like that of a slave or of a soldier in the field of battle. The sufferings of the Holy Souls are unintermittent, and so must be our labours for them. To have freed one soul is a reason for beginning to toil for the freedom of others, not for resting on our arms in the holy warfare. Thus there may be a great danger of our losing the reward of perfect faithfulness in this respect. We ought to help the Holy Souls every day of our lives, in all the ways we can, and at every time that we can. As a general reviews his forces, or as a merchant looks into his accounts to see that no part of his capital is allowed to be idle, no occasion of gain passed over, no market for his goods neglected, so must we review the means which God has given us of practising the necessary works of charity, and endeavour to use all, to use them always, and to use them in the best possible way—prayers, vocal and mental, Masses, Communions, visits to the Blessed Sacrament, acts of corporal and spiritual mercy, mortifications, indulgences, devotions, and penances of every kind. It ought to be a matter of scruple to those who take up this holy and blessed devotion, to have left any-thing undone for the Holy Souls which they might have done for them.

4. As our Lord so frequently uses the motives of hope or fear in His exhortations to the practice of virtue, and not least in His admonitions about the value of good works and almsdeeds, it may be well to fortify ourselves from time to time, in any exertions which we may make for the relief of the Souls in Purgatory, by reminding ourselves of the very great blessings which may be obtained in return for this charity. There can be little doubt that all who

help the Holy Souls must by that charity render themselves very pleasing to God, especially if they give away what might otherwise be applied to themselves by way of satisfaction, as is done by those who make what is called the " Heroic Act," and by the good religious to whom the blessed name of Helpers of the Holy Souls belongs as by special right, who give up their whole lives to labours which are applied to Purgatory. All the blessings which the promises of Scripture secure to alms-deeds and charity in general, or to them who "preach the good tidings of peace," or "separate the precious from the vile," or "instruct many unto justice," and the like, must surely belong to such persons. Our Lord will certainly acknowledge them as His own, as having carried on His own work, as having suffered, and exposed themselves to suffering, for Him ; they will have the blessing of unfailing support, which was given to the widow of Sarepta who fed the prophet, the "good measure, pressed down, and shaken together, and running over," of which our Lord speaks. No trafficking or investing of "pounds and talents" committed to our charge can be more lucrative in eternity than this. It is quite certain that those who are merciful in this way will very easily find mercy for themselves, as their reward will be an increase of grace in this life, which will enable them to merit very great rewards, and lay up against themselves very little of punishment. The charity which they show to the suffering souls will be abundantly repaired by the prayers which they will make, or win from the saints and Angels, for those who befriend them. Our Lord will be especially bound by gratitude to them for delivering His servants, His friends, His spouses, His children. Our Lady, the Mother of the Holy

Souls, will regard this charity as done to herself. Their guardian Angels, patron saints, and all the dwellers in Heaven, will speedily protect and pray for them.   There are many passages in the lives and writings of the saints which bear witness to this truth.   St. Bridget [1] relates a prayer which she heard made by the Holy Souls for their benefactors, " O Lord Jesus Christ, the Just Judge, send Thy charity to those who have spiritual power in the world, for then we shall be able to share more largely than now in their sacred chants and offices and sacrifices."
. . . " O Lord God, give of Thine incomprehensible goodness an hundredfold reward to every one in the world, of those who by their good works raise us up into the light of Thy Divinity, and the vision of Thy face."   St. Catharine of Bologna said that she had received very many graces by means of the intercession of the Holy Souls, graces which in some instances she had not obtained through the saints. Anne of St. Bartholemew, the companion of St. Teresa, used to recommend promises of Masses to the Holy Souls as means of securing favours from Heaven.   All the marks of predestination are said by some writers to be found in those who are strongly moved to this devotion, nor is it at all unfrequently found that temporal as well as spiritual blessings are obtained in this way.

[1] *Rev.* lib. iv. ch. xii.

CHAPTER XXXVIII.

The Angels and the Holy Souls.

(MIRACLES ON PALM SUNDAY.)

St. Matt. xxi. 14—17.

1. WE have already spoken of the relation in which
the Holy Souls of Purgatory stand towards the
Church on earth and in Heaven, towards the Saints
and the children of the Militant Church, towards
our Blessed Lady, their special Queen and Mother,
to our Lord Himself, and to God. But one immense multitude of their friends, more than the
stars of Heaven in number, and more glorious than
stars or anything that eye has ever seen or heart
imagined, yet remains to be mentioned, both on
account of the special love with which they regard
them and the commission which they have received
concerning them, and also because we have had to
mention their spiritual enemies, the devils, who are
by nature the same as the mighty and blessed
Angels of God, of whom we are now to speak.
Innumerable as are the evil spirits who are allowed
to beset us and hinder us in our path towards
Heaven, they are far inferior in power to the
glorious citizens of Heaven, to whom God has
given us in charge, and who love us with the most
intense love for His sake, and because we are intended by Him to take our places among them, and
fill up the gaps made in their ranks by the apostasy

of Satan and his companions in rebellion. The Angels were in continual attendance upon our Blessed Lord during His sojourn upon earth, and it was by their agency, we may suppose, that many of His marvellous works were wrought. Thus they are present to the eye of faith in every one of His miracles, though they are not specially mentioned by the Evangelists, as afterwards in the history of the Resurrection, and of certain parts of the Acts of the Apostles, as in the cases of St. Peter, St. Paul, and St. Philip. On account of their constant presence with our Lord, and of their execution of His behests, the Angels might have been mentioned in connection with many of the miracles on which we have already commented. But we have kept any special consideration of their interest in the Holy Souls almost to the last.

2. The miracles to which we now come are those few cures of the lame and the blind in the Temple at Jerusalem which our Lord wrought on the after-noon of Palm Sunday, after His triumphant entry into the Holy City. "There came to Him," says St. Matthew, "the blind and the lame in the Temple, and He healed them. And the Chief Priests and Scribes, seeing the wonderful things that He did, and the children crying in the Temple, Hosannah to the Son of David, were moved with indignation, and said to Him, Hearest Thou what these say? And Jesus said to them, Yea, have you never read, Out of the mouths of infants and of sucklings Thou hast perfected praise?" These miracles of our Lord must have especially delighted the holy Angels, who dwell with great love and reverence in the temples consecrated to God, and to whom the Temple of Jerusalem was very dear. For these are the only miracles which our Lord is

recorded to have worked in that Holy Place.   Indeed, the whole scene of Palm Sunday brings the
Angels before us, as that triumph was a representation of His triumphant entrance into Heaven at His
Ascension, when the Angels came forth to meet
Him as the crowds on Palm Sunday.   The praise
which they render to God in Heaven has to be
made complete by the addition of the countless
myriads of redeemed souls who are to be there, and
this the Angels especially desire in their eagerness
for the deliverance of the Holy Souls.

3. St. Paul says of the Holy Angels, that they
are "all ministering spirits, sent to minister to
them who shall receive the inheritance of salvation."[1]   These few words are enough to remind us
of their relations to the Holy Souls.   The ministering
of the Angels begins with our entrance into the
world, and, as the Apostle implies, is not to cease
until we receive "the inheritance of salvation.'
How faithfully and lovingly they watch over us
as long as our period of trial lasts, no tongue can
tell, and it will be one of the great surprises of the
next world to·learn.   It is certain, also, that the
care of the Angels increases in vigilance, if that be
possible, as the last moment of life draws nigh, that
they are standing by us in our last conflict, and
that they meet us at our entrance into the next
world, conveying our soul to the tribunal of the
Judge, or rather, as that judgment takes place at
the moment of death, being present while it is being
made.   The Angels rejoice immensely at a good and
happy death.   The Church bids her Ministers commend the soul, as it departs, to their charge.
" When thy soul shall depart from thy body, may
the resplendent multitude of the Angels meet thee,

[1] Heb. i. 14,

may the Court of the Apostles receive thee," and the rest. And again : " Come to his assistance, all ye saints of God, meet him, all ye Angels of God, receiving his soul and offering it in the sight of the Most High. May Christ receive thee, Who hath called thee, and may the Angels conduct thee to Abraham's bosom. Receiving his soul, and offering it in the sight of the Most High." The Angels stand by at the time of judgment, and defend the soul against the charges of the devils, as is found in many of the revelations of the saints. They tell us that St. Michael, the patron of the Catholic Church, exerts his power the more especially in favour of her children, and this is alluded to by the Church in some of the antiphons which are used on his feasts. If the soul be sentenced to Purgatory, the Angels conduct it thither, as St. Thomas teaches;[1] and Suarez says that this escorting of the souls to their place of exile is to comfort them, and also to show them honour as the children of God and spouses of Christ. But when the souls are once conveyed to Purgatory, we are told that the Angels, especially their Guardian Angels, visit them and console them frequently. The full enjoy- ment of the society of the Angels cannot be had until we reach Heaven, but they are not prevented from comforting the suffering Souls in their prison, any more than from suggesting to the living to pray for them and offer for them works of satisfaction or the Holy Sacrifice of the Mass. St. Peter Damian mentions a curious reason for the setting apart of the Monday in each week as a day of special devotion both to the Angels and the Holy Souls. He says[2] that on Sundays the Holy Souls

---

[1] In *Sent.* iv. dist. 11, qu. 1, art. 1.
[2] St. Peter Damian, *Epist.* ii. 14.

rest from their sufferings, and that as these begin again on the Monday, the Holy Mass is offered in honour of the Angels, to procure their powerful assistance to them, as also to others who are to die. The opinion about the cessation of suffering on Sunday may be uncertain, but the Saint's words show that the power of the Angels is constantly exerted for the Holy Souls.

4. Catholic writers seem to make no doubt of the truth which has just now been stated, that the holy Angels frequently visit and console the holy suffering souls. It may be thought that the mere presence of such blessed and glorious beings, which must be far more keenly perceived by the souls separated from the body than is now possible to us, would go far to make that mournful prison bright and joyous with the light of heaven itself. We cannot tell to what extent the Holy Souls are allowed to enjoy to the full the natural effects of the near presence of the Angels. But we may feel certain that their visits are of ineffable comfort and relief. We may take as an image of this consolation that visit which our Lord condescended to receive from one of the Angels in His Agony in the Garden, a visit which must have been the appointed means of some great strengthening of the Sacred Humanity for the terrible conflict which He was about to pass through, or rather which He had already in great part experienced, for the Agony was itself one of the greatest of our Lord's sufferings. The Angel may be thought to have set before our Lord the will of the Eternal Father as the reason for the chalice which He was to drink, the immense glory to His Father and to Himself which would accrue therefrom, the great fruit which His sufferings would produce in the souls of men, most of all in

U

those of His saints, and the whole of the marvellous counsel of God in the application of the merits of His Precious Blood. He may be supposed to have set before Him in particular the joy which was to be His in the redemption of each soul, and of the whole company of His elect, as St. Paul tells us that for " the joy that was set before Him He endured the Cross and despised the shame," [4] which He was to undergo. In the same way we may suppose that the Angels may comfort the Holy Souls by representing to them the decree of God's justice, which must be so dear to them, in pursuance of which they are for a time to suffer as they do; the glory which accrues to God from their under-going the sentence of His justice, the blessed issue of their purification, which will open to them the gates of the eternal home of God's children, and the like. We may suppose that as the Angels have so carefully watched every step of the lives of those who have been committed to their charge, they will be able to instruct them in many wonderful ways as to the Providence of God in their regard, espe-cially as to the dangers which have been averted from them, mercies of which they have not been conscious, or, again, boons which might have been theirs at the price of greater faithfulness. It ap-pears to be one of the constant and ever-fresh joys of the holy Angels, to watch the marvellous Providence of God towards His Church as it unfolds itself age after age and year after year, and in the same way they have rejoiced over His good mercies in the case of each single soul. All this they can reveal to the Holy Souls to explain to them the debt of gratitude which they owe to God, as well as the amount of that other debt which they are to pay to His justice.

<hr>

[4] Heb. xii. 2.

5. But it must be the most direct part of the consolation which the holy Angels constantly minister to the souls in Purgatory, to give them intelligence of the prayers and satisfactions which are offered for them in the Church on earth, and thus to let them know that they are not forgotten, and that the time of their detention is to be shortened. In this respect they are in truth messengers of good tidings and of peace, which they so much delight to be. Moreover, it is probable that the holy Angels are the sources from whom proceed a thousand suggestions to us to pray for the Holy Souls, sudden remembrances of them, feelings as if they were near and in need of our prayers, and the like. The visions of the saints reigning in Heaven are ordinarily the works of the Angels, and it may be that, if there be from time to time any similar visions of the souls in Purgatory, the Angels are also the artificers, so to speak, of these. Thus we get some faint idea of the work of the Angels of the Holy Souls, as of a work of active and multifarious charity, carried on with unwearied energy and vigilance, the object of the whole being to procure relief for those sufferers in all the many ways in which God allows of their being relieved. They pray for them before the throne of God, and, if the Angel of Macedonia could appear to the Apostle and entreat him to come over and help him, it is not wonderful if they now implore the saints to intercede for the Holy Souls, and also stir up the hearts of the children of the Church on earth for the same object of charity. And then at length comes the time of intense joy, both to the Angels and to the Holy Souls themselves, when the purification has been accomplished, and nothing now remains but for the souls to be presented to God by

their Guardians, at the head of whom the blessed St. Michael is placed for this solemn act of triumph. It is, then, in our power to rejoice the hearts of the glorious Angels of God by the suffrages which we offer for the Holy Souls, to make them our friends, and secure their advocacy for ourselves, by making them our debtors for the charity which we have shown to those in whom they regard themselves as relieved and succoured by our prayers. Our Lord says some terrible words about those who scandalize one of the little ones who believe in Him, on account of the simple truth that their Angels always see the face of His Father. We may turn the threat which His words convey into a most gracious promise of protection and advocacy on the part of these glorious princes of the Court of God, by praying and suffering faithfully for these Holy Souls whose Angels are always in God's presence, to bear witness to the slightest act of charity which is done for these patient sufferers.

CHAPTER XXXIX.

Fasting and Almsdeeds.

(THE WITHERING OF THE FIG-TREE.)

St. Matt. xxi. 19; St. Mark xi. 13, 14, 20.

1. THE miracle of the withering of the barren fig-tree stands by itself among the miracles of our Lord. For it is the only act of destruction for which He used His power, though on one other occasion, that of the entrance of the devils into the herd of swine, He permitted something of the sort. In ordinary cases His miracles were works of mercy, although, as we have seen, He more than once worked them unasked, and for the obvious purpose of proving or illustrating some Divine truth. The case of the withering of the fig-tree is not altogether different from these. For as in other cases our Lord wished to teach a certain truth relating to Himself, so in this instance He appears to have desired to make a kind of prophecy of the future barrenness of the Synagogue, which was represented by the fig-tree. Thus, there was something to be taught as true which it was important should be known, which was set forth by this act of our Lord's power. This is all the more clear, because the season for fruit had not yet come, and therefore it was not natural to expect that this tree should have borne any figs as yet. The miracle, therefore, is a visible parable.

It was on the day after His triumphant entry into Jerusalem and the Temple that " when they came out from Bethania He was hungry. And when He had seen afar off a fig-tree having leaves, He came, if perhaps He might find anything on it. And when He was come to it, He found nothing but leaves, for it was not yet the time for figs. And answering He said to it, May no man hereafter eat fruit of thee any more for ever. And His disciples heard it." Then, as St. Mark tells us, He went on and cleansed the Temple for the second time, arousing thereby afresh the malicious enmity of the Chief Priests and Scribes. " And when evening was come, He went forth out of the city. And when they passed by in the morning, they saw the fig-tree dried up from the roots." It is almost as if the final determination of the Chief Priests to put Him to death, which was quickened into activity by His marvellous display of power on Palm Sunday and the following day, had filled up the measure of the probation of the Synagogue.

2. In these considerations on Purgatory we are dealing with souls which have been to some extent, often to a great extent, barren of the good fruits which our Lord might have expected of them, but which by His mercy have not been " withered up from the roots," nor condemned to perpetual sterility as to the praise and honour which they are to render to Him in Heaven. We cannot, therefore, find in them anything that resembles the case of the withered fig-tree. But there are two circumstances connected with the miracle which we may use as enabling us to find in this narrative something which may be very useful to our general purpose. In the first place, the circumstance of our Lord's hunger may remind us of His constant

fasts, and of the hard treatment to which His Sacred Body was usually subjected, and this will enable us to complete in this chapter the subject which was begun in that on the Cure of the Lunatic Boy. In that miracle our Lord sets before us the peculiar efficacy of prayer and fasting for the obtaining of certain great deliverances. But our space then only allowed of our speaking of prayer. We may now pass on to speak of fasting. In the second place, there is one matter in which we may all of us sometimes be like the fig-tree, in refusing the alms which are sought of us, as our Lord sought from the fig-tree the boon of a little food in His hunger. If any self-reproach of this kind is to be found among the Holy Souls, it will be very much enhanced by the knowledge which they possess of the immense value of almsdeeds as a work of satisfaction. It can hardly be said that the subject of almsgiving has been hitherto passed over in this volume, for it has frequently been mentioned among other good works, by means of which the Holy Souls may be relieved. But there are still a few remarks to be made more directly on the subject, and these will be included in the present chapter.

3. The power of fasting as a work of satisfaction is so universally recognised in Sacred Scriptures and in the Church that it may seem almost super-fluous to insist on it at any great length. Fasting seems to have been connected with devotion for the dead among the Jews, not to speak of other nations, as we see in the fasting which was made for Saul after his death.[1] The instinct of the Church and of the saints has always been in the same direction, and if the early Fathers do not mention fasting among the means to be used for the relief of the

[1] 1 Kings xxxi. 13; 2 Kings i. 12.

departed, it is only because they include it under the head of prayer. It has the special direct power of satisfaction, all the more because it is one of the works which are most painful to the body, and it is thus one of the customary penances in all religious bodies in the Church. The lives of the saints and the chronicles of the religious orders are naturally full of instances in which the Holy Souls have either begged that fasting may be made for them, or have expressed their gratitude when they have had that aid afforded them. In speaking of the satisfactory power of fasting, it is well to join to it the other similar works of penance which are usually reckoned under the same head, such as the affliction of the body by disciplines, hair-shirts, vigils, prostrations, and the like. There is an old story of the great Emperor Otho, who is said to have appeared after his death to a near relation of his own, who was the Superior in a convent of nuns, begging the aid of her religious to free him from Purgatory. The petition which he made would startle many of those who think very lightly of the pains of Purgatory. He prayed the abbess to send letters to various monasteries in order that a great amount of penance might be done for him—ten thousand psalters, with ten strokes of a discipline at each psalm, during which the *De Profundis* was to be recited, and a *Pater Noster* and *Ave Maria* were to be added at each verse. And the historian adds that this was required for an emperor who had during his lifetime been a great benefactor of the Church and of the poor. There is an anecdote in the life of the famous Catharine of Cardona, who was the contemporary of St. Teresa, to the same effect. She was made aware of the death of the well-known Ruy Gomez at the moment when it happened, and before the news could reach the part of the country where she was in the ordinary way. She was so affected by the knowledge which she received of the great sufferings to which he was subjected, that she immediately disciplined herself so severely that the cell in which she lived was all sprinkled with her blood. There are many other such instances. We may add to such corporal austerities as these the bodily sufferings which come to us in the course of God's Providence, if they are readily welcomed and joyfully undergone, and under the same head will come the afflictions which the servants of God sometimes are prompted to ask for, in order that they may suffer more for the relief of the Holy Souls. The saints have sometimes petitioned to be allowed to bear in this life the Purgatory of this or that soul, and the prayer has been heard. The two St. Catharines, of Ricci and Raconigi, were both remarkable for this. Indeed, any suffering, of whatever kind, even though not corporal, such as the patient bearing of dryness and desolation, or, again, charity under some great calumny, has the effect of satisfying largely for sin, and may thus be beneficial to the Holy Souls if offered for them.

4. It is time to say a few words in addition as to the satisfactory power of almsdeeds, although it has been impossible to reserve for one chapter what is so obvious a means of relieving the holy suffering souls. Nothing can be stronger than the language of Sacred Scripture on the power of almsdeeds to *"deliver from death,"*[2] to *"purge away sin,"*[3] and the like. It is compared to the effect of water on fire,[4] or to that of ransom to the captive,[5] or to that of a

---

[2] Tobias xii. 9. [3] Prov. xv. 27. [4] Ecclus. iii. 33.
[5] Dan. iv. 26.

sacrifice,[6] which propitiates God. It is compared to a second baptism,[7] and is said to be more efficacious even than fasting. It would be well to remember that both almsdeeds and fastings will be more efficacious if they are done with this distinct intention of delivering the souls of Purgatory, or any particular souls in whom we may be interested. In that case, it is not only the satisfactory power of the good works which is applied to the souls, but the work as a whole, with all its merits of impetration as well as satisfaction. It is a much greater charity to undertake directly to fast, or to afflict ourselves in any other way, for the Holy Souls, than to apply to them the satisfaction of the good works of this kind which we should otherwise do as a matter of course. No one can do the first of these things without being very much in earnest in his desire to relieve the misery of the sufferers in Purgatory.

5. Another item of advice which is found in some writers relates to the question of pious foundations for the benefit of the holy departed, whether they be hospitals or convents or orphanages or colleges for the clergy or of any other kind. It is said that f the object be to benefit some one soul in particular, it is more prudent to give away all that we can in alms or for Masses at once, in order that the soul for whom we are interested may enjoy the benefit of our charity as soon as possible. But if the intention be to benefit the Holy Souls in general, then it is better to found such institutions as those just now mentioned, which may last on from year to year, and from generation to generation and benefit successive numbers of sufferers in Purgatory.

6. Another counsel, with which we may conclude,

Heb. xiii. 16.   [7] Ecclus. vii. 46.

is found in the revelations of St. Bridget, and has reference to the correspondence of the good works which are done for the benefit of a soul to the faults which he may be known to have committed in his lifetime. The saint was careful to give a great deal by way of alms for the repose of her husband's soul, and he begged her to sell his plate and horses, in which he had taken an excessive delight, for his benefit. In another of her visions[8] she heard the soul of a certain noble person cry "woe" four times, and she was told by an Angel that there might be four kinds of expiation offered for him. The first of his woes was that he had loved God but little, and to atone for this thirty chalices might be offered for him, in which the Precious Blood might be offered in Holy Mass, and God thus specially honoured. The second "woe" was that he had but little fear of God, and for this thirty devout priests were to be chosen, each of whom was to say thirty masses for him—nine of the Martyrs, nine of the Confessors, nine of All Saints, one of the Angels, one of our Blessed Lady, and one of the most Holy Trinity. The third "woe" which he uttered was on account of his pride and avarice, and for this thirty poor persons were to be taken in, clothed and fed, and their feet washed in humility, and prayers were to be made to our Lord that, for the sake of His own humility and His Passion, the sins of that soul might be forgiven him. The fourth "woe" was for the pride of the flesh in him, and this was to be atoned for by sending one virgin to a convent, and providing for one widow, and for one marriageable maiden, sufficient for food and maintenance in each case, and then God was to be prayed to forgive him the

[8] Lib. iv. c. 9.

punishment due to his sins of the flesh. These and other similar reflections may at least serve to show that, in the best Christian ages, the idea of the punishment which might be due to God in Purgatory was by no means a slight one, and that very great exertions were not thought too much for the deliverance of single souls. We might as well hope to relieve a great city, suffering under famine, by collecting the crumbs of bread after our dinners day by day, or to stop the progress of a mighty epidemic by a few bottles of rosewater, as to relieve the sufferings of the Holy Souls of Purgatory by trifling alms which cost us nothing, or slight penitential exercises which give but little pain.

CHAPTER XL.

Forgiveness of Injuries.

(THE HEALING OF MALCHUS.)
St. Luke xxii. 50, 51.

1. ALL the four Evangelists mention the incident in the apprehension of our Lord in the Garden of Olives, when St. Peter in his fiery zeal drew a sword in defence of his Master, and cut off the ear of one of the servants of the High Priest, who had joined the band sent under the guidance of Judas. St. Luke alone mentions the miracle which our Lord wrought in favour of the poor servant, who may have had no faith in Him, and even have been actuated by the hatred towards Him which would have been natural in one who heard Him so continually censured and spoken against by his own master. After reproving and warning St. Peter,

St. Luke tells us that our Lord, " answering, said, Suffer ye thus far. And when He had touched his ear, He healed him." It is as if He asked leave of His enemies to work this miraculous cure, in order that no traces might remain of the intemperate violence of His Apostle. The miracle may have been wrought partly out of our Lord's unfailing and ineffable tenderness of Heart, for He could not bear to see blood flow, except it were His own, shed for the sins of the world. But it is probable that the chief motive of our Lord was rather to show His entire want of all animosity or anger against His enemies,and to set us an example of that perfect forgiveness of injuries and insults which does not stop short at simple pardon, but adds to that any sort of active kindness or charity of which the case admits. It has been sometimes said of the Saints, that the way to secure the utmost possible kindness from them was to do them some injury, and our Lord in this miracle seems to have acted on the principle thus attributed to the Saints. He went out of His way to heal this poor man, and this is the only instance in which it could have been recorded of Him that He worked a miracle in favour of one who was hostile to Him at the time, and bent on His destruction. At the very moment of the beginning of His Passion, when He was treated with indignities and insults so great, when they were about to put Him in chains and drag Him so cruelly to the tribunals of Annas and Caiaphas, He took occasion to use His miraculous power for the last time before His death, not to serve Himself or even to deliver His Apostles— though the miracle may have had some effect in making the leaders of the armed band listen to His injunction to let them go—but to stanch the wound and restore the lost limb of one of His bitter enemies.

2. This great example of our Lord has many lessons for us in every way, but it helps us especially with regard to the subject of these chapters by suggesting to us one of the most efficacious means which are in our power of escaping the sufferings of Purgatory. We have not made those means so much a subject of direct study in these chapters as the means by which we may aid the present holy sufferers in Purgatory to a speedy release; but it is of course, clear that, in general, the same methods, especially of satisfaction, which seem to relieve them, are also available for ourselves. But holy writers on this subject often mention certain practices and virtues as having a particular power in shielding us from the danger of falling ourselves under severe punishments in Purgatory. It will be useful to set down some of these here, and to consider the miracle wrought on Malchus as suggesting them, because it suggests that one of them which has the special promise of our Lord. For He Who has taught us not to pray for the forgiveness of our own sins, except with the qualification that we are to ask to be forgiven as we ourselves forgive, has also promised distinctly that if we forgive we shall also be forgiven. Now, when our Lord speaks of the forgiveness of sins in the Gospel, He speaks of it in the fullest and most complete sense which His words will bear. That is, He speaks of that entire forgiveness as given by God, which not only absolves the sinner from the guilt of sin and from its eternal consequences of separation from Him, but which also remits the temporal punishment due to sin, whether in this world or in the next. But this remission is that of which we have had to say

so much in these chapters on Purgatory. We have His word, therefore, that it is in our power, with the help of His grace, entirely to cancel the debt of satisfaction which we may owe to His justice for our sins, and that the means by which this is to be done is the perfect forgiveness on our part of all the trespasses against ourselves by others of which we have to complain. It is very clear that our forgiveness of others must be as ample and unreserved and ungrudging as we wish that to be which we ourselves desire to receive from God. It is often the case, that we can forgive an injury, or a harsh and insulting word, or even a grave act of injustice and wrong, so far as is absolutely necessary in order not to lose the grace of God ourselves. That is, we do not bear malice or wish the person who has injured us any wrong, while yet we are unable to show him any greater marks of charity than are the absolute rights of one Christian from another. We are not ready to exert ourselves for him, as our Lord exerted Himself for Malchus, or to do for him any extraordinary and unusual charity. Such forgiveness may be enough to satisfy the commandment of God, but it is not enough to win the abundant and overwhelming grace which is in store for those who can from their hearts love those who have injured them, for the sake of our Lord, and as being their own great benefactors. In order to this we have need of very great grace, and it is this kind of forgiveness which has the power of absolutely cancelling the debt of punishment which we may owe for our sins. For those who can with all their heart, in this way, forgive their enemies, must be very closely united to God, and are indeed His true children.

3. There are two other virtues which have the

same power, and the same promises, for these are very nearly akin to that of which we have been speaking. These are the virtue of not judging others, and the virtue of perfect contrition. Our Lord has said distinctly, " Judge not, that you may not be judged; for with what judgment you judge, you shall be judged, and with what measure you mete, it shall be measured to you again." [1] This is something different from the forgiveness of injuries. In the forgiveness of injuries, there is no question about the fact of the injury; but in abstinence from judging, even the fact is not assumed. The forgiveness of injuries is grounded on our own relation to God and to those who may injure us; the virtue of abstinence from judging is based on the consideration that to God alone belongs the right of judgment, as well as the right of punishment. Other considerations, such as that of our own miseries and faults, which are quite enough to occupy our whole attention, may well come in to aid in the formation of this virtue, which requires the truest humility as its condition. But there are some blessed souls in the Church who have this special grace of always looking on others with the eyes of charity, of turning away from all that is evil so as not to see it, and of interpreting everything well, even when such interpretation is most difficult. Such persons have the promise of our Lord, that they shall not be judged, that is, that they shall either be preserved from all faults in return for their simple and divine charity, or shall at least have all their faults freely forgiven. In the case of the virtue of perfect contrition, it must be evident that it contains the perfect love of God, and where the perfect love of God exists, the

[1] St. Matt. vii. 1, 2.

sorrow which is founded upon it must be so pure and so intense, as altogether to cancel any debt that may be owing to His justice.

4. There are other things which may be mentioned under the head of the means of escaping Purgatory. Some of these may be said rather to be the suffering of Purgatory here. Such is the case of those who undergo some great trial, such as a great calumny against their reputation borne without resentment or repining or any attempt at justification. Such is the case of those also whom God afflicts with bodily sufferings and ailments, if they too are endured with perfect resignation and cheerful union with the will of God. Such is the case of those who labour long and assidously in propagating the faith among the heathen, or who use themselves up entirely in other works of charity for their neighbours, keeping up all the time their union with God and the peace of a good conscience vigilantly guarded. In all these cases, and in others like them, it may be said that Purgatory has been endured before its time. The same may be said of the satisfactory power of perfect fidelity, even in the least things, to a religious rule, which is a burthen that presses at no time with any great heaviness, but the continuity of which makes it very meritorious in the sight of God. Other means, again, to the same end are to be found in the perfect use of the ordinary means of grace, such as the Sacraments. For the Sacraments of Penance and Holy Communion have the power perfectly to purify the soul from the debt of pain as well as from the stain of guilt, and that they do not do this in ordinary cases is not because of their lack of power, but of the imperfect manner in which they are received. Lastly, we may

V

mention the careful and perfect use of Indulgences, and also a very deep and true devotion to the Passion of our Lord.

CHAPTER XLI.

The Treasure of the Church.

(OUR LORD'S LAST MIRACLE ON THE LAKE.)
St. John xxi. 1—19.

1. THE last recorded miracle of our Lord was worked after His Resurrection, during that part of the forty days which He spent with His disciples in Galilee. The narrative is given to us by St. John alone, who was himself present, with six other Apostles, his own brother St. James, St. Peter, St. Thomas, St. Bartholomew or Nathanael, and two others who are not named, but who may be conjectured to have been St. Andrew and St. Philip.[1] It is not necessary to repeat the story of the fishing of the Apostles during the night—when, as on the former occasion of which we have had to speak, they caught nothing—of our Lord's appearance in the early dawn on the shore, bidding them cast the net on the right side of the boat, then of the marvellous draught óf fishes which was immediately enclosed in the net, of St. John's discerning our Lord, of St. Peter's leaping into the water to go to Him, and of the meal which was awaiting them

[1] The four Apostles not included in this list would thus be St. Matthew, who was not a fisherman, and the three who were near relations or connections of our Lord, St. Simon, St. Jude, and St. James the Less. These might probably be with our Lady and the holy women at the time. But it is needless to say, that this is pure conjecture.

when they landed. The points on which we may fasten in this great miracle, and in the conversation which followed on it, are the following—the action of St. Peter, the Prince of the Apostles, in drawing the net to land himself, containing a certain recorded number of large fishes, "one hundred and fifty and three," and the commission which was afterwards so solemnly given to him by our Lord, and repeated thrice, in which, after asking him thrice whether he loved Him, our Lord bade him, "Feed My lambs," "Feed My sheep." It is generally considered by Catholic commentators on Scripture and by the theologians of the Church that our Lord on this occasion conferred on St. Peter, for himself and for his successors, the authority and commission to rule the Catholic Church which He had before promised to him, when he made his great confession of faith in the Divinity of his Master. Then He had said, "Thou art Peter, and on this rock I will build my Church, and the gates of Hell shall not prevail against it, and I will give unto thee the keys of the Kingdom of Heaven, and whatsoever thou shalt bind on earth, it shall be bound also in Heaven, and whatsoever thou shalt loose on earth, it shall be loosed also in Heaven."[3] Now He says, "Simon, son of John, lovest thou Me more than these? . . . Feed My lambs. Feed My lambs. Feed My sheep."

2. It is on this great commission, promised in the first of these passages and conferred in the second, that the vital Catholic doctrine of the prerogatives of St. Peter mainly rests for its Scripture proof, though there are also other texts and incidents in the life of our Lord on which it is based, and though the whole argument from Scripture embraces

[3] St. Matt. xvi. 18, 19.

also the commentary on the acts and sayings of our Lord which is furnished by the history of the Acts of the Apostles and by the Epistles. It is of course not to our present purpose to draw out the whole argument, as we can only have to deal with that part of the power which has been conferred on St. Peter and on his successors which has immediate relation to the subject of Purgatory. That part, however, of St. Peter's power is very important indeed to us, and it may very fitly be made the subject of this our last chapter on the miracles. The power conferred on St. Peter, with regard to this subject, may be connected immediately with the words of St. Matthew which have been quoted in the last paragraph. St. Peter, in the passage of St. John's Gospel before us, is practically ordered by our Lord to use his power in all charity for the benefit of the flock committed to him. That is one meaning at least of the touching question thrice put to him by our Lord, " Lovest thou Me ? " It is as if He had said, " If you love Me, and as you love Me, feed My lambs, feed My lambs, feed My sheep." But the power which is thus to be exercised according to the instinct and measure of his love to our Blessed Lord is, as has been said, that which was promised before in the words which St. Matthew has recorded. That power, then, consists, first, of opening the Kingdom of Heaven, for such is the meaning of the power of the keys; and secondly, it consists in the power of binding and loosing. By this, for the purpose with which we are now concerned, is meant the power either opening Heaven or not, and of laying down the conditions on which the power of the keys exercised, in any particular case or under any particular circumstances.

3. It is plain that the power thus conferred on St. Peter of opening the gates of Heaven must mean the power of removing all the impediments which, in any particular case, shut the gates of Heaven and prevent this or that particular soul, or certain classes of souls, from entering there. Now, it has already been said that there are two impediments to entrance to Heaven, original sin unremoved, and actual mortal sin unrepented and uncancelled as to its guilt. Either of these two impediments. while it exists, is enough absolutely to bar the gates of Heaven. The first of these impediments is removed by our Lord Himself, and the application of what He has thus done to particular souls takes place in Holy Baptism. The second impediment, that created by actual sin, is removed by the power of the keys. But this impediment, which is caused by actual sin, is twofold, and consists in the guilt of sin, and in the punishment due to it. If the guilt is not removed, the soul can never enter Heaven, and, even when the guilt is removed, the soul cannot enter Heaven until the punishment has been removed also. The guilt of sin, then, is removed by the power of the keys in the Sacrament of Penance, according to those words of our Lord, " Whose sins ye remit, they are remitted." The impediment of the punishment is also removed by the power of the keys, in the concession of Indulgences, according to those other words, " Whatsoever thou shalt loose on earth, it shall be loosed also in Heaven." And it must be said that any idea of the power of the keys which leaves out this remission of the pain due to sin as well as of the guilt of sin itself—when due dispositions exist, and under all due conditions, according to the laws of the Kingdom of our Lord—is absolutely defective

and inadequate. It has been said above that any idea of our Lord s Mission as the Redeemer of the world which leaves out His Mission with regard to Purgatory, is defective and inadequate. It represents Him, practically, as not being He Who was to come, and it implies, practically, that we must "look for another." In just the same way, the power of the keys would not be what it ought to be, it would not answer to the largeness and fulness and universality of our Lord's commission to St. Peter, if it did not include, in some way or other, the power of loosing the bonds of pain as well as the power of loosing the bonds of guilt. Our Lord, as the people in Decapolis said, hath done "all things well," not only "some things;"[*] and the power which He has left behind in the hands of St. Peter and his Successors to be exercised in charity must extend to all the needs of human souls waiting at the gates of Heaven. But it would not so extend, unless it had some provision for the removal of the impediment of pain, as well as for the removal of the impediment of guilt.

4. The provision of which we speak is exactly that which Catholics know as the power of Indulgences. An Indulgence is a remission of the pain due to sins, of which the guilt has already been forgiven. This remission is made by the same power which imposes this or that work of penance as an accompaniment of absolution, that is, the power of the keys of which we have just now spoken. By this power the "treasury," as it is said, of the Church is opened, and the merits of our Lord, the Blessed Virgin, and the Saints are applied in satisfaction to the souls to whom the Indulgence is granted, by the authority of the

[*] St. Mark vii. 37.

Chief Pastor of the Church, the Successor of St. Peter, and to a certain extent, of the Bishops.[4] The doctrine of the Church on this point is summed up in the decree of the Council of Trent (Session 25), which declares that the power of Indulgences has been granted by Christ to the Church, and that they are useful and salutary to the faithful. It would not fall within the scope of the present work to argue the point as to the doctrine of Indulgences against those who deny it. It is enough to say that it is, in principle, contained in the famous passage of St. Paul about the incestuous Corinthian, whose penance had been forgiven him by the Church,[5] and that there are traces of the practice in the earliest times, though it is undeniable that the great use of Indulgences, and particularly of the very large Indulgences which have been granted in the late centuries of the Church, is a development which has grown with the decay of penitential rigour and, in fact, with that great increase of human infirmities which characterises modern times. The comparative ease with which Indulgences may now be gained is a great blessing to the faithful of our times—a great blessing to those who avail themselves of it largely and diligently, while it may turn out to be a cause of severe self-reproach to those who neglect to avail themselves of the immense benignity of the Church. The causes for which Indulgences are granted are quite independent of the conditions assigned to them, and it is not necessary for us to

[4] Benedict XIII., *Trigies. II.* Serm. 24, teaches that Archbishops in their Provinces and Bishops in their dioceses may grant Indulgences of a year on the dedication of a church, and of forty days at other times. But he adds that they have greater powers in the private tribunal of penance, in regard to their own subjects.

[5] 2. Cor. ii. 5—11.

know them,—it is sufficient that the Pope has a reasonable ground, of which he is the judge. The great reason of all, no doubt, is the extreme tenderness of the Church, which desires that we should know her love for her children, and so be moved to praise the mercifulness of God, and which uses, in these days of corporal weakness and feeble virtues, an immense gentleness to the generations which have not the strength or courage to accomplish the severe penances of the ancient Canons. But at no time was it necessary that the works prescribed for those who are to gain Indulgences should correspond to the latter in importance. For Indulgences rest on the merits of our Lord, and not on those of the person who may gain them.

5. We have hitherto spoken of Indulgences indifferently, without distinguishing between their application to the living and that which is made of them to the dead. The Indulgences which the Church distributes to the living are given to them directly, those which are applied to the dead, only indirectly and by way of suffrage. Hence it follows, that if a living person is truly sorry for all his sins, venial as well as mortal, and if he performs accurately, with all the due dispositions, the works which are enjoined as the conditions of an Indulgence, he cannot fail to gain that Indulgence, our Lord's fidelity, of which St. Paul so often speaks, being pledged to him in the matter. This is what is meant, as it seems, by the theologians who speak of an Indulgence as granted by way of absolution, in which case the Church exercises her jurisdiction over own direct subjects, that is, the living faithful, granting to them the satisfactions which they require out of the merits of our Lord; whereas in the case of the departed, they are no longer directly her

subjects, and so the Indulgence is granted by way of suffrage. And, to return to the former point, a soul in Purgatory cannot perform any of the works which are enjoined as conditions of an Indulgence, and is no longer in a state to merit anything. There is, therefore, no tie of fidelity on the part of God which may bind Him to grant the Indulgence to such a soul, even though the works prescribed be performed by the living, and though the Indulgence be made by the Church applicable to the holy departed. This application, again, which is an exercise of the power of the keys, cannot be made by any but the Church, and unless she makes it, no one can benefit the Holy Souls by such an application.

6. It should also be remembered that the remission of the pain due to sins, which is the fruit of an Indulgence, can only fall on those sins the guilt of which has been already forgiven, that is, on those which have been truly, in some way or other, re-tracted. This it is which makes a Plenary Indulgence so difficult of perfect acquisition. But it does not follow, because some venial sins may not have been forgiven as to their guilt, that therefore the fruit of an Indulgence is lost, as to other light sins which have been forgiven. Again, it is taught by theo-logians that light sins committed at the time when a person might be receiving the fruit of an Indulgence, do not hinder the fruit of that Indulgence as to the other venial sins on which it would fall, though it is otherwise with sins committed at the time of performing the works which are exacted as conditions of the Indulgence, if those works are truly vitiated thereby. Again, it must be remembered, with regard to the Indulgences which are applied to the Holy Souls,

that their venial sins which may have remained unforgiven before their death, on account of their never having retracted them, are cancelled as to their guilt at the time of death, by the perfect conversion of the soul to God, which takes place in all who die in a state of grace. As to the remission of the pain due to these sins, it must be remembered that the effect of Indulgences does not come from the devotion of those who gain them, or from the labour to which they put themselves, or from the alms which they may give as their condition, but from the abundant treasure of the merits of the Church. Thus St. Thomas teaches that the essential conditions requisite for the fruit of which we are speaking, are simply authority on the part of those who grant the Indulgence, piety in the cause for which it is granted, and charity or the state of grace in those who are to receive the benefit thus bestowed.[5] Nevertheless, although all the Holy Souls are capable of receiving the fruits of Indulgences, because all are in the grace of God, it remains true that some are more capable of profiting largely in this way than others, because the fruit of this kind is shared by them according to the greater or less degree of their charity. Thus it may be necessary for some souls that a great many Plenary Indulgences should be gained for them, while others, to whom God allows a single Plenary Indulgence to be applied, may by virtue of that alone be delivered from all the pain which they owe to His justice.

7. It is certain that the blessed provision of Indulgences is one which conduces very greatly to the glory of God. It is surely to His glory that the abundant treasures of satisfaction which have been

[5] St. Thomas, *in Sent.* iv. dist. 22, qu. 1, art. 3, 2.

accumulated in the Church should be used, that piety and religion should be served by their use, that the rulers of the Church, who succeed to the throne of St. Peter, should exercise every part of their mighty prerogative for the good of souls, that a number of good works should be promoted, such as visits to the tombs of the Apostles and saints, or the relief of the poor, or the advancement of missions, and a thousand other good works, by being made the conditions on which Indulgences may be gained by those who also approach the sacraments worthily, and pray for the good of the Church. All these things are for the glory of God and of our Lord. All of them belong to the advancement of the great kingdom of the Incarnation, and charity, as well as the glory of God in other respects, is promoted when the faithful are urged on to them by the holding out of Indulgences so to be gained. Whenever we practically show our belief in the powers which God has granted to the Church, we do Him honour, and our faith is sometimes more displayed when it is exercised on things which do not meet the sight, and are less easy of proof; or again, when the points to which is refers are more questioned and assailed by the unbelieving world. On this account, if on no other, it would be our duty to proclaim in the face of the world our belief in these powers of the Church, and we might expect a greater blessing from God in proportion to our boldness and simplicity in this respect. But in truth, few things would be more to the glory of God in our generation than a great increase of devotion to the Holy Souls in Purgatory and to their interests in general, and of diligence and zeal in helping them by means of Indulgences in particular. When we review all the means of aiding them which God has put into our hands—prayers, Masses, Communions, almsdeeds, mortifications, pilgrimages, the Divine Office, the Office of the Dead or of our Blessed Lady, the holy Rosary, works of active mercy, the teaching the Christian doctrine, the attending of funerals, and a thousand more, we can find none more powerful in themselves, if the fruit be really gained, none more honourable to God and to our Lord and to His Church, than this of holy Indulgences. And besides, the mind of the Church is expressed by the fact that she makes this most loving and beautiful exercise of her prerogative go along with and accompany all other aid to the Holy Souls. For there can hardly be found any one of those named or alluded to which is not enriched by her with copious Indulgences, which are thus placed by her within the reach of all who can do any one of those other works, while she gives them besides for many a short prayer or pious practice which requires the very slightest exertion or expense of time.   And yet it is not a little thing that we do, or that we neglect to do, when we either impart to these holy sufferers a portion, be it large or small, of the inexpressibly precious merits and satisfactions of our Lord Jesus Christ and His saints, or leave them without that solace and assistance— often, we may fear, because we have not ourselves the intelligent faith to appreciate duly the needs of those who are detained in Purgatory, or the ineffable glory which results to God from the devout and charitable use of the exhaustless treasures of the Church, which He has purchased with His own Blood, and to which He has left the exercise of the powers in Heaven and on earth which were won by His Passion.